Christina

Wopila

Trusted

W9-APZ-072

BY JAMES CARROLL

The Cloister

Warburg in Rome

Secret Father

The City Below

Memorial Bridge

Firebird

Supply of Heroes

Prince of Peace

Family Trade

Fault Lines

Mortal Friends

Madonna Red

Christ Actually: The Son of God for the Secular Age

*Jerusalem, Jerusalem: How the Ancient City
Ignited Our Modern World*

Practicing Catholic

*House of War: The Pentagon and
the Disastrous Rise of American Power*

Crusade: Chronicle of an Unjust War

Toward a New Catholic Church

Constantine's Sword: The Church and the Jews

*An American Requiem: God, My Father,
and the War That Came Between Us*

*The Truth at the Heart of the Lie:
How the Catholic Church Lost Its Soul*

THE TRUTH
AT THE HEART
OF THE LIE

In memory of
James Parks Morton
and
Joseph F. Carroll Jr.

THE TRUTH
AT THE HEART
OF THE LIE

*How the Catholic Church
Lost Its Soul*

A memoir of faith

✠

JAMES CARROLL

RANDOM HOUSE

NEW YORK

Published in the United States by Random House, an imprint and
division of Penguin Random House LLC, New York.

Random House and the House colophon are registered trademarks
of Penguin Random House LLC.

Biblical quotations are from the Revised Standard Version unless otherwise noted.

Brief portions of this work were originally published in "To Save the Church,
Dismantle the Priesthood," *The Atlantic*, June 2019.

Hardback ISBN 978-0-593-13470-2
Ebook ISBN 978-0-593-13472-6

Printed in Canada on acid-free paper

randomhousebooks.com

2 4 6 8 9 7 5 3 1

First Edition

Book design by Victoria Wong

When we are stripped down to a certain point, nothing leads anywhere any more, hope and despair are equally groundless, and the whole of life can be summed up in an image. A man's work is nothing but this slow journey to rediscover through the detours of art those two or three great and simple images in whose presence his heart first opened.

—Albert Camus, 1937

Contents

✠

THE TRUTH
AT THE HEART
OF THE LIE

In the Portico

Whan I was perhaps five years old, I encountered a monk. My mother loved to tell the story. She did not pick up on its creepiness, but at an early age I did.

We were standing in the so-called Rosary Portico of a monastery on the outskirts of Washington, D.C., where I grew up. Apart from sepia tone images encountered in movies or museums, what is a monastery today? Or a monk? Or, for that matter, a rosary? In the twentieth century, they were important to many of us, many more of us then than now. Today, in the twenty-first century, there are some good folks who keep votive candles lit in the alcoves of a few actual monasteries, but those figures can seem like curators of the past. Yet that was the world into which I was born, and I see now how strongly it shaped me.

I began by loving every corner of the Catholic Church, monks and rosaries included, and the monastery is an image to which I return still, associated as it is with my mother and, therefore, with love. For many decades, the Catholic Church has been a pillar of my identity. That pillar is now cracked.

The Rosary Portico, when I stood there with my mother decades ago, was the columned arcade that enclosed the cloister—the inner garden and courtyard—of the monastery. The monk who greeted us was a stout Franciscan, a member of a religious order founded in 1209 by Francis of Assisi, the saint of the poor. That iconic figure from the Middle Ages has currency now mainly because of the present pope, who has the poor in mind, too. Alas, the good Pope Francis, for all his works of mercy, lays bare the Church's failure.

The monk's robe and the dangling beads that hung at his side had snagged my attention. My head did not quite reach the level of the white rope that encircled his ample waist. The rope, too, struck me because its draping vertical length was marked at intervals by three carefully placed knots. Then I noticed the sandals out of which his pudgy toes protruded. I'd never seen sandals on the bare feet of a grown-up man before. When my gaze lifted, I was transfixed by something else: The monk's head was bald, and from the lower part of his face a slew of wispy gray tendrils hung—the first beard I'd ever seen. When I later learned it was called a goatee, I understood at once: I'd seen such facial hair on billy goats in my picture books.

The man's grin—moist lips, yellow teeth, dancing eyes—seemed odd but not frightening. A figure so unlike any I'd encountered before, he struck me as a sort of friendly ghost. At last I spoke. "Why," I asked, "do you have hair on your chin but not on your head?"

My mother yanked my arm disapprovingly, but she relaxed when the monk, joviality itself, laughed out loud. His hand, I recall, went to his shelflike stomach, a self-satisfied petting. He said, "Just call me Brother Upside Down."

I wasn't sure what his remark meant, but I sensed that it pleased him to have made it. His other hand dropped to my head, the briefest caress.

He and my mother laughed together then, exchanging glances above me. Since I had asked my question in earnest, I was mystified. What was so funny? I might have asked him why a man wears a dress. Or why that beaded necklace hung from his belt. Or, speaking of his belt, what was with that sash of white rope at his waist, with its knotted dangling end. I probably asked about the hair on his chin because that was only the last of several oddities to strike me.

Soon enough, the incident became a chestnut of family lore — a yarn endlessly repeated in our house. For a long time, as I listened to my mother regaling friends and relatives with what I'd said, I failed to get the joke. But the story always put me in mind of the complications of the monastery moment—how my mother had instinctively reacted by rebuking me with that jerk of my arm before the brother's laugh let her see my query not as the insult she'd feared it was, but as the bright quip of her charming five-year-old Jimmy. In an instant, I'd gone from being the object of reprimand to being a point of pride—a change in status that left me feeling uncertain about myself.

But one thing was very clear from the first moment in the portico to the subsequent retellings: The power of the monk was absolute. He had power over my mother, and therefore over my own standing in her affection. My mother's double-barreled reaction had taught me that my simplest words could have two meanings—one bad, the other good. And her reaction also taught me that the authority in charge of which meaning applied was the man in the brown robe.

That made me wonder, *Who is he? And why is Mom so ready to support him, to take her cue about me from him?* My mother, of course, was a kind of deity to me, which made the moment a religious revelation. That she deferred to the figure in sandals meant he was even more exalted than she.

I sensed that this higher status of his was a function of the place in which we were standing. Therefore, I was drawn not so much to the monk as to the enigmatic milieu from which I felt his power came. The Church. I never became a monk myself—not quite—but I was a monastery man from then on.

It would be years before I was initiated into the mystery of the three vows a monk takes—poverty, chastity, obedience—symbolized, as I would learn, by the three knots in the man's dangling cincture. But I had already grasped what was essential to the monk's vocation. Surrendering every claim to the normal happiness of money, family, status, and mobility, the monk stakes everything on the existence of God—God understood as individualized, immediately available, and radically committed to those who call upon His name.

The monk's God was not the philosophical abstraction with which I would later wrestle—Aristotle's Prime Mover, Thomas Aquinas's being itself, Paul Tillich's ultimate concern. Nor was the monk's God the rarefied haze of goodwill in which I would eventually be tempted to lose myself, a woo-woo transcendent aura that forces no proposition, receives no petition, requires no obedience, but is vaguely thought to live benignly as the inner life of life itself. No, the monk's God was a God who could number the few hairs on the monk's head, know the monk's name, require kindness, demand justice, offer salvation, uphold both the vast cosmos and the monk's own pulse. A God who was a most intimate personal presence, to be compared, at that point in my life, only to a parent.

I learned, well before having words for it, that the Catholic religion is a religion not of mystical union in which the self disappears into an ultimate quietude—Nirvana, as the Buddhist's

emptiness or the Hindu's release from cycles of birth and death—
but a religion of conscious relationship, in which one's fulfillment
comes from knowing and being known by the One who is radically apart, the source of everything. Not just known—but loved.

If that loving Other does not exist—if that God does not exist—
the vowed life of the monk, priest, or nun makes no sense. I got
that. I intuited, even at age five, the radical thrill of the monk's
gamble, a roll of the dice on which his—or on which anyone's—
whole life is bet. For the first time, I saw God, even if indirectly,
which is, of course, the only way it's done. And having seen, I
heard, too. I would not know what I'd heard until much later. I'd
heard the whisper of a kind of call.

So, yes, that brown-robed monk was, for me, the first of those
"great and simple images" of which Albert Camus wrote, images
in the presence of which my heart opened. The monk's monastery
was another. So was that string of beads at his waist, which I soon
learned was the rosary for which the Rosary Portico where we
stood was named.

HERE AT MY desk in my home office now, I raise my eyes to the
yellowing card that has been pinned to the wall above me for years,
on which are printed the lines from Camus: "A man's work is
nothing but this slow journey to rediscover through the detours of
art those two or three great and simple images in whose presence
his heart first opened."[1] Circling back in memory, I am in a late
stage of that journey, with the pillars of the Catholic Church
crumbling on every side, shaking the very structure of the faith. Of
my faith. Yet these images—monk, monastery, portico—still mark
the way.

The word "rosary" comes from a Latin word meaning "circle of
roses," the flowers that make us Catholics think of the mother of

Jesus—the one we call Our Lady. We say our most important prayers to her, and we use the fifty beads of the rosary as a way of counting them. When, at age seven or so, I was given my own beads, I somehow knew, from then on, to think of myself as Catholic. I knew who God was, and I knew that I was His.

From the gooseneck lamp here at my desk hangs a rosary to this day. That says something important about me, but so does the fact that, as I see now, I will not likely recite its prayers again. Still, the God I met in the Rosary Portico when I was five—the God I associate with love—remains the only God in whose presence my chastened heart can hope to open yet again. Whether it will or not is the question.

In this book, I aim to tell three stories. One is a saga of history, of how the Catholic Church, from the days of the Roman Empire through the feudal Middle Ages, reinterpreted Scripture and the meaning of Jesus to become a bastion of male supremacy and theological doom, one empowering a clerical elite—priests—who became, for the believers, the self-serving gatekeepers of eternity.

The second story tells of how the malignity of that clericalism has been laid bare in recent years by the scandal of priests sexually abusing children, while bishops have protected the predators instead of their victims—a deviance so deeply driven into the Catholic culture that not even the brave and charismatic Pope Francis has been able or willing to uproot it.

And the third story is my own—how Jimmy, how I, became a priest; then a writer, and an op-ed columnist for *The Boston Globe*, even as that paper's Spotlight team broke the Church's sexual abuse scandal; and, finally, a shattered believer forced to confront the corruption at the heart of my faith.

I have undertaken this work of history, memory, conscience, and identity—the deconstruction of a self—prompted by a crisis of faith that I see now has been long in coming. Yet a forthright grappling with one's inner turmoil can itself be an opening to transcendence. This book, therefore, also aims to be the tribute that the excavation of one person's quite particular consciousness pays to the experience that may be shared with others—an experience of the unseen world of faith and imagination that lies just beyond the ever-receding horizon of our longing.

I was inextricably woven into my mother's unarticulated sense of that world beyond: She made me an intimate sharer of her faith. Her unuttered prayers were answered when, as a young man, I entered the religious life of the Church and, after seven years in seminary, was ordained a priest. My priesthood, though, was caught up in the political and cultural typhoon of the 1960s and 1970s, and lasted only five years. From 1969 until 1974, I was the Catholic chaplain at Boston University, presiding over a modest bowfront student center called Newman House, which aimed to be a tranquil oasis for young people caught in the crush of a frightening time. Celebrating Mass was the crux of what I did each day. I was not that much older than the BU students I served, but they loved the calming still point of the Eucharist, and so did I.

Ironically, the priestly ministry, in sponsoring my civil rights work and prompting my enlistment in the peace movement during the Vietnam War, made me a radical. Soon enough, I was in conflict with the conservative Catholic hierarchy, being called on the carpet over minor matters (not wearing the Roman collar) and major ones (what, actually, had I said in my sermon?). It only gradually dawned on me that there was a tragic flaw deep inside the institution to which I'd given my life, and that it had to do with the clerical culture I was part of—a decadence in the priesthood itself. *My* priesthood.

The nub at the center of the notorious Roman Catholic sexual predation is an idolatry of the priest and of the priestly status that goes by the name of "clericalism." It is a malignity marked by a cult of secrecy; a high-flown theological misogyny that demeans all women and fosters an unbridled male supremacy; a suppression of normal erotic desire; a hierarchical domination of priest over laypeople; and a basing of that power on threats of a doom-laden afterlife, drawn from a misreading of the Gospel of Jesus Christ. The inbuilt rank-obsession of the clerical system also thwarts the virtues of otherwise good priests, and perverts the message of selfless love that the Church was established to proclaim.

Generating a neurotic pathology in many priests, and prompting many others to protect themselves and the institution instead of victims, clericalism, I will argue in this book, is both the root cause and the corrupter, the ongoing enabler of the present Catholic catastrophe. The priesthood itself is warped. Against such a sweeping indictment, defenders of the Church as it is insist that a distinction must be drawn between the still admirable priesthood and the degeneracy of those clergymen who have betrayed it.[2] But by now it is clear that the entire milieu within which priests live and exercise ministry—its theology, aesthetic, lifestyle, heritage, values, and structure of authority—is the issue.

Without remotely understanding its bite, I saw such clericalism up close. Indeed, I lived it. In the confessions I heard in the early seventies, young people were racked with guilt not because of authentic sinfulness, but by a Church-imposed sexual repressiveness I was expected to affirm. Just by celebrating those cozy Masses, I was also helping to enforce an unjust exclusion of women from equal membership in the Church. I valued the community life I shared with my fellow priests, but I sensed the crippling loneliness that, for many, was the flip side of the priestly fraternity, the insubstantial cronyism that the priesthood offered.

In protest marches meant to question authority, it was my clerical status that gave my participation weight, and on the streets it was my fellow demonstrators who wanted me to be there because of my Roman collar. Yet in encounters with my Church superiors, I saw that submission was the virtue that counted most. My surrendering of my will was, theoretically, to God. In practice, it was only to the boss.

I realized that the price of my idealized power as a priest was the actual powerlessness of an existential humiliation that went with my place: I was low, low down on the clerical pyramid that privileged the higher-ups—monsignors, bishops, archbishops, cardinals, and the pope. That sacred hierarchy established a pattern of kissing up and kicking down, with every priest, including me, licensed to regard the disempowered laity—especially women—with paternal condescension. Clericalism *is* the pyramid, a structure of domination that must be protected at all costs by everyone occupying a niche in it—which is why bishops and most priests so routinely shield the clerical abusers instead of their victims. The clerical pyramid is the predator's safe house; the Church's sanctuary is *his* sanctuary.

That I soon enough quit the priesthood is part of what follows, but if I had stayed a priest, I see now, my faith, such as it was, would have been debased by the very same clericalism that drove me away.

But this is far more than one man's story, for Roman Catholicism has broken faith not only with its members but with the world. The ethical collapse of the Church must be seen in the context of the twenty-first century's undermining of social cohesion everywhere: the hollowing out of journalism; the evaporation of civic movements; the broad discrediting of political authority; the unsettling of traditional norms of meaning before the onslaught of digital media, screen technologies, and artificial intelligence. Stressed by manifestations of white supremacy, predatory capitalism, nationalist populism, and mass migration, liberal democracy itself, so apparently ascendant at the end of the twentieth century, is undergoing a crisis of confidence. As if such cultural traumas were not enough, environmental degradation and a reignited nuclear arms race have brought the prospect of human self-extinction out of the realm of science fiction and into the province of the possible. The human condition itself is undergoing transformations that no one understands, much less controls.

All of this was brought shockingly to the fore by the coronavirus pandemic that swept the world in 2020, just as I was finishing the writing of this book. The criminally inadequate responses to Covid-19 of many governments, especially the United States, not only led to the unnecessary deaths of tens of thousands, but also showed how essential human norms had already been betrayed.

The Catholic Church's upheaval is part of this large human problem, but the Church has made things worse for the world community with its twenty-first-century disqualification as a major center of moral value—what it had been, despite its failings, for two millennia.

The Catholic Church was the soul of Christendom, and that positive legacy, too, was on display during the coronavirus pandemic. Something precious could be seen in the timeless figure of Pope Francis standing in the rain alone in the deserted St. Peter's Square, an icon of suffering that spoke to and for the world.[3] Images of Italy's empty churches during the lockdown epitomized a global sense of loss. Ironically, that loss itself hinted at the way an unnamed legacy of Roman Catholicism was still sacred to the broad culture, even if that culture could not normally perceive it. Why should such images—the pope alone in the rain, the vast basilicas vacant—have registered so widely during the crushing health crisis? Perhaps because Christendom was an unacknowledged source of the secular humanism that replaced it, and the bequeathals of Christendom remain a buried touchstone of worth, even for a post-religious society. That such a bastion of the common good had been breached by the dereliction of priests suggests that the stakes in the Catholic sexual abuse catastrophe are enormous not just for the faithful but for everyone.

But recognitions tied to the scale of suffering caused by the pandemic, itself a transcendent challenge to meaning, made the self-defilement of Catholicism in this era seem worse. The grief that many Catholics feel for their ethically wounded Church has merged with grief for the wounds of the very planet. How does belief stand up to such distress? This book tracks one man's experience of that trouble—in my religion, my nation, my era, and my life. This is a journey from broken faith to chosen hope.

BEFORE ANY OF that, though, there were, yes, those "great and simple images" Camus wrote of, early images in the presence of which my heart first opened. What drew me to God was my mother's love and her religious devotedness: her respect for the monastery, Our Lady's rose, Our Lady's beads, the monk with his vows, the portico, the Church. *Those* images.

But as years passed, and the sepia tones of those early religious encounters were washed by experiences of the real world, I began to sense the rough dimensions—struggle, disappointment, grief—that shot through the actual lives of the Irish who'd come to America, the people among whom I grew up, including Mom. There was far more to their devotion—to her devotion—than mere piety. Eventually, I learned of my mother's actual experience: how her Irish-born father carried the post-traumatic weight of the Great Hunger, the mid-nineteenth-century Irish Potato Famine, which drove him and millions of others from Ireland and home; how he had been broken by life in America, becoming a drunk who abandoned his family and disappeared—a story so common that there was a name for it, "Irish divorce." Without her father to support the family, my mother quit school at thirteen or fourteen to go to work, a precocious breadwinner. To land a job at the phone company, her reliable, if substitute, father figure—the priest at her parish—had given her permission to lie about her age, a lesson in the ethics of what mattered most.

With rescue like that behind her, why shouldn't the Church, centered on the priest, have been the indestructible bedrock of her identity? The Church was the ground of her survival and of her strength, an experience she had in common with everyone she loved. In the way her faith underwrote her lifelong sense of self-worth, she was Irish to the bone. So, even in America, my mother's love for the ould sod was absolute, and I inherited it. And that's why this reckoning with the Church, and with myself, begins in Ireland. It was once unthinkable that I could ever feel relief that my mother is no longer alive. But then came the Ryan Report.

My historical and personal journey begins there, but—because of all that report betokened—it turns now on a question I cannot avoid: *What if the beating pulse of those first "great and simple images" of myself and of my life was a lie?*

PART ONE

✠

Ireland, Ireland

Ireland, Ireland! that cloud in the west,
that coming storm.

—William Gladstone, 1845

✠

CHAPTER 1

The Murder of a Soul

We showed no care for the little ones; we abandoned them.
— Pope Francis[1]

Ireland is ground zero for the Church's current moral implosion,[2] beginning a decade ago when, in 2009, the findings of an Irish government commission chaired by Judge Sean Ryan, called the Ryan Report, were released. The Catholic Church's sexual abuse scandal had been ignited in Boston some years before that, but in Ireland the calamity was even more catastrophic. By every measure, the Church in Ireland was in ruins by 2018, but that year Pope Francis arrived there for a major papal visitation as if everything were fine.

Even before *The Boston Globe* began publishing its predator priest stories in 2002—the Spotlight series that became the basis for a hit movie released in 2015—the government of Ireland had launched an investigation into rumors of child sexual abuse in the island nation's residential institutions for children, nearly all of which were run by the Catholic Church. The inquiry took most of a decade. Finally, in 2009, its results were revealed in the Ryan Commission's 2,600-page summary of conditions in more than

250 Church-run institutions. Despite a long-established tradition of government inspections and supervision, Catholic priests, brothers, and nuns had, across decades, violently tormented—tortured—thousands of children. The commission found that inmates of Catholic orphanages and reformatories were no better than slaves—and, in many cases, sex slaves. Rape and molestation of boys were "endemic."[3]

The Ryan Commission's findings were the first sign of a tsunami. Other reports were issued about other Irish institutions, including parish churches, schools, and homes for unwed mothers—the suddenly notorious "Magdalene laundries." In those institutions, girls and women were condemned to lives of coercive servitude.[4] The ignominy of the so-called Magdalene asylums was laid out in numerous documentary films and in *Philomena* (2013), the high-profile true-life movie starring Judi Dench. The scandal climaxed with the discovery in 2017 that between 1925 and 1961 at the Bon Secours Mother and Baby Home, in Tuam, county Galway, nearly eight hundred babies died, many of malnourishment and neglect. Their corpses were disposed of in mass graves and sewage pits. That revelation led to the establishment of yet another commission, which reported in 2019 that, in numerous institutions, the corpses of hundreds of babies had been routinely provided, into the 1970s, to medical schools for dissection. Many hundreds of other dead babies in the care of Church-run homes were simply unaccounted for. Not only priests had behaved despicably; so had nuns.[5]

Revelations of predator priests and complicit bishops had been rocking the Catholic world for years, but it was in Ireland that the swirling scandal now touched down, making that country the eye of the storm. Before, during, and after his arrival in the Emerald Isle for his 2018 visitation, Pope Francis expressed, as he put it, "shame and sorrow," but during his time there, in a series of public statements and private meetings, he showed no real sign of understanding the need for significant Church reform, not to mention authentic acts of penitence. There was a terrible pro forma quality to the pontiff's actions, as if the festering scandal had been reckoned with, becoming one more item on the Church's regular agenda.

Yet after Francis left Ireland, returning to Rome, the tempest of Catholic sexual abuse continued to shake the Church. In Germany, a leaked Catholic bishops' investigation revealed that in the years 1946 through 2014, 1,670 clergy had assaulted 3,677 children.[6] In the United States, a Pennsylvania grand jury found just then that, over the course of seventy years, more than a thousand children had been abused by more than three hundred priests, with Church authorities successfully silencing the victims, deflecting law enforcement, and shielding the predators.[7] The grand jury charges told of a ring of pedophile priests who commonly gave their young targets the gift of a gold cross to wear so that other predator priests could recognize an initiated child who would not resist an overture. "This is the murder of a soul," said one victim who offered testimony before the grand jury.[8]

While the pope traveled to Ireland and shortly thereafter, attorneys general in fifteen other American states announced the opening of investigations into Church crimes, with the U.S. Department of Justice following suit at the federal level. Soon, in several states, teams of law enforcement agents, with jackets emblazoned with the word POLICE and armed with search warrants, would burst into diocesan offices and seize records, as if they were raiding the dens of mobsters. This all amounted to an unprecedented campaign by civil authorities, who crossed previously sacrosanct boundaries of church-state separation to prosecute priestly abusers and enablers.[9]

Confronted with the mounting evidence of priestly transgressions everywhere, Francis finally issued, in the late fall of 2018, a meek call for a four-day meeting of senior bishops to be held in Rome the following February under the rubric "The Protection of Minors in the Church." To jaded Catholics, this seemed like putting Mafia chieftains in charge of a crime commission. Events would prove such skeptics to be right.

The complacency of the Catholic hierarchy seemed unshakable, even as horrible revelations of abuse continued to come in. Take the rape of nuns by priests and bishops, for example. Such a crime was once an unthinkable abomination: *Priests raping nuns? What could that be but the foulest slander put out there by an anti-Catholic bigot?*

But then, when Pope Francis did indeed acknowledge, in answer to a reporter's question in early 2019, that such heinous crimes do occur in the Church and remain a mostly unaddressed problem, he did so with maddening equilibrium—despite it being a global phenomenon. In Africa, as the AIDS epidemic had taken hold, priests had coerced nuns into becoming sexual servants because, as virgins, they would not be likely to carry the HIV virus.[10] It was reportedly common for such priests to sponsor abortions when the nuns became pregnant. Nuns had come forward in India to publicly charge priests with rape. "It's true," Francis said calmly in January of 2019. "There are priests and bishops who have done that."[11] The following April, a bishop was charged by Indian officials with rape and illegal confinement of a nun, whom he allegedly assaulted regularly over two years in the southern state of Kerala. The bishop denied the charge. The nun said she reported the bishop to the police only after having appealed to Church authorities repeatedly—and being ignored.[12]

In February, a *Washington Post* report suggested that beginning early in his pontificate, Francis knew about the systematic priestly abuse of institutionalized deaf children in Argentina that had occurred when he lived there. The pope apparently had cooperated in keeping the horror secret. Following the long-established pattern, the abuse had been finally brought to light not by Church officials, but by civil authorities and the secular press. Deaf victims reported that they were discouraged from learning sign language in their Catholic institution. A hand sign they came to know, however, was the one often used by the abusive priests—the forefinger to the lips: *Silencio!*[13] That silence had belonged to Pope Francis, too.

Meanwhile, that same February, Cardinal Theodore McCarrick, a former archbishop of Washington and one of the Church's most powerful prelates, having been exposed by press reports, was finally found guilty by a Vatican tribunal of abusing a minor. He was being punished, the Vatican announced, by being stripped of his clerical standing.[14]

This "reduction to the lay state" was described as a priest's equivalent of the death penalty, but the supposedly humiliating punishment actually amounted to McCarrick's being forced to assume the status of every other non-ordained person on the planet—a subtle revelation of the clerical caste's disrespect for the laity. That manifestation is essential to the corruption of clericalism, which I was being forced, through all of this, to confront in full.

McCarrick was shown to have been a harasser of young men and boys, and his homosexuality sparked a broad scapegoating of gays as the source of Church dysfunction. A sensational book claimed that a cabal of gay priests and bishops dominated the Vatican itself.[15] Still, in that same February of 2019, gay priests from the Netherlands openly objected to being blamed for the sexual abuse scandal, while on the front page of *The Washington Post*, beleaguered gay priests in America described themselves as living not in a closet but in a cage.[16] Gay priests are imprisoned, they explained, by the very dysfunction they are expected to uphold.

The shameful revelations would not stop. The Vatican just then acknowledged that it had long-established secret protocols for handling "children of the ordained." According to this policy, a priest who violated his vow of celibacy and fathered a child was encouraged to resign from the priesthood to "assume his responsibility as a parent," but he was in no way required to do so. A Vatican expert explained that a priest's fathering of a child was "not a canonical crime." Estimates put the contemporary number of priests' children in the thousands.[17]

As fresh torrents of the priestly sexual abuse crisis cascaded in these ways, Pope Francis clung to the idea that his upcoming "Protection of Minors" meeting was all the response that was needed. The four-day gathering of senior bishops was held in Rome that February. A signal of what to expect had come on its eve from Francis himself, who in his opening remarks turned his outrage not on predator priests, but on those he called "accusers," the people who were bringing these charges against the Church. He said, "Those who spend their lives accusing, accusing, and accusing are . . . the friends, cousins, and relatives of the devil." Francis had repeatedly referred to the devil as "the great accuser," but his spray-shot diatribe seemed aimed as much at victims seeking justice as at his own right-wing critics, who had clearly gotten to him.[18]

As the Rome meeting unfolded, the bishops dutifully employed watchwords like "transparency" and "repentance," yet they seemed to be establishing no new structures of prevention and accountability. Nor did the meeting force a reckoning in regions where Church denial and obfuscation still rule, enabling criminal behavior to flourish. This is especially true in the Global South, including Brazil, India, and Africa, but it also includes Italy itself, the seat of Roman Catholicism, where abusive priests and enabling bishops still mostly go unchallenged.

Then, in his concluding remarks to the bishops gathered in Rome, Pope Francis called the abusers of children "tools of Satan," a denigration that seemed to be undercut by his having just called "accusers," including some of those self-same victims, "cousins" of the devil. To his credit, Francis called for "an all-out battle" against priestly abuse and said the Church must protect children "from ravenous wolves"—an apt description. But he said nothing about what breeds such wolves or who sets them loose. Worse, he deflected the particular Catholic horror by emphasizing that child abuse and sexual malfeasance happen everywhere, as if to say the crimes of Catholic clergy are not so bad.[19]

The formal results of the prelates' meeting would be slow in coming, but already it seemed clear that what had been promoted as a world-historic reckoning by reform-ready Church leaders had completely failed to tackle the deep-seated sources of this massive Catholic malpractice—and had failed even to ask what those sources might be. It was one thing for grotesque betrayals to be manifest, and quite another for the radical inability—or simple unwillingness—of the institution to correct itself to be so powerfully exposed.

Coming like a punctuation mark, on the day after the Vatican gathering adjourned, was the full report from Australia of Cardinal George Pell's earlier conviction by the criminal court in Melbourne. Formerly the head of Vatican finances and one of Francis's closest advisors, Pell had been found guilty of sexually violating two altar boys in a sacristy—a crime alleged to have been committed right after he presided at the Eucharist.[20] In 2020, Australia's highest court would overturn Pell's conviction on the grounds that his guilt had not been proven beyond a reasonable doubt,[21] but accusations against Pell had drawn attention to the cases of more than one hundred other Catholic prelates who were accused of sexual misconduct.[22]

Within days of the adjournment of the "Protection of Minors" meeting, an unprecedented Vatican edict finally made it mandatory for bishops to report allegations of abuse, but the promulgation applied only to officials of Vatican City and its diplomats—not to the broader Church—and the reporting was not to be made to civil authorities but to other Vatican officials.[23] That deflection from the pope's own civic jurisdiction, coming on the heels of all the other ecclesiastical bobbing and weaving, was a forecast, in fact, of the formal worldwide policy that was then officially rolled out as the much-touted result of the "Protection" convocation.

Claiming to be an unprecedented "milestone" response to the abuse crisis, the new promulgation, titled "Vos Estis Lux Mundi" (You Are the Light of the World) and finally issued in May of 2019, was shot through with the same old Church evasions.[24] It once again required bishops to report allegations of sex crimes to other bishops and not to civil authorities;[25] it mandated no penalties for offenses; it required no public transparency; it established no lay participation in the process. Yes, it amounted to the age-old system of Mafia chieftains supervising Mafia chieftains.[26]

That definitive failure to establish a serious process of Church accountability under the much-admired Pope Francis might have seemed like the apogee of Catholic catastrophe, but then, only weeks later, Notre-Dame de Paris caught fire, and the world added to the insult of that conflagration by immediately turning it into a metaphor of the Catholic Church's own condition.[27]

WHICH BRINGS US back to Ireland. One of the astonishments of the pope's visit there was his claim, made to reporters as he returned to Rome, that until that trip he knew nothing of the Irish

Magdalene laundries or their scandals: "I had never heard of these mothers, they call it the laundromat of women where an unwed woman is pregnant and goes into these hospitals," he said. "I don't know what they call them."[28]

Never heard of these mothers? When I read that, I said to myself, *A lie. Pope Francis is lying.* In fact, he may not have been lying—he may merely have been ignorant. But this was one of the twentieth century's worst instances of Catholic transgressions. To be uninformed about the long-simmering Magdalene scandal was as bad as lying, a display of denial and evasion laying bare the true shame—and the true sorrow.

In the broader context of monstrous priestly predation, the pope's ignorant statement should count for little. Why expect him to know everything? And why not cling to the positive significance of his papacy, which stands against so many of the dark currents threatening the world? I have no good answer to those questions. All I know is that at that particular papal disclaimer, a taut wire in me snapped. Pope Francis's Magdalene denial did it, and in an instant my core belief was called into question and my entire life changed.[29]

CHAPTER 2

✠

Taut Wire

Critical Mass: in nuclear physics, the point at which
a self-sustaining chain reaction is achieved,
triggering an explosion

The taut wire within myself had begun to stretch a quarter of a century earlier. At that point, I had long left the priesthood and was just starting out as a *Boston Globe* op-ed columnist, a role I subsequently played for almost twenty-five years. Twenty years before that, while still a priest, I had been preoccupied with war, social justice, and religious reform—questions that went on to define my work for the *Globe*.

One of my first columns, published in September of 1992, was a horrified reflection on the child sexual abuse crimes of a Massachusetts priest named James Porter.[1] I argued that Porter's predation had been enabled by the Church's broader culture of priest-protecting silence. Earlier that year, responding to the *Globe*'s stories about Porter, an infuriated Cardinal Bernard Law, archbishop of Boston, had hurled an anathema that seemed to come from the Middle Ages: "We call down God's power on the media," he said, "particularly the *Globe*."[2] It would take a decade, but the one God's power would come down on was Law himself.

In tandem with the *Globe*'s famous Spotlight series and other stories thereafter, my columns on sexual abuse by priests ran on the op-ed page. Among the titles were "Priests' Victims Victimized Twice" and "Meltdown in the Catholic Church."[3] By the summer of 2018—the wire-snapping summer for me—I harbored no illusions about the Church's grotesque betrayal, even as a still practicing Catholic. It took some doing to bring me to the breaking point that prompted this book. Pope Francis—whom in so many ways I admire, and in whom I had placed an almost desperate hope—is the unlikely person who made the wire snap.

When I say snap, I mean snap. For the first time in my life, and without making a conscious decision, I simply stopped going to Mass. I embarked on an unwilled version of the old Catholic tradition of "fast and abstinence"—in this case, fasting from the Eucharist and abstaining from the overt practice of my faith. I have not been to Mass since then.

Advent, Christmas, Ash Wednesday, Lent, Holy Week, Easter—without these liturgical milestones, I have been adrift in time, unable to shake a profound sadness. What I feel is akin to depression, but I know just what's missing in my life. The cool of the air inside the parish church, the gliding surface of the pew, the velvet pressure of the kneeler at Communion time, the clenched fingers, the bowed head at rest on my forearm—without these sensations I have felt, in some ways, lost in space. Willfully unchurched, I am aware that some may share this response of mine; others might think, *Who cares?* or *About time!* But for me the moment—the snap—is a life marker. Even having reached this point, I still carry an ocean of grief in my heart. When the Covid-19 pandemic struck in 2020, the social-distancing lockdown obliterated the communion of Church rituals for legions, and the heartbreak took on a global aspect. But for me its crippling power was primordial, and its solitary anguish remains.

Out of desolation, after that snap, I had to ask myself: *Who am I if I am not largely defined by Catholic belief and practice?* And, more problematically: *How did I come to believe in the first place—to believe what I now see as the lie at the heart of the religious institution's hierarchy? How did that lie shape me? How does that lie stamp me still? And is there, despite everything, a truth at the heart of the lie?*

To WRITE IS to learn what I think, and that, in part, motivates me here. What do I make of my life, now that I am growing old, and what, in fact, do I think of the Catholic Church after all? How does the horror of such betrayal by priests and bishops involve the larger population of the Catholic people?

I think of everyone who has been appalled and disheartened by the clergy scandal, a multitude far exceeding Church membership. That the stakes are high for our broad culture in the contemporary collapse of Catholic meaning and morality was shown by the way Francis himself, early in his pontificate, so compellingly emerged as a figure of global hope, including for non-Catholics of many stripes, caught as we all are in an age that often seems unmoored.

For me the stakes are higher still. I need to understand who I am. How did I come to this place of profound personal dislocation and disenchantment? In the thick of advanced age, I am existentially adrift for the first time in my life. How? Why?

To answer those questions, I first had to go back in time, into memory, tracking through a story of one man's faith as I have lived it. Having seen what the Catholic priesthood has become, I feel the shock, also, of what it has in some way been all along. I had to ask myself how I could have embraced the priesthood myself—an act that came from the very heart of my youth, and one that, though I left the priesthood a mere five years after being ordained, turns out to define me still. If the priesthood is carried along in heretofore unseen currents of malice, where have those currents taken me? What disorder, in my own self and life, has been unseen until now?

I do not know where the exploration sparked by such questions will ultimately lead. But I do know that it began with Francis, and it began with Ireland—the wire that snapped when he went there, the lie or denial he voiced. The pope's apparent detachment from the depth of Church-caused Irish suffering, capped by his disclaimer of any knowledge about the crimes of the Irish Catholic sisters—"the laundromat of women"—brought me to this starting place. The extraordinary Pope Francis—precisely because he is extraordinary—was the instigator of my crisis, and Ireland was its incubator.

ACROSS THE TWENTY-FIRST century's first two decades, the people of Ireland responded to what was being laid bare about the Church—the lechery of priests, the sadism of nuns, the deceit of bishops—with a mass exodus from their religion. The count of those attending Mass weekly dropped by two-thirds, leaving mainly gray heads in the pews. The number of men presenting themselves for the priesthood each year dropped from many dozens to a literal handful. Large majorities of Irish voters, in 2015 and 2018, swatted aside the pronouncements of the Irish hierarchy to approve the legalization of gay marriage and abortion.[4] In 2017, the Irish elected an openly gay man as their prime minister.[5]

Ireland's ardent Catholicism had not been merely a matter of faith. After the sixteenth-century Reformation and its brutal wars of religion, spiritual domination by the pope in Rome offered a counter-colonialism with which to reject the violent dominion of

the English Protestants, and Catholicism became the island nation's boiling wellspring of resistance, its fiercest source of identity.
But Catholicism was also Ireland's tenderest source of consolation, which was never more valued than during the decades-long
nineteenth-century famine when the potato crop failed—the
event that drove my mother's father to America.[6] Among the Irish
who stayed behind, their priests and nuns—teaching, encourag-
ing, burying, blessing—were inexpressibly beloved. So why
shouldn't words fall short of the anguish caused by their betrayal
in schools, sacristies, orphanages, and workhouses? And why
shouldn't the Emerald Isle have become, with the Ryan Report
and the other revelations that followed, the quintessential vale of
tears?

When Pope Francis at last visited Ireland in 2018, less than half
as many Irish people showed up to greet him as had greeted Pope
John Paul II four decades before, in 1979. And no wonder. The
confirmable number of priest abuse victims in Ireland, across two
generations, is reliably put at about 18,500, a figure that is certainly low. But that figure matches almost exactly the counted
number of victims in the United States, which is also certainly
low.[7] Those numbers suggest a density of abuse in Ireland—where
the number of Catholics is less than one-fifth of the number in the
States—that is universally traumatizing. The odds are overwhelm-
ing that everyone in Ireland is personally connected to a victim of
a priest. And Pope Francis, arriving there, had to know it.

Yet, with his every word of attempted consolation having rung
hollow, he left the shattered nation more mired in hurt than ever.
And why shouldn't the anti-clerical bitterness of the Irish have become as militant as their devotion had once been? A Benedictine
abbot, one of the leading figures of Irish Catholicism, showed that
a taut wire had snapped in him, too. Mark Patrick Hederman,
abbot of Glenstal Abbey in county Limerick, in reflecting on the

thousands of victims and the nihilism of those who should have been their protectors, used the most extreme image imaginable to deride his Church for, as he put it, turning "this island into a concentration camp."[8] Razor wire squeezes the Irish soul.

And I felt it. I was never more Irish than when I felt, with the whole beleaguered nation, the crushing disappointment of the tepid responses of Pope Francis. It left me with this personal mission: to dig deep into myself, and into the history of the Church — its embrace of power, the sources of its clericalism. Most of all, I had to search my past and my memories to ask how the innocent boy I was grew into the restless believer I became and the heartbroken man I now am.

PART TWO

✠

What Child Was This?

But consolation from imaginary things
is not an imaginary consolation. On the
contrary, it is the only real consolation
that modern people have.

—Roger Scruton, 2004[1]

✦

CHAPTER 3

Near the House

How precious did that grace appear
The hour I first believed.
— "Amazing Grace"

Amazing grace: I remember the hour I first believed. It happened in 1950 or so, in a vivid, well-lit classroom—tiny wooden chairs right-sized for children; a crucifix on the front wall; the blackboards trimmed with eraser ledges below and penmanship posters above; windows so large it took a pole to open them. Sister Rita Elaine cruised through the classroom, placing a holy card on each of our desks. It displayed a gauzy portrait of a woman in blue, arms outstretched, floating on clouds, wearing a crown of stars—Our Lady, Queen of Heaven.

Sister explained that Our Lady had a name and that her name was Mary.

That news landed with an unprecedented jolt, because Mary was my own mother's name, though she was only ever Mom to me. The Queen of Heaven was Mary!

Around that same time, I learned that Mary, during her time on earth, had a husband—a kindly carpenter whom we were carefully instructed to think of as the stepfather of Jesus, not the father.

The second jolt came when I was told that Mary's husband was named Joseph. Holy cow! Joseph was my dad's name! Joseph and Mary! Jesus and me! Amazing grace indeed!

So, starting when I was learning to print letters, I began to think that Jesus, the son of Mary and Joseph, was a kind of brother to me, since I was the son of Mary and Joseph, too. After that, I began to take in—really to hear—what passed in my mother's censored argot for a curse: "Jesus, Mary, and Joseph!" She would exclaim the phrase when she couldn't find the keys or when the toilet overflowed, and so it should have had a negative weight, but it was always a lyric of uplift to me. With my stub of a pencil, tongue through my lips, I carefully formed the letters "JMJ," as Sister instructed, at the top right corner of every page of practice penmanship. Jesus, Mary, and Joseph were a family to which I belonged. How simple it seemed. Those three initials are not at the top of this page, but the blankness of that upper right-hand corner, as much as anything, defines where I came from and what is now missing in my life.

I think not just of my mother, but of the cosmos she embodied, the safe haven into which she ushered me at the start. To recall the golden aura of my mother's love, and by extension the glow that clung to the Irish Catholic parish of my youth, is to establish a measure by which to grasp the depth of what I experienced as betrayal by our clergy.

Our parish—St. Mary's in Alexandria, Virginia—had its school, bazaars, picnics, Holy Name Society for the men, Sodality and altar guild for the women, and CYO ball games for the kids. The parish priests, often Irish-born themselves, were chain-smoking and hard-drinking, but they nevertheless stood as trustworthy images of intellect, erudition, holiness, and, with some exceptions, affability. And, of course, as with Sister Rita Elaine, the parish had its nuns, who taught penmanship, oversaw the playground, and embodied the virtue of freely chosen selflessness. Above all, the parish had Our Lord and His mother—both figures simultaneously of transcendence and of intimacy.

The parish church located us Irish Americans in space—not only in a country we were otherwise unsure of, but in the universe itself. On our knees before the tabernacle—the gold treasure chest that held the sacred Host—or the bank of blue votive lights arrayed at Mary's feet, we knew exactly where we were and where we belonged. At the grand moments of deep significance—birth, death, illness, marriage, passage into adulthood—as well as the more mundane yet pointed moments of failure and success, the parish, through its simple sacraments administered by its priest, assured us that we were not alone. The taste of an unleavened wafer; the sound of a warbling soloist; the aromas of candle wax, stale incense, and altar wine; the male odor of a priest's cassock; the scent of soap on Sister; the feel of a tattered bingo card—it all meant home to the Irish in America. Indeed, as I would learn years later, the word "parish" itself comes from the Greek words meaning "near the house."

But in addition to space, the parish located us in time, providing a felt sense of history that extended back beyond the rough immigrant arrival on the shores of the New World; beyond the dread old-country colonial past, the Irish Famine and the Protestant Reformation—all the way back to the glories of Catholic triumph: the Gothic cathedral, five proofs of God's existence, illuminated Scriptures, tapestries and Gregorian chant. Such treasures seemed to belong even to laborers and housemaids, to us common people kneeling together in church.

Not only did the past belong to us, but so did the future, which could seem trustworthy because, however undefined, its promise of "beatitude" was already being kept in the "beauty" of parish life. For all of this, we Irish American Catholics could be scorned or ignored by people outside the boundaries of the precious turf, but we could take such Protestant condescension as a sign of veiled envy. After all, what our parish and its priest most proudly and loudly proclaimed was that there was *No Salvation Outside the Catholic Church.*

Oddly, the effect of that negative exclusion—since as a young child I knew no one to whom it applied—was only positive. It reinforced the coziness of our circumscribed world, its trustworthiness.

As I would much later understand about St. Mary's School, it wasn't called parochial for nothing.

✢

A Close Presence, My Spirit Twin

But who is that on the other side of you?
—T. S. Eliot, "The Waste Land"

I thought of Jesus as a brother when I was six, a connection prepared for by feelings I had for my own brother Joe. He was two
years older and as close to me as the bottom bunk was to my bunk
on top. The bond Joe and I shared—an unbreakable primordial
interdependence taken utterly for granted, an absolute mutuality,
radical trust, pals forever—was how I began to feel, cryptically,
about that carpenter's son from Nazareth. But not even my tie to
Joe equated to what I came to feel for Jesus.

Jesus was a boy, and then a man, with whom to identify as
readily as one does with the face in the mirror. I would later learn
that mountain climbers and solo sailors and long-distance run-
ners sometimes experience what's called a feeling of a close presence, an awareness of someone else unheard, unseen, but there!
In the normal circumstances of an unremarkable childhood, I
had some early version of that sensation of Jesus as my invisible
companion—my, if you will, imaginary friend.

Every connotation of His name, in the milieu of midcentury Irish Catholicism, made this intimacy seem a treasure of absolute value. Jesus was my Spirit Twin.

When I described the sensation to Joe, he shrugged and said he had no idea what I was talking about. Instead of disappointment at that, I felt relief, since Joe's indifference meant I'd been singled out; singled out in a way that my brother had no reason to envy. Joe had been left lame by polio and would continue to be ravaged by the disease through our growing-up years. So my every advantage over him was edged with guilt—unless it was an advantage he did not want. Joe did not want my new friend. I'd stumbled onto a double-edged solace.

My faith, from the very start, involved a feeling of being chosen, but with a complication. I now believe this deserves emphasis. Unknown to me back then, that bright light of election, of feeling chosen, cast a shadow. However universal the longing for some such sensation of being singled out—does it not undergird the magic of romantic love?—there is a dark seed in this impulse. In society, it can be an excessive yearning for status, giving rise to structures of discrimination, with the chosen ones licensed to leave all those others behind. Aristocracy is an obvious instance of this impulse, but even the so-called meritocracy, lately put forward as the more democratic alternative, breeds an equally elitist caste system, one that regards itself as deserving of its privilege—status that is not inherited but earned. Status squared. This ranking is false, of course—especially when, as so often, it stands on assumptions of white supremacy.

In the Church, which remembers Jesus himself as saying "Many are called, but few are chosen,"[1] such anointing is typically claimed for the clerical elite—an essential aspect of clericalism.

The ordained hierarchy often forgets that Jesus said this at the end of a parable about the heavenly king preferring the nobodies on the street to the rich and powerful—a repudiation of status. Yet the idea of "being called" is central to the priesthood; indeed the word "vocation" is used as a synonym for it, so being singled out as special goes right to the heart of the priest's identity. But does that make him better than everybody else? In reckoning with clericalism and its deficits, I have seen again and again how this very human impulse has gone wrong once it has taken root in the soil of the Church's male-dominated cloister of inequality.

But recognizing that primal sense of being chosen in my childhood does not mean I was merely passive in this, which suggests perhaps that instead of designating Jesus as my "imaginary" friend, I should say He became my "imagined" friend—a verb, not an adjective. If the active voice describes a sentence where the subject performs the action stated by the verb, I was the acting subject. I see now that I had a choice in Jesus's being intimately present to me, and I made that choice. Invited to do so by an inspiration I cannot identify—tied, perhaps, to a wish for distance from my brother's impairment and for a special connection to our devout mother—I imagined Jesus at my side.

And there He was, and there He would stay.

BECAUSE I EXERCISED a certain agency in this awareness, my Imagined Friend, unlike the "imaginary" friends of other children, would steadfastly remain beside me as that close presence, preparing me to answer what I eventually took to be His call, which in turn, almost despite myself, ultimately made me a Catholic priest.

And it is why, I suppose, the essence of my crisis of faith today, long after I left the priesthood but not the Church, boils down to a feeling of connection with all those victims of priests—of being tossed aside, the opposite of being chosen. What remains of a con-

nection to Jesus once the connection to the encumbered apparatus of the Church is broken? That is one question for this old man.

But what of myself as a child? Back then, I went right on having that sense of Jesus's nearness even when I began, on cue, to
think of the young Galilean man—my friend—as the actual Son
of the Almighty and Omniscient God. So that was why the role of
Joseph—St. Joseph—was limited to stepfather!

These things, which might have seemed outlandish to another
little boy, simply fell into place for me. I was told it, and I accepted
it—until I finally understood that Jesus was not just the Son of
God, but God Himself!

But Jesus, son of Mary, somehow remained my brother. My
heart had opened to Jesus, and Jesus made His home within my
heart's chambers.

I would continue to feel some such innermost attachment to
Jesus as I came of age and childish notions of "God" began to fall
away. Once I started to entertain ambitions for my own life, Jesus
emerged freshly as an image of the man I dared to want to imitate:
love over power; mercy over condemnation; compassion itself.
Jesus remained a still point of my faith, even when it wavered, for
Jesus, too, could be thought of as doubting and as lost. Jesus got in
trouble. There was a presence of God with whom I could identify,
since I got in trouble, too.

Later, when I was a priest and war came to define my preoc-
cupations, I discovered Jesus, the Prince of Peace. As social justice
made its demand, the prophetic Jesus was there ahead of me.
When the prospect of an apocalyptic end of history unsettled my
young adulthood, I found Jesus claiming authority over the absolute future. When pleasure began to attract more than penitence,
there was Jesus at the banquet table, lifting a cup of wine, declaring "L'Chaim!" Whatever the language of divinity came to refer
to, I continued to understand that backwater Jewish nobody as the

embodiment—yes, the Incarnation—of what mattered most about the Holy One, however defined. And what mattered most was a love that saved you.

THAT I BECAME a Catholic priest in 1969 is one story, but another unfolded as the crush of war and protest took me out of the priesthood in 1974. Beginning then, a feeling of close intimacy with Jesus should have been impossible, since ex-priests in that era were ipso facto banished from the easy fellowship of the Jesus people, the Church. Yet, banished though I was, my connection to Jesus held. The Catholic Church had introduced me to Him, but the institution had little to do with what sustained that bond—or so I thought. I was not precisely a believing Catholic (no infallible Roman pontiff for me!), but I was a practicing Catholic, living the faith by what I did more than by which rules or dogmas I held to.

What I did, as an ex-priest, was present myself for Communion, without worrying what those around me made of my stubborn presence at Mass. As far as I was concerned, we were all alike in our hidden personal complications when we approached the rail.

The deepest secret of the monastery had stamped itself upon me. Jesus was the "great and simple image" in whose presence my heart first really opened. He was my brother, my dear companion, my second self—my, yes, Spirit Twin.

As I grew older and questions naturally unsettled the assumptions of childhood and young adulthood, still Jesus was there, a permanent presence of what had drawn me: justice and peace, certainly, but the wrenchingly personal, too. When failure imposed itself as an iron law of life, including mine, Jesus was there. When the ultimate forsakenness of death showed itself to me—my father's death, and my mother's soon after; the infant daughter my wife and I lost in 1986—Jesus was there.

And how? Not through doctrines that seemed more and more obtuse; nor in the once magisterial authority of a discredited hierarchy; nor even in the embellishments of ordinary faith—those cloistered arcades, rosaries, holy cards, votive candles, novenas, confessionals. No, Jesus was there in the "great and simple image" of the Mass—where we and millions met and were fed.

Across the nearly half century since leaving the priesthood, I went to Mass week in and week out. I was always conscious of my status in the Church as one sent to stand in the corner, but that spurning only made my place at the Communion rail more precious to me. That even I, an ex-priest who'd broken his vows, could be there defined Christ's great unconditionality. Jesus did not care what my clerical status had been, or what, actually, made up the doctrinal content of my belief. He was the close presence beside me on my long-distance run, my trek up the frozen mountain, my solo sail across the ocean of life. The close presence was the Real Presence. And the people on their knees beside me made it plain that I was not so solo after all.

What I did not sufficiently comprehend across the years was that this barely surviving connection to what had braced my imagination from childhood forward depended absolutely on the figure of the Catholic priest.

Without the priest, there is no Mass.

Long after "the Church," referring to the Vatican and its global minions in chanceries and diocesan offices, had ceased drawing my loyalty, I depended still on the Church's order of ministry—its Holy Orders, its clericalism. In some strange way, my having been a priest prepared me to take utterly for granted the enabling function of the man at the altar.

Though as a priest myself I had never comfortably claimed the exalted status of being an alter Christus, "another Christ," as a layman that is precisely what the priest, the celebrant of the Mass, had become to me. Having embraced the secular thinking that made the idea of "God" elusive, I still found that the rooting symbol of the ordained priest, the liturgist, remained constant and wonderfully available wherever I found myself on Sunday. Rural parishes, big-city cathedrals, school chapels, my own neighborhood church—these places were always there, and so was I. And so was Father What's-his-name. My felt connection to Jesus as more than a biblical abstraction or mythical hero of social justice depended on the ordained man—always a man—who bent over the bread and wine and repeated the words of the Consecration. Again and again, I presented myself to a priest, receiving Communion as a way of touching—and being touched by—the core of what mattered most to me: my Imagined Friend, my Spirit Twin. Because of the priest, I could draw close to Jesus, full of trust.

But now?

CHAPTER 5

✝

Disabused

And immediately something like scales fell from
his eyes, and he regained his sight.
—Acts 9:18

The verse refers to the conversion to Christianity of St. Paul,[1] but the fallen scales in my case prompted a very different vision, the story I am telling here. The recognition that snapped open in me, in connection with the pope's visit to Ireland in 2018, forced a deeper confrontation with the real meaning of what I'd somehow suspected or known all along: that again and again, the clerical system had been grotesquely betraying us. Its own essential corruption had been laid bare. Because of revelations driven by the secular press and civil authorities—never by the men in robes—the Catholic priest had emerged as suspect, and often as an avatar of sexual abuse, with the preferred victim a child.

The sexual abuse of children is an ancient and pervasive crime, one that is committed wherever adults have power over the young. Schoolteachers, scoutmasters, other clergy, family members, even fathers and mothers are known to physically exploit their vulnerable charges. The home can be the cockpit of abuse. Defenders of the clerical status quo insist on this broader context, as if predation in the sacristy is no big deal. Alas, as I noted earlier, Pope Francis himself displayed this impulse to relativize the priestly crime.[2]

But the exploitation of children by Catholic priests stands apart—in its worldwide range, in the enabling complicity of Church authorities, and in its deeper meaning as sacrilege—because of how God is so often invoked to seduce and coerce victims. The crime of sexual exploitation, especially of children, has shown itself to be endemic to the priesthood. Throughout my youth and middle age—throughout my own time as a priest and after—I did not see it. Then, slowly but surely, the full weight of this dark truth imposed itself, beginning, as I said, in the early 1990s, but coming to a demonic and doubly shocking climax in 2018 and 2019, under Francis, the pope who'd renewed our faith.[3]

It was when Francis repeatedly failed in his response to the unchecked current of accusation and revelation—not just regarding priests as predators, but especially with bishops as enablers, and with bishops and cardinals as predators, too—that I was forced to undertake a deeper and more comprehensive reckoning.

I had been one of the Argentinian pope's staunchest defenders in his campaign to change the Church.[4] I'd saluted him for "Laudato Si'," his historic encyclical calling for urgent action on climate change.[5] I'd celebrated him as the champion of migrants, and as the archetypal antagonist of Donald Trump and this era's other neofascists.[6] And then, during the Covid-19 outbreak in 2020, Pope Francis emerged even more as a global figure of empathy and justice. But Francis has a tragic blind spot—the corruption of clericalism—and finally I have to admit, regarding his complicity, that his blind spot had long been my own.

POPE FRANCIS ROUTINELY expresses his "shame and sorrow," but he instinctively defends the accused;[7] he denounces the clerical culture in which abuse has found its hospitable niche,[8] but he does nothing to dismantle it.[9] Indeed, in his instinctive protective responses to the corruption of clericalism, he embodies that culture, even while seeming to criticize it.

That the papal predecessors of Pope Francis behaved in this way seemed unsurprising: Pope Benedict XVI, acting as a Vatican official before his elevation to the papacy (he served as pope from 2005 to 2013), forbade bishops in 2001 ever to refer cases of predacious priests to civil authorities, binding them under what he called the "pontifical secret."[10]

The revelation was that an otherwise revolutionary figure like Pope Francis displayed in himself the indestructibility of this abusive clericalism. The magnificent Francis revealed the depth of the silence, the denial, the rot. For years, I'd refused to give up my faith even in light of the corruption of the institutional Church. But Vatican bureaucrats and self-serving inquisitors were not the issue now. The priests were.

THAT HUNDREDS OF priests abused thousands of children in the proudly Catholic city of Boston was thought, in the beginning, to be a purely local problem, born, say, of a neurotic Boston Irish insecurity in response to condescending Boston Brahmins. But neurosis was too benign a diagnosis for this pathology, and cued by *The Boston Globe* Spotlight investigations, the press began to uncover it across the entire United States. Within a few years, sexual abuse lawsuits and their mostly secret financial settlements have cost the Church more than $3 billion and sent one of every ten U.S. Catholic dioceses into bankruptcy.[11]

In Europe, meanwhile, the scandal was at first derided as a peculiarly American decadence, but that perception did not last. Soon enough, a worldwide Catholic debauchery was exposed, with many thousands of priests all over the globe found to have abused tens of thousands of minors and with the episcopate universally protecting the predators instead of the young people. From the Americas to Africa; from Europe to New Zealand; from Australia to the Philippines, Guam, and India—wherever there were Catholic priests, there were children being preyed upon and tossed aside.[12]

Church authorities in the Global South may still be mostly in denial, as noted, but even in the North they have responded, as in their February 2019 Vatican gathering, with pro forma bromides of regret and little else. That is why the bishops have been preempted as investigators by lawyers and grand juries, as in Philadelphia. Here is the most important point: But for crusading journalists and intervening lawyers, the sexual abuse of children by Catholic priests would still be hidden—and rampant.

When Jorge Mario Bergoglio was elected pope in 2013, taking the implication-laden name of the thirteenth-century St. Francis of Assisi, it seemed certain that he would lead the Church out of this morass, but the mire has only thickened. If "a fox knows many things," as the ancient Greeks had it, "but a hedgehog knows one important thing,"[13] Francis was the hedgehog whose one important thing was mercy. At the beginning of his pontificate, that seemed the perfect antidote to the cruelty of the way his predecessors had deflected priestly crimes. But such omnidirectional mercy proved inadequate for what confronted the Church, since predator priests merited, first, not mercy but judgment—and a child-protecting banishment, if not imprisonment.

Across several years, and through multiple moments of truth, Francis proved to be powerless to deal with the ignominy, much less with its deep causes. He may denounce the culture of clericalism, calling it "our ugliest perversion,"[14] but what, actually, does he mean? He has stoutly protected the twin pillars of Catholic clericalism: the Church's misogynist exclusion of women from the priesthood, a subject that he calls a "closed door";[15] and the Church's almost universal requirement of celibacy for priests. When, in 2020, bishops from the Amazon region of South America formally asked Francis to address a desperate priest shortage by allowing the exceptional ordination of married deacons to the priesthood, he ignored the request. No.[16] He had earlier said he would rather die than change the celibacy requirement for priests. He meant it.[17]

Equality for women as officeholders in the Church has been resisted precisely because it could bring with it a broad transformation of the entire Catholic ethos, especially as it applies to sex—what the writer Garry Wills has called the Church's "general sex-craziness."[18] That would mean yes to female sexual autonomy; yes to love and pleasure, not just reproduction, as a purpose of sex; yes to contraception; and a fresh consideration of the whole range of questions reshaping the ethics of human reproduction, from stem cell research to artificial insemination to genetic engineering. Such a recasting of Catholic sexual obsessions would bring other transformations, too: no to the automatic association of sexuality with sin; no to male dominance; no, ultimately, to the sovereign authority of clerics.

The debasement of Catholic morality when it comes to women, power, and sex is perfectly captured in the fact that the Church's canon law provides for the ex post facto excommunication of a woman who attempts to say Mass. There is no such penalty for a pedophile priest. On the contrary, canon law is rife with due process protections of an accused cleric, and nothing prevents even those found guilty from being returned to the ministry. A woman at the altar, by contrast, is automatically cast out of the Church.

It is deeply ironic that the dilemma facing Pope Francis, while caused in part by his own clerical myopia, has been made exponentially more pressing by his conservative opponents' weaponizing of Church confusion about homosexuality. The alarm signal of danger that Francis sent to conservatives was his early refusal to condemn homosexuals when he posed his famous question "Who am I to judge?"[19] In response, the pope's critics among his fellow prelates engaged in intrigue, rumormongering, leaks, and open defiance—an urgent attempt to roll back the change Francis seemed to represent. If the pope wouldn't condemn homosexuality, what would he condemn? And if the pope was renouncing the moral superiority of one empowered to officiate, criticize, and pronounce, where would that leave the other prelates, whose sway depended precisely on their authority to issue rules and enforce them? Soon enough, the pope's critics in the hierarchy were blaming him for "the plague of the homosexual agenda" in the Church.[20] If Francis was prepared to tolerate gay priests, they insinuated, he could be tarred with tolerating the rape of children.

That Catholic conservatives so pounced on a murky conflation of homosexuality and pedophilia threw Pope Francis further on the defensive about both—perhaps prompting him even to reverse himself on homosexuality and begin to denigrate the very gays he had at first defended.[21] Such conservative pushback seemed to succeed in scapegoating gays for a broad Catholic dysfunction—a tragic setback for civil society, where the affirmation of gay rights has been a signal achievement.

Francis is at the mercy of an incoherent Catholic morality about all kinds of sexual expression, and he seems incapable of bringing the needed moral clarity and essential new structure of accountability. That incoherence in ethics and morality is itself essential to the malignant culture of clericalism that imprisons many, including the pope.

. . .

ONCE UPON A time in the history of the Church, the selling of indulgences sparked a vast reformation of the Christian religion,[22] yet what was that corruption compared with the systematic rape of children everywhere? When even Pope Francis joined his fellow prelates in responding to this crisis with business-as-usual platitudes and a pro forma meeting of the crimson-robed men in Rome in 2019, the true dimension of the crisis was made clear at last. Ethically speaking, the Catholic Church has collapsed into an ocean of ruin. If concrete blocks had been chained to our limbs, we Catholics could not have been plunged more efficiently to the bottom of a moral abyss.

For Catholics, the priest is the living sacrament of Christ's presence in the world, delegated above all to consecrate the bread and wine that define the soul of the faith. The priest lives as a symbol — one that transcends the ordained individuals who are priests. That the majority of those men are virtuous does not undo the fact that the clerical culture has itself become an emblem of malevolence.

While a relatively small number of priests are pedophiles, a far larger number of priests have been prepared to give their twisted colleagues a pass. That may be because many priests have themselves found it impossible to keep their vows of celibacy, whether intermittently or consistently.[23] Such men are thereby profoundly compromised. Gay or straight, many sexually active priests uphold a structure of secret unfaithfulness, a conspiracy of imperfection that inevitably undercuts their moral grit. The contradiction between official Church condemnations of homosexuality and the massively flourishing company of quietly gay priests, even if they are consistently celibate, only adds to the problem.[24]

At a deeper level, Catholic clerics may be instinctively reluctant to judge their predatory fellows because the priest, even if he is a person of full integrity, is always vulnerable to a feeling of having fallen short of the impossible ideal of being that alter Christus figure. Here is the feeling: *In secret, we are all compromised.*

I remember retreat masters exhorting us priests in training during our seminary days with a line from Scripture: We were to "be perfect, as your Heavenly Father is perfect."[25] Moral perfection, we were told, was a vocational mandate. That such hubristic claptrap came from blatantly imperfect men did nothing to lessen the weight of this admonition. I know from my own experience how priests are primed to feel unworthy.

Whatever its cause, a guilt-ridden subculture of clerical moral deficiency, layered with silence, has licensed, protected, and enabled those malevolent men of the cloth who are prepared to exploit the young. The culture of the priesthood itself is toxic, and I see now that my priesthood was, too. At the very least, priests have the habit of looking the other way when it comes to the predations of their fellows. That habit is general enough to have taken hold in me back then.

When I was the chaplain at BU, one of my campus ministry colleagues, the chaplain at Boston State College, was a priest named Paul Shanley, whom most of us saw as a hero for his work as a rescuer of runaways. In fact, he was a rapacious abuser of runaways and others. After being exposed by *The Boston Globe* Spotlight series, Shanley served twelve years in prison. It haunts me that I was blind to his predation, and therefore complicit in a broad structure of willed ignorance and deceit. I am appalled now at myself.

IT HAS BECOME routine for Catholics today to denounce clericalism—the supernatural status claimed for priests. Clerics themselves denounce it.[26] But what is suspect, finally, is the priesthood as such. It's an illusion to pretend that "clericalism" exists apart from the entire culture defined by the sacrament of Holy Orders, which is the formal name of the priestly ordination rite. And indeed, the very "order" of the Church is at issue when the priest himself emerges as a figure of deviance, or of complicity with deviance, that was never openly seen before.

The deviance that makes the priest a contemporary archetype of harm, however, is rooted in something very old. That deeper dysfunction of the clerical culture is only now being laid bare. Most Catholics take for granted the denigrated place of women in the Church, yet that injustice, too, is finally being shown up for the generating corruption that it is. In the age of the Me Too movement, at last the Roman Catholic priesthood—considered as a whole—must be understood, quite simply, as a male supremacist institution.

And intertwined with that problem is another: the inhumane Catholic ethic of sexuality to which I referred before—the rat's nest of obsessions about everything from divorce to premarital sex to homosexuality to contraception to masturbation to in vitro fertilization. That entire cluster of Catholic moral fetishes must itself be confronted as essential to this crisis.

But questions of sex and gender aside, a theology of the priesthood that establishes a clerical elite with a privileged status conferred in heaven—and unchallenged institutional authority over the Church on earth—cries out to be jettisoned. Such elevation makes something sacred of that primal longing to feel chosen that I have mentioned before, and that may be a mark of the human condition. But here the ranking is decreed to be the will of God, applied not to everyone but to a caste apart. We've already seen how, even as a child, I was myself drawn to the priesthood by that very note of feeling chosen. As a child, that is, I was ushered into this misconstruction of virtue. And I stayed there.

CHAPTER 6

A Chosen People

The text has finally disappeared under the interpretation.
—Friedrich Nietzsche, 1886[1]

O ne surprise, and deceit, in the history of the Catholic Church is the way Scripture has been used for power—has been misinterpreted to mean the very opposite of the "good news" that Jesus Christ came to preach.

One New Testament text, written to refer to all the people of God, came to be understood to refer to clerics alone. The text, from the First Letter of Peter, is "But you are a chosen race, a royal priesthood, a holy nation, God's own people."[2] Indeed, the original Greek term *kleros*, the word that gives us "clergy," has been translated as "chosen" in that text. But in the New Testament, *kleros* was usually applied not to an ecclesial elect, but to the whole community of Jesus people, which understood itself, like Israel before it, as the "chosen people."

In the Roman Empire of the fourth century, after the emperors became Christian, the elite status of chosenness came to be applied exclusively to those who ministered in the Church. Such figures were originally known as presbyters, or elders. A new "clerical" class was constructed not by divine mandate, but by legislation of the Roman Empire. It was only then that the word "clergy," in our sense, was invented. And it was only then that the clerical aristocracy was established.[3] The corruption of clericalism is embedded, therefore, in the historical perversion of the word's very root and meaning.

It began as a misinterpretation of Scripture, at the service of the Roman Empire's established political power. It created a structure in which a new class of "priests" were, in effect, designated office-holders in the empire—wielders of imperial power. Then it was institutionalized in, and backed up through, a reinterpretation of theology and philosophy, including that misinterpretation of Scripture. The special status of the clergy was made to become a matter of deep religion.

Thus the Church began to speak of an "indelible mark imprinted on the soul" of a priest—an essential re-ordering, through ordination, of the man's very being.[4] As Roman Catholic canon law still puts it, "The character imprinted by ordination is forever. The vocation and mission received on the day of his ordination mark him permanently."[5] No matter what he does, a priest can never be an ordinary layperson again. "You are a priest forever," as the ordaining bishop tells each man he consecrates.[6]

This status relies not on function—what a person does—but on being. That's why even predator priests like the disgraced Cardinal Theodore McCarrick, convicted by Church tribunals and forcibly defrocked, retain all priestly powers and can, for example, offer absolution of sin to the dying.

This transformation of the ordained, in the phrase coined in the thirteenth century by St. Thomas Aquinas, is an "ontological change"—a change in the man's core metaphysical makeup.[7] He becomes a being set apart from—and above—everyone else.

Why shouldn't men invited to think of themselves this way get lost in a wilderness of self-centeredness? And why shouldn't the Church find it difficult, or nearly impossible, to subject men set apart from and above others to the rules and consequences—and civil laws—that bind the rest of us?

But the "ontological" superiority to other human beings that is routinely claimed for ordained men looks absurd in the present circumstance. Absurd, deeply wrong, and perilous. Yet this extraordinary eminence of priests is nowhere questioned in Church circles even now. Indeed, official explanations about McCarrick's "reduced" but still "ontological" status after his punishment only brought this absurdity to the fore and more clearly into focus.

Hence the scales have fallen from the eyes of many Catholics and non-Catholics alike. Hence, as it were, we have been disabused of the lie by the abuse scandal.

A 2019 Gallup poll found that two-thirds of American Catholics declined to rate as "high" the honesty of Catholic priests.[8] Such disregard poses another world-historic institutional question: If the ethical standing of the Church of Jesus Christ can be so crushed, what can't be?

To ASK ABOUT the deep causes of this crisis in the Catholic Church is not to deflect immediate blame from abusers and enablers, but to confront the essential pathology that has masqueraded for centuries as Catholic virtue—and from which the evil of abuse has arisen. In some ways, this deviance involves not just clerics but the whole of Roman Catholicism. Millions of Catholic laypeople hold official Church positions of one kind or another, as religious educators and so-called pastoral ministers in parishes, but also as professionals working in Catholic schools, social service agencies, colleges, and hospitals. As a group, these people have passively accepted the hierarchy's decades-long refusal to engage them in dealing with the abuse crisis, and with few exceptions, they have declined to organize themselves to demand real reform of the clerical caste.

Such Catholics have declined, that is, to engage in the politics of the Church, as if that were somehow forbidden. Given that many thousands of minors have been put at risk by Catholic dysfunction, this refusal by the inner circle of the so-called faithful to do more than squirm as the scandals proliferate amounts to a grave failure of Christian responsibility.

But many among the whole Catholic laity have found a kind of moral deflection to be necessary—their way of protecting a primal allegiance to the Church and to God. For example, across the last two generations, Catholic birth rates make clear that the "people in the pews" have turned a blind eye to the Church's solemn condemnation of artificial contraception as a grave evil. Such a reaction is understandable, yet it involves a towering institutional deceit by all parties, with popes and bishops pretending to condemn birth control as intrinsically immoral; with priests pretending to censure penitents in the confessional; with Catholic sexual partners pretending to respect Church authority. No one dares to say out loud that this Church teaching is at best hollow and at worst a lie.

The baleful culture of "preventing scandal" has infected everybody. It is a disorder played out at the Communion rail, where mass disobedience is ignored by all concerned. The full-bore institutional hypocrisy on birth control has inflicted a mortal wound on the soul of the whole Church. Many of us Catholics have perfected the art of looking the other way.

But in addition to a pressing institutional question, a habit of Church deceit has also posed an overpowering personal challenge to many Catholics, myself included. Speaking for myself, I never knew until now what the hackneyed phrase "crisis of faith" referred to. Now, with my thinking upended and my feelings in turmoil, I am forced to ask questions that are as urgent to me today as they were urgently avoided all my life: What does it mean that for five years I myself was a priest? Seeing much of the priesthood for what it has become, how could I have embraced it as my life's project? What does it mean that, theologically, the "ontological change" claptrap still applies to me? What does it mean that for fifty years I have preserved my reverence for the priest as an uncriticized ground of significance? And why should my distress not be edged with the dreadful knowledge that I have somehow been complicit?

A whole new reckoning is in order—not so much with the Church and the corruptions that once appeared as virtues, but with my own personal history. I want to understand—from that "child in the monastery" moment forward—how I could have so fully handed myself over to what today seems a culture of transgression.

Now when I think of Brother Upside Down, the monk with hair on his chin, I remember the soft weight of his pudgy hand on my head, and I wonder: *Was there anything lascivious in that Franciscan's petting of his paunch, his liberty in touching the head of a child? What, actually, did my mother make of his wink and nod in my direction? What would she have made of it if I had been twelve? Or fifteen? How far would she have entrusted me to him? Who was that man, anyway? What was he up to?* Even as a young child, didn't I sense something creepy in his touch? And were there undercurrents of seduction attached to my own juvenile charm?

Even to ask such questions of myself is to wave a soiled surrender flag. For me, the heart of value has been devalued. Having once been defined by the priesthood, how can I not fiercely hate its corruptions now, with every fiber of my being?

To answer that, I go back to the beginning, with that wish to be "chosen," elevated above my brother, and I continue with the nuns who hinted that my elevation could be absolute if only I accepted the call to the priesthood that was on offer for one tapped like I had been. My life as a priest began years before I knew it, when, in all innocence, I grasped the stakes of the religious bet— one's whole life staked on the existence of God—and trembled to think I might make it. Or might not.

I long ago stopped believing in miracles, but it seems a kind of anti-miracle now, a transcendent volte-face, that having opened to the core truth of my life in the presence of that happy Franciscan tumbler—Pope Francis with a beard—my Catholic heart should now shut down in a reversal that, for starters, makes me distrust the memory of that monk touching my head when I was five.

Now, remembering my story of choice-and-consequence in light of what the world has learned from priestly abuse—and what I have learned from my study of the history of what shaped the Catholic Church, leading to its betrayal of the Gospel—I see how, as I grew into manhood, a primordial Catholic mistake, a cult of status based on an exploitation of suffering, became so fully my own mistake. The misinterpretation of Scripture and the adoption of a Roman imperial power structure were only the beginning of an iniquity at the heart of Catholicism, culminating in the crushing corruption of today's clericalism. I am starting to see through the shadows of the past that the priesthood has been not my exaltation, as I first thought. No. It has been my lifelong curse, even as it is a curse on the Catholic faith as well.

✠

PART THREE

Nulla Salus: "No Salvation Outside the Church"

Furthermore, we declare, we proclaim, we define that it is absolutely necessary for salvation that every human creature be subject to the Roman Pontiff.

—Pope Boniface VIII, 1302[1]

✦

CHAPTER 7

Please Call a Priest

Now let us try for a moment to realize, as far as we can, the nature of
that abode of the damned which the justice of an offended God has
called into existence for the eternal punishment of sinners.
—James Joyce, 1916[1]

The Irish Catholic Church, with its unchecked abuse of Ireland's young, was condemned in the most extreme terms, as we have seen, for turning "this island into a concentration camp." The Benedictine abbot who hurled that expletive went on to say that the Church's purpose in loosing such mayhem was "to control everything . . . and the control was really all about sex."[2] Essential to that control, as Catholicism practices it, is the denial that power over people and control are the real motives, as well as the denial that sex is the mode.

I was well educated in the art of such an inner lie, but in my case that lesson came well before sex had anything to do with it. As I look back now, I see that it was in the "near the house" parish of my childhood—that happy St. Mary's in Alexandria, Virginia, with its nuns and Irish priests—that I absorbed the perverse mechanism of clerical domination.

Like legions of other U.S. citizens, my mother and father had come to the nation's capital during what was referred to simply as "the war"—World War II. That's what had us settled in the Virginia suburb across the Potomac River from the District of Columbia. My father had left a rough blue-collar job in the Chicago stockyards to begin, after eight years of night law school, a career as a spy-catching FBI agent. With the onset of the Cold War and the birth of the national security state, his counterespionage experience was a sudden qualification, and he was brought as a spymaster into the nascent U.S. Air Force, commissioned directly to the rank of brigadier general. It's a story I have told elsewhere.[3]

During World War II, narrowly identified Americans from widely different backgrounds had been thrown together in the foxholes, cockpits, and tin cans of the battlefields, skies, and oceans of the Pacific and Europe. Just so, in the postwar boom all over the country, these veterans found themselves moving into newly built suburban tracts, housed cheek by jowl with people they would never have met—much less befriended—a mere decade before. Our new suburb in Virginia was not far from the Pentagon, where my father went to work six days a week for most of my growing-up years, until he was transferred to an air base in Germany when I was in high school. Judging from surfaces, my parents had shrugged off the "near the house" parochialism of their native Chicago, but surfaces were not what mattered most.

Our housing development, known as Hollin Hills, was a so-called modernist phenomenon: boxy homes with butterfly roofs, vertical wood siding, expansive glass windows, brick floors, and oversailing second stories. The style had originated in prewar European design, a conscious repudiation of old-fashioned aesthetic mores that the war then reduced to rubble in cities across the continent. In transit to America, the popularized midcentury modernism of houses like ours starkly overthrew the traditional colonial and Georgian styles that should have defined the homeownership dreams of conventionally minded people like my parents. That they fell instantly in love with such radically unornamented architecture showed how their imaginations, too, had been unknowingly upended during the war, preparing them for wholly new ideas of what was beautiful. That their ideas of the good were upended, too, was not clear yet, but a hint of that transformation could be found in the facts that our nearest neighbors were Jewish and that, within my hearing at least, that was unremarked upon by my parents. My best friend in those years was the boy next door, a kid named Peter, and his Jewishness, as I came to appreciate much later, would offer me an opening into a new understanding of myself.[4]

But for all the ways our new world was different, its center for my mother and brothers, if not as much for our Cold Warrior father, was still the parish. For me, as a beginner in the parochial school, the parish was quite simply the realm of those nuns who gave me my first holy cards and my first idea of the Holy Family—that other Mary and Joseph and their little boy, my Spirit Twin. The nuns were Sisters of the Holy Cross. Their stiff white headdresses looked like halos, which was, to a six- or seven-year-old, signal enough of their elevated status.

At some point surprisingly soon, the nuns tapped me with the insinuation that I might be a special boy, which had the momentous implication we have seen. The feeling jibed with the sense of being chosen—or "elected"—that I had because of the close presence of Jesus, my Imagined Friend. But even more, to be a designated favorite of the nuns was to be an acknowledged favorite of God's. Here began my initiation into the much-layered-over malignity of clericalism.

I associate this sister-given invitation to self-aggrandizement with that visit to the Franciscan monastery in Washington, where my encounter with Brother Upside Down offered the first hint of the existence of God and the possibility of an affinity for Him that would set me apart from my brother, who did not want it anyway. The moral complexity of this summons, now that I recall it, was breathtaking in its reach, stretching from selflessness to solipsism and back.

For me at St. Mary's, though, the thing was simple. I quickly understood that earning and maintaining the approval of the nuns was the essential purpose of my young life. Clapping erasers, sitting in front, raising my hand, sharpening pencils—the routine of teacher-pleasing came naturally to me. When the sisters fixed on me the beam of election—I did not yet know of it as *kleros*—I felt a first blast of an actual ambition for my future, which was to join them in the company of God's elite, the clergy.

In those early years, it was never quite made explicit to me that this approbation involved what I would learn to call a "vocation." But it nevertheless transformed my inner assessment of myself from then on. Set apart from my brother, I would be set apart from everyone else as well.

IN THEIR BLACK religious garb—their "habits"—the sisters glided so smoothly across the linoleum floors that it took a leap of faith to believe they had legs and feet like the rest of us. Long chains of rosary beads hung from their belts, like those of that Franciscan monk, but where he had been jovial and kindly, the nuns were uniformly stern. They carried metal clickers, one crack of which could jolt an entire bustling classroom into silence. Their most emphatic instruction concerned the Catholic catechism, and I took in its absolutes absolutely. *Question: Why did God make you? Answer: God made me to know Him, to love Him, and to serve Him in this world, and to be happy with Him forever in the next.*

This life, next life: As soon as I heard of it, that distinction fixed my economy of time and quickly defined the brackets of comprehension within which I located every thought, every desire, and every fear. *This life, next life.* To my ear, the loudest note of the faith was rendered in that bicameral structure of existence, but I grasped in its promise of eternal life and happiness, ironically, the threat of its opposite. There was happiness in the next life, or there was doom in the next life. One or the other.

Understanding that, I was primed to personally embrace what was already familiar to me as a kind of Catholic mission statement, that parish mantra: *No Salvation Outside the Church.*

I remember the illustrating diagram that Sister Rita Elaine drew on the blackboard: a pair of circles that did not overlap. Across one, she scrawled a vivid X, and above it words that I would later recall as *Nulla Salus*, which she explained was Latin, the language in which God spoke to His chosen people. *No Salvation Outside the Church* was almost certainly the first phrase I ever memorized. That this, of all Catholic maxims, was the one to lodge first and most firmly in my nascent consciousness was surely tied to that word "salvation," which took on its deepest meaning when I was ushered to the lip of the high ledge that overlooked the pit of hell. Salvation was escape from hell.

Gripped by the gulf between this life and the next, my childish imagination was entirely taken over by the threat—the fear—of an infinite and eternal ruination. I am sure the first renditions I saw of naked men and women were picture-book images of the tormented damned: Dante's Inferno meets Dracula's lair—rendered for children. Even the anguish of impossibly twisted bodies might have remained abstract as a fate threatening me, but for the gruesome detail that defined every illustration I saw—fire.

Hell was a lake of fire, a terrifying image I would later find in the Bible.[5] There would be infinite pain, as the nun explained it to us, and the damned would have the infinite capacity to feel it. In the afterlife, Sister said, our flesh would burn but not be consumed. The fire would never go out.

The fire! And we would never get free of it.

I would later realize that the nun, whether consciously or not, was imitating the vivid sadism of the Jesuit retreat master whom James Joyce presents as the torturer of Stephen Dedalus in chapter 3 of his 1916 book, A *Portrait of the Artist as a Young Man*. But Joyce's hero has an advantage: He is an adult. The horror of hell was presented to me at an age when perceptions are acute precisely because one is unable to distinguish between the actual and the imagined. So of course I took Sister's every word as a literal description of the real. I felt the heat. The fire! I smelled the sulfur. I heard the shrieking. Obsessed, I tested my fear and dread one day by putting my finger to a candle flame to see if I could stand the pain. When my skin blistered, I hid it from my mother, certain that I had committed a sin.

As these horrid perceptions were beginning to really haunt me, they were made more pointed still when I was initiated just then into what was presented as the solution to such trepidation—the grim rituals attached to the sacrament of Penance, aka Confession. Alas, my trepidation grew worse.

I see, in looking back on all this, that below the surface of religious observance, what we children were most powerfully being brought into by this Irish stew of dread and expectancy was the potent mystique of the ones who stirred it: the clergy. That the Catholic priest was charged both with espousing a fear of the next life in hell and providing, through his sacramental power of absolution, a conditional release from that fear is what, at bottom, makes the mechanism of this core priestly function so toxic.

First, we become convinced that our situation is hopeless. Then we are offered a way out of that hopelessness, a way over which the priest—and the priest alone—presides. Here is the black seed of what is meant by "clericalism."

"As the Father has sent me, even so I send you."[6] This was Jesus, speaking to the Apostles after the Resurrection, but in what was perhaps our first instruction in Holy Scripture, we children were told that Jesus was expressly addressing this commission *to the priest*—not to the Apostles. The priest who was in that darkened booth over there—the confessional. The priest who was waiting for us on the other side of the screen before which we would kneel.

"And He said to them, 'Receive the Holy Spirit. If you forgive the sins of any, they are forgiven; if you retain the sins of any, they are retained.'"[7]

This verse establishing the charter of the sacrament, formally known as Penance, was affirmed as such only by the Counter-Reformation Council of Trent in the mid-sixteenth century. We, of course, could have no idea that the Confession ritual was completely unrelated to anything Jesus was first believed to have said or done. There is something profoundly ahistorical in the assertion that the sacrament of Confession as we know it was "instituted" by Jesus. The ahistorical, in fact, defines this entire history.

Certainly, the promise of forgiveness was essential to the ministry of Jesus (and essential already to my gratitude for His friendship), but was God's compassion meant to be transformed into an impersonal instrument of a clerical border patrol? Looking back, I recognize that this overpowering threat of doom, coming from One we were taught to call "God," efficiently trumped the former ease I'd felt in the company of my Imagined Friend, the Son of God, who now seemed only partially able to temper the divine menace of God, His Heavenly Father. Suddenly, as a source of hope, the priest had more salience than Jesus did—a marker of my first induction into the priesthood.

I recognize also that an essential deceit marked Catholic instruction in this doctrine of priest-mediated salvation. How were we to know that the one-on-one penitential rite of Confession, empowering the ordained priest to "retain" the unforgiven sin that could send a person to hell forever—empowering him also to free the sinner of that sin and its consequences—had its actual origins in the Middle Ages, when popes were consolidating political power and feudal-lord clergy were imposing Church controls on the Catholic laity? The priest's self-designation as the next-life gatekeeper of heaven and hell served to bolster his claim to primacy over this life on earth.

If this sacred invention of Confession was not a building block of the clericalism that even Pope Francis would denounce as a source of the Church's priest sexual abuse scandal, what was? The problem, as it came to me, began then, with the sacrament of Confession.

Essential to the priest's power, of course, was the cult of secrecy in which this sacrament came wrapped. True, the "seal of Confession," the priest's solemn obligation to disclose nothing of what is said in the confessional, could console a penitent with the confidence that his or her worst admission was being made to God and not to a man, enabling a true reckoning with conscience. And true, there is something beautiful in the idea that a guilt-racked sinner can confide the worst secrets of a shattered heart to a trusted priest, who will articulate the forgiveness of God and of the community, and never relay the secret to anyone else. Where else is trust like that to be found?

But this ecclesiastical obsession with secrecy, bleeding out from the sacrament of Confession itself, became the hierarchy's tool for protecting its own power, ultimately at the expense of children. Indeed, it became a mode of sexual assault—abusers exploiting the sacrament's intimacy; their enablers using the sacrament as an excuse for not reporting them. "We couldn't tell you," an abused child explained to his mother, as *The Boston Globe* Spotlight team learned, "because Father said it was a confessional."[8]

The predators did this, but so did their protectors. The late Cardinal Bernard Law of Boston, before being forced to resign because of his support for priest-rapists, attempted to silence an abuse victim with the sanctified seal of the sacrament: "I bind you by the power of the confessional," Law said, with his hands pressing on the man's head, "never to speak about this to anyone else."[9] With such sacred silence, victims were victimized again.

Even now, when clericalism is sometimes derided by clergy themselves as a source of the abuse scandal, no one in Church authority is prepared to revisit the "seal of Confession" as one of its bastions.

The bottom line of what we children were taught about that darkened booth could not have been clearer: We were desperately in need of the priest who stood between us, damnation, and eternity.

WHEN, IMMEDIATELY AFTER my first Confession, I made my First Holy Communion, I was presented not only with my first fancy clothes—a white suit with long pants—but with a much-desired gift, my first wallet. In its leather fold I found a card that was neatly printed with the words "I am a Catholic. In case of an accident, please call a priest." I would carry such a card for years, convinced that the last-minute ministrations of a priest, if I was lucky enough to have one at my side at the moment of death, would save me from hell. The first hint of a growing disillusionment with this base system came, eventually, with a joke card that read, "I am an important Catholic. In case of an accident, please call a bishop."

When the idea of *No Salvation Outside the Church* was first explained to me, I took it as mainly good news, since "salvation" was the essence of rescue from that frightening eternal lake of fire, and we Catholics were assured of being "saved." The catch, of course, was that first we had to be "absolved" from our sins. In Confession, we could be. Hence the absolute necessity of the priest in our lives and in ensuring our lives in the life to come.

The eternal beatitude of heaven was never as vivid to me as was the relief of being spared from hell. This joy, of course, was a version of pleasure at not being hit by a hammer anymore, but upon glimpsing this promise, I nonetheless loved the Church for it. I fully grasped the priest's urgent importance. It did not dawn on me, at first, that our positive Catholic fate was paired with the infinitely negative fate of others—"non-Catholics"—probably because I had yet to reckon with who, precisely, the wretched figures of the inevitably damned might be. I remember the chill on my neck when, one day, it dawned on me that one of them would be my chum next door, Peter. I wanted to warn him but did not know how.

It seems hard to imagine that the Roman Catholic Church would subject children to such guilt-ridden brooding about sin at the age of six or seven years old. Again, we are below the surface of religious observance here, recognizing only now what dark institutional purposes this grim apparatus of salvation served. Ironically, it was precisely that happy First Holy Communion rite that most clearly conveyed the perverted implication of transcendent clerical power. In Church discipline even to this day, Confession, the sacrament of Penance, is treated as a mandatory prelude to Communion, and no exception is made for kids.[10]

So, beginning with that initiation in our white suits and dresses, we children learned that Communion and Confession were halves, as Sister might have said, of the same walnut. On Friday afternoons, ahead of the Mass on Sunday at which we would "receive Communion," we were paraded to the church and lined up in its dark aisle to await the burst of red light above the confessional, a signal for the next child to approach, push back the velvet curtain, and enter the torture chamber of God's judgment. It all seemed normal, since according to the primitive developmental psychology of Catholic piety, we second graders had reached "the age of discretion," marking us not only as capable of committing sins, but—like all fallen humans—as inclined most gravely to do so.

Just how gravely I myself was so inclined became clear to me exactly then, a recognition tied to what I actually felt in that spooky booth and that inevitably spoiled the pristine pleasure of being in the "state of grace," as we were said to be after Confession. The sacrament of mercy turned out to be unmerciful to me. As part of the sacramental protocol, I was required to learn by heart the Act of Contrition, the Catholic catechism's rote antidote to eternal damnation, to be recited by the parishioner as the climax of the penitential rite of Confession. I recall it to this day: "O my God, I am heartily sorry for having offended Thee, and I detest all my sins, because I dread the loss of heaven and fear the pains of hell, but most of all because they offend Thee, my God, Who art all good and deserving of all my love." In the exactly repeated formula, that expression of sorrow for sins could merit God's forgiveness—which came in the form of the priest's equally rote formula recitation, called the absolution.

All of this should have been a consolation. But in my case, the antidote was a new poison, because the Act of Contrition required me to declare that my repentance was motivated not mainly "because I dread the loss of heaven and fear the pains of hell"—the fire!—but "most of all" by my pure love for the offended God. Yet in my heart of hearts, I knew that such dread and fear were precisely—exclusively—what made me sorry! That devout "most of all" had nothing to do with it. I even remember making a joke with some friend that instead of being "heartily" sorry, I was "hardly" sorry. But it wasn't funny. And anyway, how could a damning God be "all good and deserving of all my love"? Even in my penitence, I was telling a lie, yet another sin. Despite my feeling of friendship with Jesus, I was a candidate for hell.

ONCE I WAS introduced to this image of a possible future of damnation, I began to experience it as a present desolation—especially in the middle of the night, when I would be jolted awake by that classic dream of falling. In my case, the falling dream—doubly terrifying because I was on the top bunk—was always falling into the pit of fire.

The terror was compounded when I pictured my friend Peter, the Jewish boy next door, falling into that same pit, too—but through no fault of his own. That was not fair! "Not fair"—the child's ultimate moral insight. Whatever awaited me, liar that I already was, such a fate awaiting Peter was simply wrong.

Who would want to sit blissfully for all eternity at the feet of a monster God who would inflict such punishment on Peter, the undeserving? But such a question brought fresh horror. Was I choosing Peter over God? This fear, of which I could speak to no one, not even under the "seal of Confession," was my first deep secret.

Our secrets make us who we are. That this one, in looking back, appears so trivial only underscores the demonic force of such Church-induced scrupulosity. My conviction of my unworthiness would drive me from then on. I made desperate efforts to disprove it. But the more I seemed to succeed, drawing praise as a "good boy"—ultimately as a "fine man"—the more certain I remained that I was damned.

Am damned.

CHAPTER 8

De Profundis: "Out of the Depths I Have Cried unto Thee"

I don't even maintain that faith makes loss easier; it just,
if I may say so, improves the quality of the suffering and
makes it sometimes fruitful instead of useless.
—T. S. Eliot, 1940[1]

A t St. Mary's School, at age nine or ten, I had my first success.
But, naturally, it came with that shadow of my furtive unworthiness, known to me alone.

Promoted from grade to grade, I went from being the nuns' medieval page to being the parish priests' full-fledged squire—an altar boy. Indeed, I was eventually singled out as one of the chosen few "heads"—the senior Mass servers who, a notch above the school patrol, occupied the pinnacle of parochial prestige. That I was esteemed by nuns and priests—and that my parents knew it—was a source of quiet self-satisfaction, but its underside was pointed. The more affirmed I was, the more I felt undeserving of affirmation.

What began in Confession as an awareness that my contrition was imperfect, though I claimed otherwise, grew into a whole web of secret feelings that I believed were wrong. That my brother Joe was ineligible to serve Mass because of lameness caused by polio covertly pleased me. Indeed, despite a pretense of empathy toward

Joe, I felt nothing but gratitude that the disease had infected him, not me. My wicked thankfulness, in turn, convinced me that I was somehow responsible for his disability. My every relationship seemed morally fraught like this, especially my friendship with Peter, my neighbor. If I chose his side against God, where did that leave me with Jesus?

The list of transgressions went on. Secretly I thought that Sister Rita Elaine, with her temper, was too mean to be holy, but I sucked up to her shamelessly. When Mom gave us the silent treatment, I hated her—and dared to savor the spiteful feeling as a first source of independence. At another friend's house down the street, I stole glimpses of his father's girlie magazines—abashed by delight and a thrilling new guilt. No one had a hint of any of this, and I certainly never mentioned such grappling in Confession. Despite the earnestness with which I'd begun, I was a pious fraud, and I knew it. I would never quite shake this inner feeling of inauthenticity. I have it now as I write.

But being in the altar boy elite assuaged my uneasy conscience, and the status came with perks. For example, I was regularly tapped to serve funeral Masses, which were typically held in the middle of weekday mornings at the church down the street from the school. Serving those special liturgies was a privilege that often got me excused from class and tipped a quarter by the funeral director, lucre with which I always beelined across the street to the corner store and its Hostess Twinkies.

But at some point, puerile detachment failed, and the experience of funerals began to weigh on me, a kind of initiation into the solemnity of the human condition. Once tuned in, I found the Mass for the dead to be wholly riveting: the priest's ghoulish black vestments; the stripped-down altar; the black-silk-draped casket at the head of the aisle; the lugubrious organ, with the balcony soloist trilling through Schubert's "Ave Maria"; and always a clutch of red-eyed family members in the front pew. I was the robed young fellow—black cassock, white surplice—leading the way in with a candle; then drifting around the sanctuary, carrying the missal from one side to the other; presenting the priest with cruets and finger towel; ringing the bells at the Consecration; holding the incense pot when the time came to wave the thurible around the casket, a ritual of a final farewell. No one in attendance at these funerals noticed me, and once I was confident in knowing exactly what rubrics applied and when, my mind was set free to actually pay attention—real attention—to what we were doing and why. Those funerals changed me.

Unlike other Masses for which the words of Consecration served as the hinge, I experienced the Requiem Mass as pivoting on the priest's recitation, in Latin, of Psalm 130, the first verse of which I found myself knowing by heart, even in the esoteric Latin language: *"De profundis clamavi ad te, Domine."* It was a phrase I took in, and I made a point of following along with the translation in the funeral missalette: "Out of the depths, I have cried unto Thee, O Lord."[2]

Young as I was, the anguished words spoke to me. In Mass after Mass, I waited to hear them, until I understood somehow that the words were speaking for me. I had depths of my own—unspoken, unspeakable. They were a matter of remorse attached to my fakery, but I sensed that my painful dislocation was only part of the trouble. I was burdened by a mysterious grief over nothing I could name, which only made the torment worse. I dared to imagine that whoever wrote that psalm had versions of the same desolation.

What's the Bible for if not to help us feel understood? *De Profundis:* "Out of the Depths." Yes, this prayer was a response to death, hence its place as the hub of the Requiem Mass, but I was glimpsing the mystery that there is death in the midst of life. *I am already dying* was my feeling. And it left me speechless.

Now, of course, the Latin phrase *De Profundis* is associated more with Oscar Wilde than the book of Psalms, having served as the title of the wrenching self-examination he pursued while serving two years in prison for the crime of "gross indecency with other men." Wilde writes, "There is not a single wretched man in this wretched place along with me who does not stand in symbolic relation to the very secret of life. For the secret of life is suffering."[3] When Wilde's *De Profundis* was published in 1905, one critic commented, "We see him here as the spectator of his own tragedy."[4]

That succession of funerals at St. Mary's, several times a month across my last three years of grade school, made me an intimate witness to—not spectator of—the tragedy for which I had no words: the bleakness of mortality. Those Masses opened me also to the reliable consolation of the faith, despite everything. Only much later did I appreciate what an unusual experience this confrontation with transcendental loss was for a child. Indeed, it is only now, as I enter old age and weather the deaths of peers, that I find myself experiencing an equivalent succession of funerals and memorials, when the inner state of focused melancholy takes me back to those midmornings in St. Mary's Church when I was young.

At the Requiem Mass, I saw up close the very essence of our religion: how God accompanies suffering, and how, in that, while not removing suffering, God changes suffering's meaning. "The secret of life is suffering," said Wilde. On my knees, focused on the tormented figure of Jesus on the cross, with His lacerated legs calling to mind my brother's, I recognized my old Imagined Friend—imagined, still—as a new kind of companion. For it was He, not the psalmist, who most eloquently let go that cry. *De Profundis.*

Jesus on the cross had hurled those words to heaven—not only *for* us but *with* us. "My God, my God!" He cried. "Why hast Thou forsaken me?"[5] Who has ever more clearly articulated the depths of mortal dread? At funerals, Jesus was with us as our fellow mourner. In a surprise that I plumb fully only in looking back, my inchoate sense of that fellowship in suffering was enough for me to grasp something essential about the much-touted miracle of the Resurrection, which until then had been a meaningless magic trick to me—something to do with the Easter Bunny bringing eggs. What, in fact, is the Resurrection, though, but a simple proc-lamation that life can be found in death? On my knees, as a boy, I grasped that.

Here it is: Jesus was God, and God died. He did so not "for" us, as the doctrines say, but "with" us. That Good Friday turn in the story was all the "good news" one needed. The dead body's post-mortem magical mystery tour—its being "raised" from the tomb three days later—was not the point. Rather, Jesus, as our faithful companion through everything, even brutal death, was the point. Jesus, with us in death, changed death's meaning. I would not be able to articulate this intuition until years later—Resurrection was not resuscitation—but I finally saw what it really meant to believe. This made me see with fresh clarity the place of Jesus in my life— but not only Him.

Just as crisply, I saw the unsullied power of the priest—power for good! If I later overcame a complex of contradictory emotions to become a priest myself, this must be why. Those funerals sealed in me an unbroken sense of the use to which human longing can be put. At funerals, it is, above all, longing for life that we feel— "life," as Jesus put it, "to the full."[6] And what I sensed was that such longing carries within itself the promise that it can be fulfilled. Why else do we feel the longing—the desire—so intensely? The priest, if he does anything, speaks to that longing, and to its inbuilt promise of fulfillment. The priest. Yes.

. . .

YET THE ACTUAL priests who spoke to that longing for life, in those poignant funeral liturgies, live now in memory as images of something quite other. There is the priest ideal, and there are priests as they are. Two of those priests stand out especially, at least one of whom emigrated from Ireland, and perhaps the other did as well. Each of their voices carried more than a hint of the harp. I cannot think of what the Church in Ireland has become without thinking of them. And I think, freshly, of the altar boys in Ireland with an empathetic vividness. I should have felt such empathy for victims long before this.

First, Monsignor Stevens. Above the confessional where he sat waiting were the red light and the placard that read simply THE PASTOR. It was into his lair that we children were herded on Fridays week in and week out.

Bless me, Father, for I have sinned. I would mutter the phrase to myself ahead of time, rehearsing that and other lines. I trembled to pull back the purple velvet curtain and enter the darkness, trying to remember what to say. The stink of the monsignor's halitosis always hit me, and I had to focus. *I accuse myself of* . . . I dutifully enumerated my offenses, as instructed by the nuns: *I failed to say my prayers. I disobeyed my parents. I lied. I was unkind.* To my knowledge, in fact, I never did any of these things. But, as already explained, I was guilty because of the sacramental formula—the Act of Contrition—that I was then required to recite. To Monsignor Stevens, again and again, I affirmed that I was "heartily sorry," while meaning "hardly"; that I repented not mainly because I dreaded "the loss of heaven and fear[ed] the pains of hell," but because I'd offended God who was "all good and deserving of all my love." My true lie.

I'm sure that Monsignor Stevens never gave a thought to what he heard from me, and I always felt that I'd gotten away with something when, after telling me to recite three Hail Marys to make up for my sins, he mumbled through the words of absolution.

But then something happened that made me wonder. One early morning at Mass, I was the expert altar boy at the monsignor's side as he distributed Communion. In sync with each other, he and I moved rhythmically along the ornate brass rail. He placed the Host on each communicant's tongue, and I dutifully held the paten, the gold plate, under the person's chin. We had done this together hundreds of times. But then he stumbled, just at the wrong moment. Lurching, he let go of the sacred wafer an instant too soon, and it began to fall away from the receiver's mouth. This was precisely the mischance that I was there to guard against, but I froze. By the time I tried to catch the Host with the paten, it was already fluttering to the floor. I'd missed it—a sacrilege!

I reached down to the unleavened white disk on the black linoleum, intending to rescue the Body of Christ from the unclean floor by picking it up—an automatic, unthinking response, fueled by my horror at having, after all my years as an altar boy, failed in this, my gravest responsibility. But if my unconsecrated fingers had touched the Host, the sacrilege would have been compounded. Seeing that, Monsignor Stevens brought the heel of his stout, high-topped, Irish peasant brogan down on my hand, smashing it. I remember looking up at him, and the expression on his face— perspiration on his brow, hot ferocious eyes, twisted mouth—was one of such massive disapproval that I believed at once he'd seen through to the very core of me.

He did not release his boot, and I understood that the pain in my hand was punishment, pure and simple. Not just for the sacramental taboo I'd nearly broken—I'd nearly touched the Host!—

but for all the times I'd lied to him in Confession. I thought he knew what I was. I thought he was right. And why should I not remember him and that moment to this day?

THE OTHER UNFORGOTTEN priest, coming later in my time at St. Mary's, was—let's call him—Father George, who arrived from Ireland at the start of the year I was in eighth grade. Young, shy, and movie-star good-looking—the first man I ever heard referred to as a "black Irishman"[7]—he quickly became the pride of the parish. The mothers loved him, especially my own. I was riding high as the head acolyte and felt an unusual sense of assurance when I first met him in the sacristy. His handshake was soft. He wore cologne, tasseled loafers, and French cuffs. He carried himself like what I would later learn to call a dandy. But mostly it was his kindly demeanor that set him apart from the other priests. He was the first one to offer to drive us altar boys the short distance back to school after midmorning Mass. Even in the rain, the other priests never did that. I thought he wanted to show off his new car, a shiny black Ford Fairlane that put Monsignor Stevens's clunky old Buick to shame.

Soon enough, in sacristy encounters and in the hallways of the school, I felt singled out by Father George. To everyone else I was Jimmy, but he called me James, which seemed, oddly, an expression of intimacy. At first, I liked it. He had a way of placing two stretched-out fingers on my shoulder when he spoke to me, a fond drumming. Looking back, I recognize in the kindnesses he showed me a sort of courting. Such attention pleased me at first—doubly so when I saw how it pleased my mother. In his presence, a lilt came into her voice, an unconscious aping of his Irish brogue that even I recognized as a mode of flirtation. Something new was at work with this priest.

Eventually, Father George was speaking to me about my priestly vocation, and he did this without the sly indirection I'd grown accustomed to from others. I'd been artfully tapped by the nuns, for example, to give a school assembly speech for which they supplied the title: "Fishers of Men," the phrase with which Jesus had recruited his Apostles. Duh.

But Father George just came right out and said that I had the "call." I was mature beyond my years, he said. I was above average. In serving Mass, I appeared born for the sanctuary. I had the natural gift of holiness. That I demurred when he said this, he assured me, only proved that it was true. And most momentously, Father George was the first to explain that a vocational summons from God carried the obligation of acceptance: "Not my will, but Thine be done."[8]

The priest explained what he referred to as "holy discernment." It was he who made me see the bold typeface in which I was meant to read the line "Many are called, but few are chosen."[9] Once discernment had been accomplished, according to the disciplines of spiritual direction—which he was offering—one simply had no choice of one's own in the matter. To refuse God was blasphemy. "Lord, what wilt Thou have me to do?"[10]

It speaks volumes, as I remember this, that I also remember with what secret dread I received the news. I'm sure I said nothing to Father George, but I responded, inside, with a visceral refusal. That was when I began to feel uneasy around him. Still, the dynamic between us had been set flowing. When he identified himself as my spiritual director, I wondered why I had no say in the matter. Yet it flattered me to be taken so seriously, and I tried hard to put aside my reluctance. I took refuge in the evident complications of that word "discernment," but when I tried to speak of my confusion to my parents, they were alike in telling me that Father George, in having been recently ordained himself, knew more about perceiving God's will than anyone. Though reluctant to overtly push it, my parents did not conceal their pleasure at what they clearly took to be a Church-sponsored unfolding of my, yes, vocation.

I was left feeling guilty about yet more dissembling—a new version of my old defect. The distance grew between my barely acknowledged inner truth and the pious posturing to which I felt obliged. Father George had a stilted way of talking, a penchant for big words that, instead of impressing me, turned me off. Even his calling me "James" instead of "Jim" began to seem phony. My secret disdain, speaking of being a phony, was becoming sinful.

With my parents' blessing, Father George took me to the dinner meetings of a Washington-area laymen's group called the Serra Club, named for the California missionary Junípero Serra and dedicated to the recruitment of boys for the priesthood. When Father George first mentioned it, I thought he meant the Sierra Club, which was famous then for lawsuits stopping the construction of dams out west. The first dinner we attended was in a restaurant with a view over the Potomac River, and the introductory speaker pointed to the river and made a joke about the Sierra Club campaign against a Colorado dam—which must be why I remember the connection. Other awkward lads from various parishes were present, each with his priest-escort. As I recall, we boys avoided making eye contact across the linen tablecloths as we listened to stilted lectures from Catholic insurance salesmen and dentists about the glories of the consecrated life, participation in the priesthood of Christ Himself. One man said that in heaven the angels genuflect to priests. It was news to me that angels had knees, but the odd assertion was, in fact, a first explicit indication of the supernatural claims routinely made for Catholic clergy, the lethal preferment that would so backfire in the end.

Father George took me out one night for pizza, a dish I'd heard of but never tasted. I was happy for the chance. He brought me to a drive-in restaurant, the Hot Shoppe, on Washington Street in Alexandria. We were sitting in his fancy Ford, which still had the new-car smell. A nearby loudspeaker blared, with Elvis singing "Hound Dog." The peaked-hatted carhop, a girl, attached the pizza tray to the slot of my window. I noticed what was called in those days her figure. I have no memory of eating the pizza or whether I liked it, because Father George chose that moment to broach the subject of the minor seminary, the diocesan boarding school for which I'd be eligible in a few months. I'd get to wear a cassock every day, he said. I'd be like a junior cleric. I'd be on my way to the inner circle of heaven. I knew I was being rushed. I didn't think it was right. I distinctly remember the long, mute awkwardness of my not replying.

It may or may not have been that same time, but one evening Father George brought me to the rectory where he lived. I do not remember why. He parked the Ford out front. As instructed, I followed him up the stairs from the street. I was struck by the shadowy interior of the house and felt uncomfortable being there. He asked if I wanted to see his room. I followed him up the interior staircase, at the top of which was a closed door. He opened it. I looked inside. I saw a desk, a chair, and a carefully made bed with a crucifix placed just so on the pillow. That was it. We left the rectory. Father George drove me home.

Even as a naïve eighth grader, I knew that the priest's bringing me to his room was odd. Perhaps he was only trying to give me a glimpse of the priest's actual life, part of his recruitment. But really. That I spoke of the weird encounter to no one suggests that it left me with an edge of remorse, as if I'd been part of some misdeed. Here was a hint of the way in which the sinister underside of clericalism could have a collusive consequence. Looking back now, of course, I cannot help but feel that I dodged a bullet of some kind.

What I do know is that in telling my parents what the priest had said to me about my "vocation," without putting into words how he had begun to creep me out, I managed to make clear my feeling that the so-called minor seminary was absolutely not an option to be discussed. Whatever pull I'd felt during those funeral Masses toward our religion's precious function as a refuge from death and grief—a suffering God who changes the meaning of suffering— was readily trumped by a visceral, if mostly unacknowledged, repulsion toward Father George.

Not repulsion toward Jesus, I insisted to myself. But I was confused. Now I would say that I intuitively sensed in the priest the exploiting inner mutilation that would drive many of his kind to inappropriate emotional connections with the vulnerable, if not to outright criminal acts. I did not know what to do with the incipient recognition. With my mother and father, I referred neither to that discomfort nor to the other feeling that began to well up in me with power—the shadowy guilt that engulfs those who say no to God, who is "all good and deserving of all our love."

Here is the odd part. The consolation of the Catholic liturgies that taught me how to live with suffering—that God shares it with me—was undercut by my initiation into a whole new kind of suffering: radical anxiety about the permanent impossibility of fully authentic virtue. So, yes, God suffers with us. But, no, God cannot possibly enter into the suffering of being constitutionally unworthy of God.

Later, I would apply the language of sin to these feelings. And I would remember the figure of that priest, Father George, as one who somehow introduced me to them. That he never touched me inappropriately did not prevent my every association from returning to him when I learned much later what other priests had done to other boys. The abyss into which those fellows were thrown— a pit of suffering—amounted to the depths from which no cry could be heard, not even by the God to whom we were commanded to address it.

✠

CHAPTER 9

Good Boy No More

You're tearing me apart!
—James Dean as Jim Stark in *Rebel Without a Cause*

My older brother, Joe, was brighter and more studious than me. Introverted and impaired from young childhood by the ravages of polio, he had long channeled his energy into academic achievement. Two years ahead of me, he had been admitted to a selective all-boys Catholic prep school—there were only about a hundred students—on the far side of Washington. It was not a boarding school, and the long commute from Virginia was arduous. My mother's stern will that Joe should go there, despite the bus-and-trolley sojourn, reflected her determination to support him in what advantages he had. A superior school for a superior boy.

The place was called St. Anselm's Priory School, and it was attached to an English Benedictine monastery. The monks, cowled and hooded, were the teachers. Some of them were from England, and others pretended to be. The Anglophilia of the place meshed with its proudly snobbish cult of excellence. Because of my sibling's advantage—and only that—I was admitted to St. Anselm's, too.

The trek from the far side of Alexandria and across the District of Columbia, an hour and a half or more each way, made after-school activities problematic for my brother and me, but it was a socially isolated school in any case. The academic demands were intense, the discipline firm, coats and ties the rule. We students were addressed by teachers and one another by last name only, an implicit edict of impersonality. I quickly understood that St. Anselm's Priory School was not to be Archie and Veronica's Riverdale High—the school I longed to attend.

As if the St. Mary's nuns had tipped them off, though, the monks, too, soon made me feel singled out, with, for example, a freshman year—or, rather, third form—invitation to join the monastery's junior order of Benedictine Oblates—a kind of lay auxiliary. I still found it impossible to deflect the thrill of being chosen, and so once a week or so, letting Joe make the early bus trip home alone, I happily joined in with the after-school Oblate exercises of vespers, followed by work in the monastic print shop. *"Ora et Labora"* (Prayer and Work) is the Benedictine motto.

To sit in the shadowy chapel while the monks chanted the psalms brought me back to that experience in the Rosary Portico when I'd instinctively grasped the power of the monastic bet, how everything depends on the existence of God. Seeing my high school teachers as cowled mystics intoning prayers began to prompt a change in the way I saw myself—not as their pupil but as their confrère. The resistance to holiness that I'd habitually, if secretly, felt in myself at the parish in Virginia began to fall away before an innate attraction to what I would later learn to call the contemplative life. The aura of that first monastery, experienced when I was five years old, came back. At St. Anselm's, there was a card in the pew, a picture of Jesus, with His words "Go into your inner room, shut your door, and pray to your Father in secret."[1] I welcomed the chance to quicken my friendship with Jesus in this new setting. I felt at peace in the chapel. It would not last.

After vespers, I would go down the spiral stairs to the cramped room in the monastery basement, a low-ceilinged brick vault with cabinets and tables organized around a large black machine, a primitive printing press. I began my initiation as a typesetting apprentice, put to work organizing the broad trays of tiny lead letters and blanks. Fairly quickly, I learned to set type, spacing the blanks among the letters to rectify the margins. I remember helping to produce a pamphlet titled *The Pope Speaks*, which featured a Vatican diatribe against atheistic communism. In truth, I would have preferred going out for the basketball team, but the friendly monk-printer nevertheless made me feel like an athlete being groomed for a sport I could not identify.

That St. Anselm's was a world entirely without women confused me. At St. Mary's, there'd been dances for the boys and girls, and in the summer there were parties at the country club and at nearby houses afterward. Spin the bottle, cheek-to-cheek dancing, and holding hands were our timid rites of initiation, and if I gave a friendship ring to a girl in the eighth grade, I did not mention it to my parents. For that matter, I never brought up the subject of my budding sexual interest when I went to Confession, either. I knew that sex and sin came as a package, but my first stirrings had yet to feel wrong to me.

Still, I sensed how that early fear of doom, tied to my acute sense of being a fake, was shifting into the even more dangerous territory of "sins against the Sixth Commandment," which famously forbade "adultery." That word, I'd come to understand, applied as much to teenagers as to adults; it applied as much to girlie magazines displayed on newsstands and to the sight of curvy girls in sweaters as to actual fornication, which I could only vaguely imagine. "Mortal sin" was becoming an especially weighted phrase, carrying a certain prospect of peril to which I felt unaccountably vulnerable. To speak of such dread to others, even a priest, would have meant acknowledging it to myself, and I simply could not do that yet. I was ripe for implicit instruction in the puritanical arts of sublimation and repression.

If all-male St. Anselm's represented an abrupt interruption of my introduction to adolescent romancing, in truth I think I welcomed it. Sex was not mentioned within my hearing at the school, not even by my otherwise randy classmates. That surprising assertion probably says more about me than about the reality of a high school that certainly had its locker rooms. But it did not have girls in the hallways, slim ankles to notice, swaying pleated skirts to be drawn by, or those curvy sweaters. In the year I am remembering, the only coed social for us third-form youngsters was an insufferably awkward tea dance in the afternoon, with St. Anselm's boys and imported convent-school girls clinging to opposite walls, munching powdered-sugar cookies.

Ironically, perhaps, the physical absence of girls abetted the vivid arrival of the female form in my imagination. The SILENCE PLEASE sign in the school library hung above not just the tables and chairs but also the very subject that began to take me there in my spare moments. In Bible class, of all places, I was introduced to the phrase "carnal knowledge": "Now Adam knew Eve, his wife, and she conceived."[2] This fresh definition of "knowing" threw me at first, and then it drew me. That carnal knowledge was essential to Bible study presented a sanctioned opening through which I was happy to pass. The library was my passageway.

Aiming at an appearance of casual randomness, I surreptitiously stalked the shelves that held the art books and anatomy texts that featured naked female bodies. Soon I knew just where they were. I was especially drawn to one particular portrait of Adam and Eve, those delicate little fig leaves balanced at the deltas of their legs, drawing the eye there every time. The reproduction I'm remembering was almost surely of the totemic engraving by Albrecht Dürer, although his name would have meant nothing to me at the time. His portrait of the primeval pair epitomized the Renaissance glorification of the human body, male as well as female, but it was the figure of Eve who made me catch my breath. Her small breasts held a particular allure, as if this woman, unlike the buxom movie stars of the day, could be chastely gazed upon.

In looking back from the vantage of one who has fully rejected the theological denigration of women that began with a perverted reading of the Genesis myth and its scapegoating of Eve, it strikes me as a momentous prognostication that that woman should have been my first imagined love object.

If I noticed Dürer's Adam, it was only to imagine myself in Adam's place with his woman. I was as lean as Adam, if less muscled. The male and female figures were so exquisitely drawn, both as types and as particular individuals, that it was possible to see them equally as Romeo and Juliet on their one night together—or even as James Dean and Natalie Wood, whose brooding complications made the innocent Adam and Eve seem the ultimate rebels without a cause.

But, in truth, it was a relief not to have to measure Dürer's modestly voluptuous Eve against an actual girl. As the idea of sex came more steadily into focus, I was properly fascinated and dreadfully afraid. I knew that, as one being tracked, whether willingly or not, toward the elite status of one "chosen," I was headed toward territory in which open sexual expression would be forbidden. As early as that, I felt the load of repression that must be carried by ordained men, the weight under which all too many break. The elite call to "celibacy," heard only by some, confounded and compounded what I already knew as the mundane call to "chastity," addressed to everybody—the rules against "petting" and "going all the way" and anything else "outside of marriage." So the shadow falling on my budding sexual interest was double-layered, and why should I not have wanted out from under it? This emotional crosscurrent sealed my secret longing, my secret foreboding. Secrets were defining me more than ever.

Soon enough, owing mainly to a succession of disappointments in the classroom—failed exams, blown answers when called upon, red-slashed homework papers—I found it impossible to deflect the inner awareness of my broader alienation at St. Anselm's. Unlike my brother, I was a misfit there. I was being invited for the first time to take on a really serious intellectual challenge. The monk-teachers conducted their classes with unforgiving rigor and made their high expectations explicit. The school's academic demands were proving to be a bridge too far for me. Joe was able to focus on his homework during our long bus rides to and from school, but I was not. With my other three brothers underfoot at home, I found it impossible to get my class assignments done. It showed in my grades.

My participation in the after-school Oblates dwindled, and once again, sitting in the shadowy monastery chapel, I was undermined by a feeling of inauthenticity. Who was I to pretend to be a junior monk? Whether I knew it or not, my initial embrace of that identity had come from the old habit of pleasing religious overseers, and I realized at last that I did not have to do that anymore. My teachers' disapproval of my below-standard schoolwork had begun to register, and all the monks seemed to know of it. By Thanksgiving that first year, I had stopped showing up at the print shop. I do not remember the brother making an issue of it. The pope could speak without me.

. . .

As if putting on new clothes, I found myself donning a new self-image and presenting a new face to others. No longer the good boy, I became the kid in the back of the classroom hoping not to be called on. By midyear, my alienation began to show in my behavior. I ran in the hallways. I was caught with a pack of cigarettes. I organized a boycott of the greasy French fries in the cafeteria, offending Brother Dominic, the cook. I lost one library book, then another. I threw chalk. I was late for the weekly Mass. I imitated the way one of the monks scratched himself and held my nose to mock another's body odor. Busted. Busted. Busted again.

Oddly enough, I recall feeling relieved at my new status. It's pretty clear to me now what I was up to. A stumble into bad deportment and underperformance could lead away from my fate as one "chosen," and, unconsciously, that had become a central purpose of my young life. I found myself periodically getting "sent up," dispatched by teachers to the headmaster's office. And there I confronted a monk-administered callousness that not only shocked me but came to define the heart of my experience at the Benedictine school. It's an experience that has always come to mind when I remember my time there. And it's an experience that has haunted me in recent years as I've struggled to understand how my Church could have been so taken over by deviance.

One day, in Latin class, I was exchanging a goofy note with the kid in the next chair when Father Raymond, the Latin teacher, surprised me from behind. He clapped my head, a not unusual form of discipline from that stout monk. Instead of shaking the mild blow off, I fell to the floor, pretending to be hurt. I feigned unconsciousness. Father Raymond ordered me up, but I ignored him. He repeated the command. I did not move. He knelt at my side with sudden alarm. "Carroll! Carroll!" He shook me. I remained limp, unresponsive. I sensed the stunned silence that fell over the room as the dozen other boys craned to see what was wrong with me.

Father Raymond, leaning over me, grew frantic. "Jimmy!" he said now—an unprecedented use of the diminutive, which fully displayed his panic. "Jimmy!" But I felt a panic of my own, as I realized what I'd done. I'd never imagined that the priest would be so vulnerable to my prank. I began to stir, wanting to appear to slowly regain consciousness. *Where am I? What happened?* I nearly pulled it off. Instead, I burst out laughing—an expression, of course, of that panic getting the best of me. I laughed and laughed. I covered my face with my hands, unable to stifle my wheezing giggles. I was literally rolling in the aisle. Father Raymond drew himself up, realizing he'd been had. His face reddened. He threw his arm toward the door, screaming, "Get out! Get out!"

I waited on the bench outside the headmaster's office. Father Austin, short and bald, was a stern Englishman, or so he presented himself. We students did everything we could to avoid even passing him in the corridor. I was wholly intimidated. St. Anselm's Englishness included a "public school" attachment to corporal punishment, and I was braced for my first taste of it. After Father Raymond came out of the office, stalking away without a glance at me, Father Austin stood at the door, command enough. I entered. He closed the door. "The desk," he said, as he flipped the folds of his monk's habit away from his arms. Somehow I knew that he was instructing me to bend over the desk. I did as I was told, arranging my hands just shy of the inkwell and blotter.

I glanced back and saw the paddle. It looked like a cricket bat but was thin enough to flex. The priest struck my buttocks multiple times. I lost count at five. In one memory of this nightmare, I was ordered to drop my pants, and the priest was striking my bare skin, but I find it impossible to credit that. Whether my ass was exposed or not, the pain was excruciating and the indignity unspeakable. What most registered, though, was the priest's coarse grunting. When he finished, he said simply, "Go." Desperate to hide my tears, I was resolved not to look at him but couldn't help myself. I looked. I was taken aback by what I saw. His face was flushed. His eyes, waiting for mine, were ardent. I did not know what to make of his fiery expression, but in recalling it in the context of today's broad priestly dysfunction, I recognize a kind of hatred, as if Father Austin blamed me for something he disapproved of in himself.

That I remember the priest as somehow deviant is probably unfair, but the near universal disapproval of such beatings now, even in the United Kingdom where it was entrenched, indicts the untoward punisher's effervescence that commonly marked the practice. In my case, an inchoate sense of the priest's emotional agitation as he hit me, more than the physical sensation, was what stamped the experience in my memory. I can't help but interpret the thing anew, as if an undertow of gratification was welling up in him from the great unspoken energy of taboo—a hint of the perverse.

Whatever it was to the monk, that rush of the forbidden was the very thing I unconsciously feared in myself in the quite separate realm of the school library, where I secretly lingered over the naked figure of Eve in the garden.

But there was one thing of which I was fully conscious as I left the headmaster's office that day—the crystal clear feeling, as I might put it now, of *Screw you! I will not be cowed by shit like this!*

My deportment did not improve. Perhaps I was somehow brought into the malevolent dynamic of sadomasochism, but beginning then I asked for it, being "sent up" repeatedly during my time at St. Anselm's. Beaten. Beaten. Beaten again. If the physical punishment was intended to subdue me, it did the opposite.

In fact, I only undercut myself. In that otherwise excellent school, I squandered my chance to begin to fulfill what intellectual promise I had. Other students made the most of the place. I did not. My teachers showed little interest in me. My brother Joe continued to thrive. On the way home from school, claiming I had to do research at the Library of Congress, which was not far off our bus route, I went my own way. I stopped riding the bus altogether. Instead, with my thumb out at intersections, I hitchhiked across Washington, into Virginia, all the way home. In doing that, I was able to secretly hoard the bus fare and spend it on pizza slices and Cokes—an unprecedented and ongoing deceit of my parents. At school, I pretended to be fine with my marked status. With my classmates, I made a joke of how often I was sent up and proudly claimed the record for the number of times I was paddled. *Hot shit.*

YET—GOOD BOY NO more—I'd become wholly disoriented. Looking back, I'd say I was at the mercy of a rather desperate urge to prove my unworthiness for God's election, to prove wrong those who'd seen me as a priest-to-be. I would be like everybody else— that was all I wanted. Nevertheless, I instinctively submitted this new condition to the test of my deepest identity, one more basic than any mere question of status. What would my transformation into a troublemaker mean to the One whose close presence had defined me? My Imagined Friend did not set me above others. My friendship with Jesus had nothing to do with promotion from inferiority to superiority. It had nothing to do with others. Not even with those who disapproved of me.

It was then that I first grasped something new about Jesus, hinted at in the Gospel story of His defiance of His parents when, at age twelve, He disappeared from their caravan returning home from Jerusalem and was mightily rebuked for it. Jesus's bad behavior hit me only now, and only now did I begin to understand Him as having then grown up to be a man who kept bad company, a rule breaker, an ultimate troublemaker. Jesus could claim, of course, that He was going, as He told His distraught parents, "about my Father's business."[3] He had that all-trumping Father in heaven. There was no such excuse for me, since it seemed to be the Heavenly Father's very business that, in my resistance to God's call, I wanted to eschew.

Even in that unsettled period, the partnership with my Imagined Friend did not break. The nuns needed my comportment, the parish priests my piety, the monks my subservience. My Spirit Twin needed nothing but being near me, still.

I did not revel in my petty delinquency, but I did welcome the release from feeling like a fraud, the much-praised but phony altar boy I'd been before. Eventually, Father Austin's vehement disapprobation, which mystified me as much as I'd asked for it, proved to be yet another sort of distinction, and in that it felt familiar. It was one more way of being chosen—that's all. Across my time at St. Anselm's, though, the blatant satisfaction the priest seemed to take in hitting me made me feel despoiled. In the end, that punishment, not my bad behavior, was what made me feel ashamed. I feel shame now in recounting this.

When my father, announcing to the family that the Air Force was transferring him to Germany, apologized for making me leave St. Anselm's Priory School after only two years, I pretended to regret it. Hypocrite again.

✠

PART FOUR

A Theology of Abuse: Anselm and Augustine

But Jesus said, Suffer little children, and
forbid them not, to come unto me: for of
such is the kingdom of heaven.

—Matthew 19:14 (King James Version)

✠

CHAPTER 10

St. Anselm, God Damn

God wills it!
—Pope Urban II, 1095, launching the Crusades

The great question posed by the Catholic sexual abuse scandal is not *How could priests and bishops have done this?* Rather, given the global scale of the clerical crimes against children and the all-but-universal habit of Church denial that enabled those crimes, the great question is *What in Catholic culture gives rise to this grotesquely massive dysfunction?* And, as well, *What else has come of it?*

At St. Anselm's Priory School, without knowing it, I brushed up against the answer. The school's patron, St. Anselm of Canterbury, was one of the people who put in place an inhumane theology that has endured. The other was, as I will show, the writer St. Augustine of Hippo. (Austin, the headmaster's name, is an anglicization of Augustine.) The theology this pair of saints created has sustained belief for eons, but it has simultaneously, if quietly, promoted the denigration of both women and Jews. Now, though, their systems of thought have been revealed to have endangered children, too. Despite the range of positive contributions to faith and reason for which Anselm and Augustine are celebrated, the two were also instigators of the present Church calamity.[1]

The doctrine most associated with Augustine, captured in the phrases "the Fall" and "original sin," assumes an inescapable human depravity and at the same time puts in motion an explosively repressive theology around sexual sin. Anselm's equally influential "theology of atonement" subtly promotes an idea of a God who wills suffering because humans deserve it. This thought contradicts the clear biblical idea that God changes the meaning of suffering by joining us in it—what I grasped as a child at those funerals. Instead, Augustine and Anselm together gave to us a doom-threatening monster God who requires suffering as the precondition for His being reconciled with us—us, His own creations. From this omnipotent, sadistic God, as Catholics are taught, only a Catholic priest can offer rescue—a deep-seated theology that undergirds clericalism and its worst abuses.

Augustine's idea of what accounts for pervasive human immorality and Anselm's explanation of why Jesus Christ died on the cross have been the two most controlling works of Christian theology ever written, so much so that they eventually lodged in the Catholic imagination not as theories but as definitions: as God-given realities.

Humans are fallen. God damns sinners. God damns sex, especially female sex. To worship and obey this damning God is to enter into a compact of loathing—loathing the unredeemed. This negativity, however, comes so cloaked in false benevolence as to promote—perhaps to guarantee—a deviant cruelty.

ANSELM (C. 1033–1109) was the most famous Benedictine monk of his age. Renowned as the archbishop of Canterbury, and remembered therefore as the quintessential Briton, he was, in fact,

Anselmo, born in northern Italy and, because of vassal-liege tensions with the king of England, spent most of his last years in Rome. There he focused on writing theology. Anselm was present in that capital of the Latin West as the First Crusade was launched in the year 1096 by Pope Urban II. Urban was Anselm's patron, and Anselm gave Urban a theology that supercharged his impulse to go to war—war against "the infidel," Muslims and Jews; in effect, war against difference.

In the autumn of 1095, in France, before a throng so vast it had to gather in a field, Pope Urban II summoned the kings, princes, and common people of the Latin West to march on Jerusalem in order to liberate the Holy Land from the Muslims, who had controlled Jerusalem for four centuries, since 637. Pope Urban is remembered for having concluded his bellicose sermon with the cry, "God wills it!" With that began the Christian holy war, the Crusades, which would rage intermittently for two centuries, from 1096 until 1291. After that, Church-supported wars against Muslims would rage on the Iberian Peninsula until 1492. But the essential meaning of the Church's campaign against "the infidel" showed itself at once.

The Crusaders sacked Jerusalem in 1099, mercilessly slaughtering all the Jews and Muslims of that city. But on the way to Jerusalem, those Crusaders, in the spring of 1096, attacked others they encountered en route—the infidels near at hand, Jews living in towns and cities up and down the Rhine River. This was Christian Europe's first pogrom, resulting in the deaths of thousands of Jews. Those mobs of fighters marked by crosses were convinced they were carrying out the will of God in attacking Jews. *God wills it!*

For the first time in Christian history, acts of violence were formally deemed to be holy. Those enacting such violence were assured of salvation. In previous Church-related wars, such as the conversion campaigns waged against Germanic pagans by Charlemagne three centuries before, priests accompanied combatants to offer them absolution for the wrongs they did in battle. In the Crusades, priests were there not to forgive the fighters but to bless them.

Essential to this outbreak of sacred violence—underwriting it, if not igniting it—was a newly promulgated theological rationale that was embedded in Anselm's attempt to explain the Incarnation. His theology transformed the Catholic imagination by providing the crusading Church with a sanctifying ethic. In effect, Anselm's theology described God as inherently violent, not only in relation to His creation but also in relation to "His only begotten Son," Jesus. That assertion was the deep, perhaps unintended, nub of Anselm's treatise *Cur Deus Homo* (*Why God Became a Man*), published in 1098. Divine violence licensed Christian violence.

The Incarnation, a term drawn from the biblical verse asserting that "the Word became flesh,"[2] is the belief that Jesus Christ is "truly God and truly man." Anselm set out to explain why the Incarnation had to happen—that is, why the Son of God had to appear in the form of a man. Anselm's answer cut to the chase: The Son of God took human form in the person of Jesus Christ precisely to die on the cross, in obedience to God's will. The drama of the Crucifixion of the God-man had to be enacted if the fallen human race was to be "saved," brought back into the good graces of God. Only the God-man's death could right the wrong of human sin.

This deserves emphasis: The salvation of fallen humanity required the death of God's Son in fulfillment of the will of God the Father. "Not my will," a terrified Jesus prayed the night before his Crucifixion, "but Thine be done."[3] *God wills it!*

The obedient death of Jesus was the sole mechanism by which God restored the order of the disordered world. For Anselm, the other "saving events" of which tradition speaks—the life of Jesus, the teaching of Jesus, the example of Jesus, the Resurrection of Jesus, and the ongoing Real Presence of Jesus in the Church—were all irrelevant when it came to accomplishing the first and final purpose of the Incarnation.

Anselm argued that the obedient death of innocent Jesus was the ransom required by God the Father as the price of the redemption of sinful humanity. Jesus died to save us. The saving act was His violent death, obediently embraced. And what made it saving was His being God's Son, in full submission to His Father. The extremity of this way of thinking about God is captured by a Jewish observer who found it "incomprehensible."[4]

Anselm's assertion overturned a thousand years of Christian understanding. The death of Jesus had been described as ransom before, but when, say, St. Paul used the image,[5] he was describing *a ransom paid to the devil,* who had ensnared vulnerable humans. Now *the ransom was being paid to God,* who had turned against those humans because of their sinfulness. Specifically, God rejected humanity because of the sinfulness of Adam and Eve, whose defiance of Him had transformed them and their progeny, in effect, into His hostages.

Since Jesus's freely offered obedient and bloody death was itself the means of universal salvation, the feast of that death—Good Friday—took preeminence away from Easter as the high point of the Church's liturgical calendar. Death trumped life in the Catholic imagination. It was no accident that Anselm was writing in the eleventh century, the millennial era in which cults of death—the apocalyptic dread, self-flagellation, the Domesday Book—had come to the fore.

From then on, the gruesome, corpse-laden crucifix, which had rarely been seen in the Church before, took over the center of Latin Catholic devotion. Recall that the Great Schism, dividing the Eastern Orthodox Church from the Roman Catholic Church, had occurred only a few decades before, in 1054. Now the Church of the West would center its imagination on the battered Jesus of Good Friday instead of the glorified figure of the resurrected Christ, epitomized in the golden-hued icon face that remained the central symbol of Eastern Orthodox religion. The wretched crucifix remains the central Roman Catholic symbol to this day.

We've seen how representations of the suffering Jesus can change the meaning of suffering for the good, as it did for me during those funeral Masses at St. Mary's, or when I saw my brother's wounded legs in the battered legs of Jesus. In Jesus, God suffers with us. But the hyper-glorification of physical anguish is something else — a kind of sacred savaging of the body itself. *The body is the thing to punish, to flee, to hate.* The body is the thing to focus on. And should it surprise us that the train of thought that led Anselm to so privilege death over life was set moving by the naked figures of Eve and Adam?

That is, by their bodies.

HERE'S THE WELL-KNOWN story. "The Lord God took the man and put him in the garden of Eden to till it and keep it." This is from the book of Genesis. "And the Lord God commanded the man, saying, 'You may freely eat of every tree of the garden; but of the tree of the knowledge of good and evil you shall not eat, for in the day that you eat of it you shall die.' Then the Lord God said, 'It is not good that the man should be alone; I will make him a helper fit for him.'"[6]

In the story, there begins the trouble.

God has given Adam a command. God also has given Adam a companion, whom Adam happily calls "the flesh of my flesh."[7] But between Adam and Eve stands the tree that is forbidden. "So when the woman saw that the tree was good for food, and that it was a delight to the eyes, and that the tree was to be desired to make one wise, she took of its fruit and ate; and she also gave some to her husband, and he ate."[8] In this way, Anselm explained, Adam, "without compulsion and of his own accord, allowed himself to be brought over to the will of the devil, contrary to the will and honor of God."[9]

"Honor" is the operative word here, for Anselm is applying the feudal standard of "offense and recompense." The social ethos of the Middle Ages had a rigid hierarchy that put every person in a distinctive place. The king was supreme in the political realm. Popes and bishops were supreme in religion. Various barons, princes, and knights filled in the upper slots of the societal structure, with peasants and serfs on the bottom. The structure worked well enough except when political and religious claims overlapped, and they did so with a vengeance in the late eleventh century. In that era, Church authorities and secular rulers argued over control of vast swaths of Church property, and over the appointments of bishops, whose wealth and power could be immense. Such competitions between king and bishop could be intense.

The most celebrated such conflict was between Thomas Becket and England's King Henry II in 1170, when the king had the bishop murdered—in the cathedral. But a rehearsal for that much-dramatized dispute played out in 1093 between Anselm, newly appointed as archbishop of Canterbury, and King William II, son of William the Conquerer. William insulted Anselm by refusing to recognize his authority as archbishop, which he did as an excuse to seize Church wealth and estates. Anselm proclaimed this insult to be an insult against God, but William nevertheless forced him into exile—exile in Rome, where he wrote his treatise on the Incarnation.

In the feudal system, the vassal was subordinate to his liege lord, and therefore owed him homage and fealty. The structure of their relationship was strict and hemmed in by a rigid code of duty and honor, from king to serf. King William II defied Archbishop Anselm by claiming to be his superior in matters believed to belong to the Church. In so doing, the king sullied Anselm's honor—an additional offense—by refusing deference. Anselm's personal experience of this conflict provided him with the frame of reference for his understanding and description of humanity's relation to God, the Heavenly King. The final insult of exile only added to Anselm's sense of grievance, and he projected those feelings of affront onto the God who'd been dishonored by man.

When violations of this unbending social code occurred, they could be reconciled only through the shedding of blood ("feud" shares a root with "feudal") or through inflexibly defined rituals of compensation and restitution. In matters of offended honor, a person of lesser rank could never be reconciled with a superior except through the intercession of a mediator who shared the status of the superior and served the inferior as a kind of advocate.

Anselm applied this structure of power and honor to the relationship of God and humans in "the Fall," the grievous alienation from God that resulted when disobedient Adam and Eve were expelled from paradise. How could that alienation ever be overcome?

As beings of lesser rank, humans themselves could never redress the insult God took from Adam's sin—could never "atone" for it—since in the feudal schema, only those of equal social status could appease one another. According to this rigid code, an insult to God's honor required the absolute rejection of the inferior being who committed the offense. Thus God's attitude toward Adam and his progeny: That first sin, a direct rebuff of the Creator's overflowing love, with which the Genesis story begins, led to the stern condemnation by the Judging God who expelled the sinful humans from the Garden of Eden.

In this highly legalistic social structure, God was the ultimate liege lord, and the offending human was the unworthy feudal vassal whose only chance of righting the moral and legal imbalance caused by his offense depended on his finding an atoning substitute whose social rank equaled that of his liege. Only a lord could satisfy the debt owed to a lord. In the Middle Ages, such contractually defined status counted for everything, and that informed Anselm's understanding of humans as vassals in relation to God.

Because the Lord, offended by the sin of Adam, was divine, the only one who could possibly make restitution for Adam's sin also had to be divine. Yet because the one offending was human, the one redressing the offense also had to be human. The solution to this impossible dilemma—and the explanation of God-in-Jesus—was the "incarnation" of a being who was both divine and human, the God-man Jesus Christ. This was "why God became a man," as Anselm's treatise title puts it.

But God becoming a man was not enough. The only way in which the God-man could accomplish the expiation of human sin—Adam's sin—was to suffer and die, because only the infinite suffering of one infinitely innocent could wipe the slate clean of the infinite offense that God the Father took at the sin of Adam: an infinitely efficacious sacrifice offered once and for all. The grotesque physical anguish Jesus suffered was itself the mode of expiation and satisfaction. "O most Precious Blood of Jesus Christ, the Blood of Salvation," Catholics pray to this day, "Cover us and the whole world. The ocean of the Blood of Jesus Christ set us free."[10]

An extreme instance of restorative justice, this scheme took over the Catholic imagination and came to be called "substitutionary atonement." Anselm's *Cur Deus Homo* may rank, simply, as the most influential work of theology ever written. An innocent substitute, who in no way deserves the fate, has laid Himself down—"He laid down his life for us"[11]—like a bridge across the gulf that had formerly separated humans from their God. Eventually, Anselm's notion would be embraced, and heightened, by Protestant conceptions called, for example, "vicarious atonement" and "penal substitution." The conviction that God required the violent death of His Son as a mode of loving redemption took root in the Christian mind, and it remains the dominant paradigm of salvation.

Really? Is God the Father actually such a legalistic fiend? Does this theology quietly appeal to a strain of sadism buried deep in the human psyche? Perhaps so. Something must account for the ferocity with which this harsh idea about God took hold across the centuries. Even as a child, an altar boy at those funerals on weekdays, I experienced a hint of that other, precious vision—not that God wills suffering, or requires it, but that God joins us in it. Because of tragedies built into the human condition, we humans are already on the cross. God did not put us there. God comes to us there. Why else would we cry out to Him from the depths?

But no. Anselm's idea was that God, bound by the law of a cosmic social order He Himself had created, demanded suffering as the mode of fallen nature's redemption. This amounts to a perverse reversal of the idea of love: God so loves His Son that He will have Him killed—killed in the most grotesque way imaginable, on the cross.

In the apocalyptic climax of this theology, God so loves the world that, at the end of history, He will destroy it, a vision many find vividly rendered in Apocalypse, the final book of the Bible. Its verses lift up scene after scene of the all-devouring violence of God's wrath, with the moon becoming blood, the stars falling to earth, the sky itself split like a torn page.[12] This end-of-the-world spectacle took hold of the Christian mind at the turn of the first millennium, just in time to license the Crusades and their marauding desolation in the name of God. (The world would see apocalyptic expectation again as a licensing theology for the nuclear age, just in time for the second millennium.)

GOD WILLS SUFFERING *because humans deserve it.* Here is the root of the brooding Catholic conscience that can never shake off a certain dread of doom. I was Exhibit A of this structure of mind, tormented by the overthought compunction that troubled my dreams—that falling dream, falling into hell—from the very beginning of my self-awareness. *Suffering is redemptive. Suffering is good. Suffering can be infinite in intensity and eternal in time. God wills it!*

Even though I'd glimpsed alternatives with an eye forever peeled for a different meaning—what else was I looking for at those funerals?—I was a connoisseur of Anselm's brutal scheme years before I ever heard his name. How fitting that, when I finally encountered an actual Anselm in that Benedictine headmaster and a crib-sheet version of Anselm's thinking at the school named for him, he became the patron saint of my restless adolescence, the sponsor of my own initiation into the corporal punishment equivalent of atonement theology. In this twisted adolescent thinking, it wasn't Father Austin who beat me; it was God. And if the headmaster took pleasure in hitting me, it was due to his feeling that he was God's agent. And I was still saying no.

CHAPTER 11

✠

St. Augustine, Un-indicted Co-conspirator

Who told you that you were naked?
—Genesis 3:11

Bᵤt it was Father Austin at St. Anselm's Priory School, namesake of that second saint, St. Augustine, who beat into me a first iteration of Augustine's great and costly mistake. The consequences for the Church of St. Anselm's ideas were bad enough. But what Augustine set in motion was worse.

With Father Austin pointing the way, I joined the implicitly masochistic company of Augustine's heirs, all those Catholics primed to see normal sexual feelings as sin. Anselm asked, *Why did God become a man?* Augustine asked, in effect, *Why did God make creatures who copulate?*

The answer to both questions, and to the question driving this book, is suggested by the place women came to occupy in the lives of Catholic priests.

Fᴏʀ ᴍᴏsᴛ ᴏғ a thousand years—from the time of the Apostles in the first century to the so-called Gregorian Reforms of the eleventh century—most priests and many, perhaps most, bishops of the Roman Catholic Church were married men with families.[1] That was true, and would remain true, of the various other Catholic churches to the East—the Coptic, the Orthodox, the Armenian, and so on. But with the turn of the first millennium, universal clerical celibacy was embraced by Catholic authorities in the West. In 1123, the First Lateran Council made the celibacy requirement for Roman Catholic priests a part of Church law. This occurred just when Rome-centered theology was recasting itself around the grim idea of a damning God. As this theology led to a revolution in the ways the Church organized and understood itself in relation to war, so an equivalent upheaval transformed attitudes on the subject of sex.

The doomsday dread of hell that traumatized the Latin Catholic imagination in the era of Anselm could be assuaged, as we've seen, only through the ministrations of the clergy—the mystical maneuver of Confession, with which I became acquainted as a child. But what I could not have grasped back then was the way this annihilating claim about hell underwrote other unprecedented claims, including the material power of popes and bishops from the Middle Ages on. Here was the real point of *No Salvation Outside the Church*: power. It was a formula that, long before it haunted me, had guaranteed the absolute sway of the clergy for centuries.[2]

The pope, with transcendent authority over access to happiness in eternity, claimed to be the feudal overlord of the world in the here and now. Through the domination of this exclusivity, Europe's emperors, kings, and barons would mostly bow to the Roman pontiff. In the wake of Anselm, the logic of *Nulla Salus*—"No Salvation Outside the Church"—was simple: After the Fall of Adam and Eve, a yawning gulf opened up between every human being and God, and since only Jesus, the God-man, bridges that gulf, salvation requires connection to Jesus. But that connection is available only through the Catholic Church, with all of its members subject to the pope in Rome—and his ministers, the priests.

This theology established a pyramid of ranking, said to be divinely ordained. The hierarchy—Church over king—was not just one of politics but one of being itself, with the pope reigning supreme.

Pope Innocent III (1198–1216), for example, claimed as Roman pontiff a place for himself "between God and man, lower than God, but higher than man, who judges all and is judged by no one."[3] No longer merely the "successor of the Apostle Peter," the pope was now the "vicar of Christ"—the stand-in for God. The entire structure of Roman Catholicism was recast as a theocracy, soon to be known as "Christendom"—the cultural, social, and political hegemony that defined Western civilization, centered in Europe. Even if kings and princes regularly resisted this geopolitical system—one could call it a "theo-political" system—secular as well as religious power inevitably swirled around the papal palace and its delegated institutions.

Catholic priests, from village pastors to teachers in cathedral schools to bureaucrats of the newly established Roman Curia— the papal court—were essential agents of this social order. The official place of priests on the ecclesiastical pyramid, priests delegated to share in the exercise of this absolute power, was exactly defined just then with the first promulgation, in 1143, of what became the Codex Iuris Canonici, the Church's Code of Canon Law.[4]

At the same time, the priest's ultimate sacramental power— only the priest can change the Eucharistic bread and wine into the literal Body and Blood of Jesus—was formally established as the ground of his claim to exalted status. The Fourth Lateran Council, in 1215, declared of the Eucharist, "No one can effect this sacrament except a priest who has been properly ordained according to the Church's keys, which Jesus Christ himself gave to the apostles and their successors."[5] Note that the council would have had no need to assert the exclusive right of the priest to exercise this power if non-priests were not also doing it at the time. Where once the presence of Christ was understood as abiding in those gathered in His name,[6] now it was in the consecrated and consecrating fingers of the ordained man.[7]

But the commissioning of every Catholic priest to share in the power of the ecclesiastical pyramid required that each one of them submit to that power in a wholly new way. The unequivocal character of clerical discipline meant that the priests' long-standing but competing allegiance to wives and children could no longer be tolerated.

With violent coercion, therefore, the popes of the late eleventh and twelfth centuries forced on clergy the universal law of celibacy, formalized with that edict of the First Lateran Council in 1123.[8] Although the Catholic memory hardly registers this, the enforcement of this rule had drastic practical consequences, no doubt including the driving of now forbidden wives and children of priests into penury, prostitution, orphanhood, and even slavery. Pope Urban II himself, the instigator of the First Crusade in 1096, had a few years earlier at the Council of Melfi (1089) ordered the enslavement of women married to priests.[9] For precedent, Pope Urban had Pope Leo IX, who, decades earlier, had forcibly brought "priests' prostitutes" as slaves into his own residence, the Lateran Palace. Bishops and princes alike were licensed to sell the wives of priests to the highest bidder.[10]

Mandatory celibacy, surviving until today as an inhuman pillar of clericalism, began, therefore, with a massive crime against thousands of innocent Catholics—especially women.[11] Although the ideal of celibacy was always put forward as a matter of high spirituality, the controlling motive for this purging of marriage from the priesthood was economic. Through networks of monasteries and feudal fiefdoms, the Church was the largest landowner in Christendom—the territory described today as western Europe. Celibate clergy, with no households to support, would lack the essential drive to accumulate wealth for themselves; nor would they produce legitimate heirs to lodge competing claims to the vast estates and treasures the medieval Church was hell-bent on protecting and expanding. That the offspring of clergy were officially declared to be *nullius filius*, literally, "the child of no one," meant they had no rights of inheritance.

But something else was at work, too. The imposition of a totalitarian sexual repressiveness on all priests reflected the hatred of the flesh that underwrote Anselm's degradation of the body, epitomized in the gruesome new iconography of the crucified Jesus. It also fulfilled a broader and profoundly misogynist puritanism that had coursed like a feverish Gulf Stream current below the surface of Catholic thought and life for six hundred years.

THAT CURRENT HAD been set running by one of Anselm's predecessors, St. Augustine of Hippo (354–430), in a revised reading of Scripture and Catholic theology. Augustine was a North African bishop and theologian. He foisted an interpretation of the Genesis creation myth on the Church and the West—and on me—as if it were the historical record of actual human beings, with dark consequences for the entire human future. As with Anselm, a perverted misreading of the story of Adam and Eve set the devils loose.

It was in Augustine's thinking about sex, erotic longing, and physical pleasure that the saint most decisively shaped the imagination of Christendom and the culture that came of it. Most important for our purposes, Augustine could be said to be the unindicted co-conspirator of the crimes of clericalism, the one who most set a malign dynamic moving in the Catholic unconscious.

This book's tracing of theological history meshes again with my own personal story when I recall those furtive periods spent in the library of St. Anselm's Priory School, under the spell of Dürer's chastely alluring couple — in particular, that pristine naked Eve. I sensed then that those moments marked an initiation of some kind, but given how filled they were with delight, I could not have remotely imagined how fraught such sensations would prove to be.

Augustine's astounding writings — he authored nearly a hundred books and thousands of letters and sermons, most of which survive — stand as the intellectual foundation of Christianity, a mainstay of Western philosophy. Augustine's *Confessions* amounts to the first true autobiography, a bold foray into memory and conscience that laid the groundwork for the elevation of individual experience. "Allow me this, I beseech You," he prayed in the fourth chapter of *The Confessions*, "to trace in memory my past deviations."[12] In some way, my journey into memory as a route to sacred meaning has a related aim.

A journey was also, of course, Albert Camus's image: "A man's work is nothing but this slow journey to rediscover through the detours of art those two or three great and simple images in whose presence his heart first opened." Camus, also North African, was writing in the twentieth century, and was a kind of latter-day, secular Augustine.

As a young man, Augustine embraced Manichaeism, an ancient philosophical movement that saw a dualism in the universe — the cosmos divided between spiritual forces of light and physical forces of darkness. A like dichotomy shaped Neoplatonism, another powerful philosophical movement of the first centuries of

the Common Era, and numerous sects in early Christianity embraced the idea that good resides only in the spirit world, with the
physical and material world the domain of evil.

Soul against body. Spirit against flesh. Such ideas had profound implications for moral thought, in nothing more powerfully
than in questions having to do with sexuality, which was taken to
be the cockpit of evil. Augustine was infected with those ideas. In
his greatest work, *The City of God*, he defined the City of God as
the world of the spirit, while the City of Man was the world of the
flesh. His infection of—let's call it—bipolarity would serve to
transmit a timeless plague to the Western mind.

In fact, the young Augustine seems to have been a Manichaean
manqué, if the repudiation of bodily pleasure is a mark of that
doctrine. He loved bodily pleasure. As he would recount in *The
Confessions*—written in his forties, about ten years after his conversion to Catholicism—he had been a man of "restless passion."[13]
He had lived with a woman for more than a dozen years and had
a son by her. On the rise as a teacher in Milan and seeking respect-
ability, he had sent his unnamed concubine back to North Africa.
But still at the mercy of what he called his "sexual habit,"[14] he had
promptly taken up with another woman. Perhaps his most famous
statement from this book is "Make me chaste and celibate, Lord,
but not yet."[15]

But once he became a Catholic, coming to prominence in the
Church, he embraced chastity and celibacy with a vengeance,
and he expounded a theology that drove the flesh-hating assumptions of Manichaeism and Neoplatonism deep into the religious
imagination of Christianity.

Like Anselm after him, Augustine's thinking took off from the
myth of Adam and Eve in the Garden of Eden. To him, it was not
just a fable. After all his years of emotional and spiritual wander-

ing, the story of Adam and Eve was, in the words of the scholar Stephen Greenblatt, "the key to everything."[16] For Augustine, as a result of that primeval, historical act of disobedience—*they ate*— the human condition was marked from then on by suffering and death.

As Augustine saw it, these wages of misused human freedom implied an admission of universal woundedness as a precondition for self-acceptance, forgiveness of the other, and authentic community. We are all in the same boat; no one is perfect. This is a profoundly humane vision. But it cast a bleak shadow.

What began in the Bible as a symbolic tale to account, after the fact, for the woes of the human condition became, with Augustine, an a priori act of divine judgment. In this reading, the loving Creator was transformed, in the moment of Adam's sin, into the damning Judge.

Adam, as Augustine saw it, embodied all of humanity. This meant that Adam's sin belonged to every person, in every era. Suffering is, therefore, deserved by all, and the infliction of suffering is justifiable. As in Anselm's later invention, violence inflicted for the sake of divine justice defined Augustine's schema. *God wills it!*[17]

Once Adam had tasted of the forbidden fruit, "the eyes of both were opened."[18] The man and woman saw what they had done, they saw their punishment coming, and they saw that it would condemn their children, too. And their children's children, ever after.

In this simple scene and what follows in Genesis, it should be noted, there is no mention of "original sin" or "the Fall," but in Augustine's reading, the burden of the narrative could not be clearer. *This happened.* Eve and her daughters, as the igniters of sin, were condemned to undergo agonies of childbirth. Adam and his sons, as the ones whose disobedience was decisive, were condemned to the misery of ceaseless labor. Adam and Eve forfeited their physical immortality. All must die, but death was not even the worst part.

For Augustine, still in the grip of that dualistic opposition between virtuous spirit and wicked flesh, a troubled conscience would be forever tied to the human person's physical existence. In that beleaguered interiority—the agonized "restless passion"—would be found the most exquisite punishment. Defining that fretting dread, Augustine's supremely consequential leap of invention took off from the next verse of Genesis: "And they knew that they were naked; and they sewed fig leaves together and made themselves aprons."[19]

Until they sinned, the innocent Adam and Eve had not noticed their nakedness. Suddenly, they were embarrassed by it. They were ashamed not so much of their nakedness as of their exposed genitals. All at once, they were not just aware of their sexual organs but obsessed with them. What do fig leaves do but draw attention? As a result of Adam's act, which followed on Eve's proposal, lustful desire took over the human will.

Augustine took his cue from those scanty fig leaf "aprons" and jumped to the conclusion that the actual sin of Eve and Adam boiled down to a fevered sexual arousal and its climax. Before the sin, as Augustine imagined it, "they felt nothing in their members to make them ashamed of what they saw."[20] After the sin, they felt lust. Before the sin, they copulated perhaps, but "by means of the organs of generation not less obedient than [their] other members, to a quiet and normal will."[21] Their genitals, that is, would have been as readily controlled as a moving hand or chewing teeth.

Genesis defines the occasion of sin only as "the tree of the knowledge of good and evil," yet for Augustine that was a matter of carnal knowledge. Yes, Adam knew Eve. Recall that the word "fuck" is commonly said to derive from the Puritan verdict "Found in Unlawful Carnal Knowledge."

Accounting for the fate of the poor banished children of Adam and Eve—all human beings banished from paradise—Augustine posited that the cursed consequence of the first couple's disobedience was passed down through the generations by means of the very act of physical intimacy that was itself the source of generation. Even in marriage, sexual arousal is evil. Marital intercourse is tolerable only for reproduction, never for pleasure.[22] Children born as a result of their parents' sexual intercourse are born into sin—original sin. Even licit sex is a moral trauma, with mortal consequences. Only the "rebirth of Baptism" could take that sin away.

So complete was the doom that followed on this legacy of original sin that, in Augustine's conception, an infant who dies without that cleansing rebirth of Baptism goes straight to hell. This grim forecast would prove to be too cruel for Catholic belief, and so the myth of "limbo" would be invented, a Last Things[23] respite for those babies. In limbo, they would never be happy in the afterlife, but at least they would not burn.

Apart from those babies consigned to hell, the lake of fire, the single most fateful note of this reading, concerned the woman, who would be reduced to her sexuality and derided ever after as the source of the sin and therefore the cause of the Fall. Bold Eve, after all, was the one who offered the forbidden fruit to weak-kneed Adam. All human suffering was pinned on her.

Augustine's dualism saw the male as spirit and the female as flesh, which made male supremacy the foundation stone of existence. Female flesh was properly held in contempt. Adam was the moral agent whose disobedience—whose defiance—was determinative, but the woman's body set the evil dynamic in motion. The woman would be the locus of punishment: She would have no sexual autonomy; no place in the exercise of social power; no independent role outside the narrow confines of family. Not to mention being trapped in the pain cave of the birthing room.

After Eve, according to the train of thought Augustine set moving, the woman would be the temptress, to be controlled at all costs. Otherwise, the man, ever weak-kneed, would be lost in a wilderness of unbridled erotic longing. If Augustine's theology as regards sex took off from his mature remorse at the rampant lust he had experienced as a young man—and, perhaps, from his regret at having banished the woman who had had his child—and if that theology also followed from the cultural assumptions embedded in the ancient world's spirit-flesh dualism, the consequent indictment of the woman as the source of sexual sin was equally rooted in the ancient world's patriarchy.

But it was not always so. The theological denigration of women was a major revision of the assumptions that had informed the Christian movement from the Gospels forward. Jesus himself modeled an egalitarian respect toward women: In Christ, "there is neither male nor female."[24] Early Christians presented a definition of morality that had everything to do with love of neighbor and nothing to do with the stifling of normal erotic impulses. After Augustine, such erotic impulses were absolute occasions of sin, and women were sin's custodians.

Augustine's reinterpretation of the Adam and Eve story amounted to an invention of a new theology. It was miles away from the simple and beautiful truth that Augustine and Anselm both would have found had they more profoundly taken in another verse in Genesis: "He created them male and female, and He blessed them, and called them human."[25] But after Augustine, that original blessedness was replaced by original sin.

Augustine's massive reimagining of the Christian tradition—he wrote definitive treatises on everything from the Trinity to the "just war" theory—came exactly as the Roman Empire was crumbling before the onslaught of northern "barbarian" invaders. His thinking was a last bulwark against the new chaos, and it made his reputation as the greatest mind in the ancient Christian world. Stamped with such prestige, his new interpretation of the story of Adam and Eve immediately led to a practical elevation of virginity as the ethical ideal, and with the Christian calendar of saints dominated ever after by putative male and female virgins.

The ritual purity codes of pagan cults—vestals and eunuchs— were reimagined as Christian saintliness. The idea that the Church's priestly elite should be radically celibate began to circulate, even if it did not take full institutional hold until the Middle Ages. But the idea of sexual repression as a mode of intimacy with God surely did.

Across the centuries, the quashing of normal erotic urges only drove such appetites into the social and psychological netherworld, where they festered with predictable results: sexual neurosis, ecclesiastical dishonesty, desire displaced into power, obsessive insistence on male dominance, demonization of deviance from unrealistic norms, scrupulosity canonized, denial of all of this as the governing instrument of clericalism.

The massive sexual dysfunction of the contemporary Catholic Church began with Augustine.

THESE ABSTRACTIONS WERE anything but abstract when I was young. I was like a tuning fork, set vibrating by the conscious and unconscious signals that surrounded my coming of age. I was a boy who could explain little but who took in much. The world around me was ever larger and more electric, but its scale and intensity were nothing compared with the world within.

Always, in that inner realm—where I was otherwise alone, ever the solo sailor, the mountain climber, the distance runner—there was the felt presence of the One who was there, just there, my Imagined Friend.

As I became more literate in belief, the Jesus of the Gospels began gradually to come into focus. I was able to give content to what had been mainly an intuitive intimacy—and, given all that I had learned from the religious authorities in my life in the parish and the school, an eccentric one.

As I learned to read literature, I was also able to read the accounts of what had made Jesus unforgettable to His first followers and what was making Him unforgettable to me. I had a pocket-sized New Testament that I began to read on my own. Soon enough, it was always in my book bag. I had no words for the sensation then, but in looking back, I realize that the figure of Jesus, now one I learned about as well as imagined, was steadily reinforcing the hidden thing in me that was pushing back against what I was getting from the Church.

In the most human of the friends of Jesus in the Gospels, I recognized myself. I identified most powerfully with Peter, who wanted desperately to be worthy of Jesus, but who regularly fell short. His habitual failure came to a climax when, despite himself, he expressly denied that he knew the Lord. He did this in Jesus's most brutal hour of need, even while He was being hauled to Golgotha.[26] Peter's lying betrayal occurred not once but, as the text puts it, "thrice": "I know not the man!"[27]

I had no direct acquaintance with the self-loathing that so gripped the treasonous Peter after the death of Jesus—"He went out and wept bitterly"[28]—but I understood it. Yet self-loathing like that could be reversed. Is that what I found so riveting about Peter?

When I finally took in the story—really took it in—of how the risen Jesus, mysteriously appearing on a beach, so tenderly forgave Peter, I was amazed to find tears in my eyes. "Peter, do you love me?" Jesus asked. "Yes, Lord, I love you." Jesus repeated the question, putting it to Peter three times—*thrice*—one time for each denial. "You know all things, Lord," Peter pleaded finally. "You know I love you." And then Jesus made forgiveness real by commissioning Peter as the shepherd of His own flock: "Feed my sheep."[29]

It did not occur to me to ask, yet I do now: What could this irresistibly human Peter have to do with the infallible popes who would rule like emperors from a gilded chair they claimed was his?

In that early time of my awakening, on another front I did take sharp notice of Jesus's warm attachment to women, something that was never spoken of in all the sermons I heard. Even as an uninitiated reader of the Gospels, I could sense the unashamed sexual undercurrent that ran between Jesus and several women: the one "taken in adultery"; the repentant prostitute whose oily ministration with unpinned hair He welcomes; Mary Magdalene, who follows Him almost everywhere, refuses to abandon him on Golgotha, and is there to embrace Him in the garden of the tomb. Was it outrageous of me to feel, if inchoately, that Jesus was by my side, even as I came into sexual awareness? He invited me with that oft-repeated refrain—"Be not afraid"—to lighten up.

My coming to the more complicated inner consciousness of young adulthood, therefore, instead of driving me away from Jesus, seemed yet another occasion for deepening my connection to Him. My old Imagined Friend was still there. Even the contradictions and confusions I encountered seemed like yet more information to be used as, well, *knowledge.* The Genesis story's insistence that the fruit of the tree was "the knowledge of good and evil" made sense to me, even if that knowledge, absent any truly evil act I might have committed, was costing me my innocence.

Augustine's term for the permanent dangers of sexual arousal and the involuntary inclination toward sin that it inevitably provoked was "concupiscence." Stephen Greenblatt says the word implies that sex has an inbuilt "touch of evil."[30] Concupiscence is classically defined as desire of the lower appetite contrary to reason. (The Latin *cupere* means "to desire.")[31]

It is a word that, when I came to it, I understood at once — going right back to my infatuation with Dürer's Eve. But my longing was for far more than Eve. The portrait of the naked woman, however much it stirred biological ardor, forced the larger acknowledgment that my desire had come to transcend every physical sensation, including nascent sexual feelings.

What was I longing for? I was longing to surpass myself. I was longing for my future. I was longing for experience in the world. I was longing for life itself. That longing defined me. And the knowledge it brought was that Jesus, with me in suffering, was with me in longing, too.

In Father Raymond's Latin class at St. Anselm's Priory School, I had learned of the *mysterium tremendum et fascinans*, the mystery that repels and attracts. Now I had an English word for it — a fancy one. At last I had a word for the knot of anguish lodged less in my groin than in my chest — the sorrowful self-doubt that had marked me for years: concupiscence.

I could not have explained it yet, even to Jesus, but I had from Him an unauthorized way to think of the concupiscence — the desire, the longing — that should have been damning me. Yet it was making me who I was.

✠

CHAPTER 12

Destroy the World to Save It

I saw a star fallen from heaven to earth . . . and from the
shaft rose smoke like the smoke from a great furnace.

—Apocalypse 9:1–2

Thus I came to the far side of adolescence, in that "sent-up"
resistance to the religious "vocation" toward which I had
been tracked. My subject in this book is the crisis in the Catholic
priesthood—what underlies it and how it relates to the Church's
effect on my life. My theory is that by telling the story of my coming to embrace the life of the priesthood, even if despite myself, I
can uncover something about the priesthood's meaning.

I would never have become a priest if the only draw were the
complicated inner currents that I have identified thus far. Despite
the all-too-human tides that ebb and flow below the surface of a
person's consciousness, the call to the priesthood amounts to an
invitation to the urgent business of making the world a better
place. I was typical of most men who wind up getting ordained in
that I heard such an invitation and took it.

. . .

THIS PART OF my story begins with a girl, and with my father's posting to Germany in 1958, halfway through my time in high school. Trailing our father by a few months, for the sake of a completed school year, my mother and brothers and I sailed to Europe on the SS *America*. That ship, in the mid-1950s, was the fanciest ocean liner afloat—our first real taste of the privilege of Dad's rank. Heading off from suburban Alexandria to live in a military enclave for the first time, we were about to be initiated into the rarefied class status attached to the stars on my father's shoulders. The swank ship was a foretaste.

One night early in the transatlantic crossing, when I had slipped away from my family to wander the promenade decks of the *America* alone, I came across a girl my age, standing by herself at the ship's rail, looking out over the moonlit sea. Her long brown hair wafted in the warm breeze of the vessel's motion. She was dressed in what I would later learn to call a twinset, but she looked glamorous to me.

"Hi," I said with as much nonchalance as I could muster. "Nice night." I leaned on the rail. With my back to the wind, I found it possible to light up one of the Marlboros I'd filched from a silver tray in the first-class cocktail lounge. She replied in a friendly way, and we struck up a conversation. She told me that she was an Army brat, traveling with her family to Germany. I remember the encounter vividly and how it left me feeling. I reconstruct our exchange here, faithful to that feeling, if not necessarily to the exact words we used.

"That's amazing," I replied with relief. "I'm an Air Force brat"—it was a phrase I'd never used before—"and we're going to Germany, too. Wiesbaden."

"Hanau," she replied confidently, "a garrison near Frankfurt." The two German place-names—Hanau and Frankfurt—meant nothing to me, but I was struck by the word "garrison," the ease with which she'd used the argot. She added, "My father is about to take up a command."

"A command?"

"Third Armored Division," she said. "That's tanks. My dad's a bird colonel. Battalion commander." I remember her saying such things with a curl of pride that embarrassed me, since I could make no such efficient description of my father's role. I'd been in the Pentagon on the occasional Saturday, a few times after school, but Dad's life in the Air Force had been a world away from mine.

As if reading that hesitation, she asked, "What about yours?"

"Mine?"

"Your father. What rank?"

And that simply, she pointed the way into the world I was about to enter. "My dad's a general."

She registered my statement with a cocking of the head, an assessing with which I would soon enough become familiar among teenagers who were obsessed with, among so much else, the military ranks of their fathers. "How many?" she asked. When I did not answer, she added, "Stars?"

"Two." In fact, Dad had been promoted from one star only a few months before, with the new assignment.

"Major general," she said, grinning. "Yes, sir!" She feigned a salute, then surprised me by reaching across to my cigarette. "May I?"

"Sure."

The ease with which she took a drag made me certain she was a veteran smoker, way ahead of me.

We met up again on subsequent evenings as the ship churned its way across the Atlantic. Once, we drifted, with feigned entitlement, into the cocktail lounge, where we were served beers, no questions asked. I remember being enthralled with her, liking the flirtation, but she was, essentially, my first instructor in the ways of military "dependents." She was a rising junior, too, and would be attending the Army high school in Frankfurt. She had grown up on Army posts, had lived in half a dozen different places, including, as I recall, Japan.

She sharpened my anticipation of Germany, and not only positively. It was this girl, I believe, who first made me aware of a possible underside to the life we were about to take up.

There were things to fear. I'd have thought they would have to do with the Nazis, leftover auras of World War II, but that was wrong. Compared with her, I felt naïve. She had a grasp of the geography that lay ahead of us. What became vivid to me, for the first time, was the Iron Curtain—the fact of it. Only beginning now did I grasp that the phrase was not a mere metaphor. The fortified border dividing West Germany from East Germany would only be an automobile drive away from where this girl and I would live.

When "the balloon went up," she told me, we "dependents" would be the first to go. The balloon going up—that is the expression I associate with her: the beginning of war. Here is what I took from her: Having American children that close to the Red Army front was Washington's way of guaranteeing the North Atlantic Treaty, guaranteeing that the United States would respond to any Soviet move in Europe. That, more than kinfolk sentimentality, was the Pentagon's reason for transporting military families to the European theater.[1] We kids were collateral. The Reds would storm west, we would die. Boom. America would have no choice but to respond, and then all hell would break loose. The balloon would go up. Us.

"We're the sacrificial lambs," I picture her saying, with the wave of a cigarette. "Our job is to be burned alive." I would learn soon enough that an Army brat's authority in making such assertions was absolute. Hers was absolute to me, and so was her sense of the shocking new imminence of war. I had no idea what to say. She noticed that. She said, "Doesn't your dad tell you anything?"

The night before the ship pulled into the German port of Bremerhaven, where we would disembark, the girl and I found each other at the rail once more. Her Frankfurt, we had discovered by then, was less than an hour from my Wiesbaden, an easy train ride. We promised to see each other again. But we never did.

That the girl's father was a commander of tanks was probably what prompted me to soon learn that Soviet armored divisions outnumbered NATO forces three to one: tens of thousands of Red tanks arrayed along a front line not far from Frankfurt—or Wiesbaden.

In addition to the delights of an American high school abroad— sock hops, pep rallies, no drinking age—I was soon to feel the heat of Cold War fever, discovering more fully what it was to be the Free World's sacrificial lambs. My first real taste of the sweetness of being young would be soured by fear. Of that, in effect, the girl on the fancy ocean liner had warned me.

IT'S ONLY IN looking back that I comprehend the breadth and depth of what took me into the Church. It is not too much to say that in Germany I found myself staring into an abyss, which stared back.[2]

It may seem a stretch, but what I am calling the "theology of abuse" extends to the broad religious attitude that underwrote the American consensus in the years of my growing up—a consensus that had its unnamed origins in the nihilist theology of St. Anselm and St. Augustine, and that enabled all Americans to live with a deeply sublimated nuclear dread. Yes, nuclear fear is part of this story, too.

It's simple, really. I briefly referred to this before. The God who chooses to save the fallen children of Adam and Eve by requiring the death on the cross of His only begotten Son is the God who, at the end of history, will save the world by destroying it. That is the vision laid out in the last book of the Bible, aptly known as Apocalypse.[3] That text is chock-full of fallen stars, obliterated cities, rivers afire, world-shattering wars between forces of good and evil. It is a handbook of an ultimate Armageddon. And its theme boils down to this: *If God, for His own purposes, can destroy His own Son, He can destroy the earth and its cosmos.*

This is the God whose bottomless love for you, as Anselm and Augustine tell it, will send you to hell for all eternity.

This is the God who, hearing the earnest petitions of an interceding saint, will interrupt the laws of nature to miraculously heal one person's fatal cancer while ignoring another's, because that other has no advocating friend among the heavenly elect.

This is less a God of love—or justice—than a God of whimsy.

I was born the very week that the atomic weapons laboratory opened in Los Alamos, New Mexico. The span of my life, therefore, matches exactly the threat-laden age when the capacity to bring about the end of history was transferred from God to human beings. We humans could embrace this capacity, even celebrate it, only because we were convinced, as the medieval popes first proclaimed, that God—somehow—wills it.

In my New Testament, I read of what to expect on the Last Day. The coming of the heavenly Jerusalem presupposed the utter destruction of the earthly Jerusalem. "The new heaven and the new earth" could come to pass only once "the first earth had passed away."[4] And it would pass away in a cataclysmic war to be fought on the fields of Armageddon, led by one "clad in a robe dipped in blood, and his name by which He is called is the Word of God.[5] . . . He will tread the winepress of the fury of the wrath of God the Almighty."[6]

So much for the Prince of Peace.

True, God's love would wipe away every tear, but only after God's wrath drank the tears of every human unlucky enough to be alive at the end. And how, exactly, would all of this occur? "Then I looked, and I heard an eagle crying in a loud voice as it flew in mid-heaven, 'Woe! Woe! Woe to those who dwell on earth.'[7] . . . And a great star fell from heaven, blazing like a torch, and it fell on a third of the rivers and on the fountains of water.[8] . . . And he was given the key of the shaft of the bottomless pit; and from the shaft rose smoke like the smoke of a great furnace, and the sun and the air were darkened with the smoke from the shaft."[9]

Here was a first whiff of the mushroom cloud. Not for nothing, as even I understood, was this vision of the End Times given as the Bible's last word, the word that gives us the synonym for ultimate mayhem.

The apocalyptic imagination came into its own by informing a new American creed during the Cold War, when opposition to what was called "godless communism" prompted the invention of "mutual assured destruction." MAD was a doomsday scenario our God-fearing nation could have purposefully embraced only with assurances of divine approbation. The leaders of Christian religion—from the evangelist Billy Graham and the theologian Reinhold Niebuhr to Pope Pius XII and New York's Cardinal Francis Spellman—were happy to provide those assurances. Yes, indeed, *God wills it!*

The slogan that gave perfect expression to this mindset, the political mantra of my 1950s childhood, was "Better Dead Than Red." It was to my America what *No Salvation Outside the Church* was to my Catholicism. But what we did not sufficiently grasp was that the "dead" would extend from each of us individually to the whole of civilization itself—perhaps, with the global catastrophe known as "nuclear winter," to the very planet. During the Vietnam

War, a decade later, an American combat officer articulated a distilled version of the doctrine when he told a reporter with unforgettable succinctness, "It became necessary to destroy the village to save it."[10]

Like most Americans of my generation, I had been schooled in the bruising trauma of an atomic bomb attack through duck-and-cover exercises, crouching under our pint-sized desks. We had been instructed to close our eyes so that the fireball would not blind us—the fireball that would incinerate everyone who could see it. As is often remarked (sixties radicals emphasized this), ours was the first generation to be reared in the knowledge that a world-ending cataclysm was lurking just outside the window. We did know that, although we knew nothing about the insane number of atomic and hydrogen bombs that were stuffing the American arsenal while we covered our heads.

The United States had nearly ten times more nuclear weapons than the Soviet Union,[11] yet we thought the thing to fear was Moscow, which, in 1957, successfully launched the first space satellite, Sputnik 1. This dramatized Moscow's shocking new ability to hit America with an intercontinental ballistic missile, and soon we Americans had convinced ourselves of a terrifying "missile gap" favoring the Reds. For the first time in its history, the United States was unprotected by its ocean bulwarks—an unprecedented vulnerability to all-out attack, made palpable to every American by the sight of a twinkling new star in orbit overhead. The sublimated fear of a coming nuclear war quietly shaped the inner awareness of legions of children, preparing us to become that sixties generation who wanted nothing so much as change. And why not?

OWING TO ACCIDENTS of my biography—above all, my Air Force father's place in the inner circle of the nuclear brass—my case of nuclear dread became acute, explicit, highly personal, and life-shaping. That had subtly begun even before we went to Germany. As a young boy, I had attended air shows at Andrews Air Force Base, outside Washington, the original headquarters of the Strategic Air Command. I'd watched airmen salute my father as we stood beside a giant eight-engine B-52 bomber. That one plane carried, as my father put it to me once, "a thousand Hiroshimas." I'd have expected to hear an undertone of boasting awe in his statement, but what I sensed was more ominous than that. As he pointed to the bomber's fuselage legend, PEACE IS OUR PROFESSION, I picked up the mournful note when he recited the deterrence dogma: "Only our readiness to obliterate the enemy keeps him from attacking us."

Still, I was thrilled at my father's going off to work in his blue uniform, and I came as naturally to the effervescence of "Off We Go into the Wild Blue Yonder" as to "Take Me Out to the Ballgame." But when, halfway through my high school years, we followed my father to Germany, my airpower romance came in for a rough landing. Once we were at Wiesbaden Air Base, I found myself in the crosshairs of the Moscow-Washington standoff. Expanding on what that girl on the SS *America* had begun, my fellow military dependents at Wiesbaden completed my initiation into the secret meaning of our overseas proximity to the Iron Curtain.

Looking only for a lark, I underwent a lethal jolt of nuclear dread in what was already dubbed "Flashpoint Berlin." There I would see the cost of the good-versus-evil bipolarity of our Cold War dogma, and I would learn that I myself could not be trusted with it.

And, with my father at a moment of fevered crisis, I would see more deeply into the nihilist heart of nuclear darkness than any boy should have to. There is nothing like a vivid sense of the approaching end of the world—that biblical "bottomless pit"—to give a man religion. That's one way I got mine. But what kind of religion?

Then, having been unexpectedly brought onto the stage of the Cold War drama, I would, even more surprisingly, be introduced to a man who would give me an entirely new way to experience it—the way of an authentic Christian faith that, once grasped, I would embrace and want to spread. Amazingly, that man would be a pope. Just when the close dangers of war nearly overwhelmed me, the Roman pontiff himself would prepare me to see those dangers, and standing against them, as essential to the kind of priest I could be.

I WOULD LOVE now to meet that young woman I met on the ship, to tell her how much that brief encounter changed me—not its hint of romance, but its first faint signal of consummate alarm.

When I look back on those days and nights of the Atlantic crossing on the SS *America*, I recognize something else, too. Someone else. My old companion was there, hovering in the shadow, the close presence. I would never have spoken of Him to that girl, of course. If my connection to Jesus had been shaped, first by a child's devotion to an "imaginary friend" who became "Imagined," and then by a tormented adolescent's recognition of a fellow sufferer, now another meaning came to the fore.

To stand on a luxury liner's teak-floor promenade deck late at night in the middle of the Atlantic Ocean, the wind howling; to stare up at the midnight-blue canopy above, shot through with a plethora of glistening silver stars never seen before; to feel the rise and fall of ocean swells, the dizzying hint of weightlessness at each instant of crest—it was, yes, to be seized for the first remembered time by the grandeur of the universe, which could mean only one thing to me.

"The world is charged with the grandeur of God." I would think of that midnight ocean sky when I came upon this line from the Gerard Manley Hopkins poem "God's Grandeur."[12] But the memory of that ocean sky, open above me as I was getting my first particular taste of the world's radical vulnerability—"*A thousand Hiroshimas!*" *My father did tell me something!*—would make another line from the poem all the more jolting. "It will flame out, like shining from shook foil."

"Flame out!" There it was. On the SS *America*, no less, I felt a premonition of the coming end, not the cosmos being snuffed by an explosion of the sun, but the earth being done in by men at war. By us.

At that point, yes, it was the Reds I feared. Yet what really brought me low was the radical insignificance of my own puny being in the face of such a prospect: radical insignificance except for—and even I could feel this—the unbounded capacity of one's own consciousness to take in such a magnificent, terrible perception.

I thought I would flame out with what I saw. My exquisite sense of how close to being lost all of this grandeur could be was precisely what made it so infinitely precious that night. On the edge of the unspeakable, I felt more alive than ever. "Because the Holy Ghost over the bent World"—Hopkins again —"broods with warm breast and with ah! bright wings."

Perhaps because, at that moment, I had no language of my own for any of this—it was literally unspeakable—I felt more intensely than ever the muteness of that close presence, the "someone there" who had, since the beginning of my self-awareness, gone by the name of Jesus.

"I have come that you might have life," He said—a rescuing promise that I found in my pocket New Testament—"life to the full."[13] His was not a coming for the sake of death—not even redemptive death, as Augustine's punitive exegesis and Anselm's medieval treatise both had it—but for the sake of life's fullness.

What was I longing for but that? Not just for myself, but for my threatened country and for the fragile world. As I had instinctively said no at St. Anselm's Priory School to the headmaster namesake of Augustine, I was instinctively saying no to the death-laden theology of the Church's greatest saints.

My longing had itself been a first opening to what I would eventually know to call transcendence, and that night in the midst of the ocean, I felt it as never before. Suffering had been my initial entrée to the faith—suffering experienced as the dread of hell, anguish at my brother's polio, the poignance of the families at those funeral Masses, the agony of a tormented conscience. But the fullness of life, paired with its radical contingency, was a different opening, a better one, to a better faith.

To life! *L'Chaim!* Jesus, a man given to wine and banquets, not hair shirts. Jesus, a man among men, a friend to women, a greeter of strangers, an enemy to none. Jesus, contentedly at my side as I embraced a new sense of myself. Jesus with me during a loaded shipboard flirtation with a pretty girl—a girl who invited a plunge into depths from which I've yet to emerge.

I Want to Live! was the title of a hit movie that year. It starred Susan Hayward and told of a prostitute sentenced to death for murder. Nuclear obsessive that I was about to become, *I Want to Live!* was a movie title made for me, one I would never forget. *I want us all to live!*

CHAPTER 13

✣

Some Damn Fool Like You

Berlin is the testicle of the West. When I want
the West to scream, I squeeze on Berlin.
—Nikita Khrushchev[1]

N o sooner did we arrive in Germany in the spring of 1958,
taking up life in the American enclave at Wiesbaden Air
Base, than U.S. military forces shifted to high alert, a nerve-racking
hair-trigger status that would outlast my more than two years there.
That fall, Nikita Khrushchev, the Soviet premier, gave the three
Western powers—the United States, France, and Great Britain—
six months to withdraw their forces from West Berlin.

In addition to the dread sparked by Sputnik twinkling overhead, the terror attached to the imagined "missile gap" was on
the rise. Moscow's nuclear edge seemed commanding. Yet it was
not real. In 1958, in addition to its vastly larger warhead arsenal,
the United States had dozens of ICBMs, while the Soviets had
four.[2] Yet that perceived Soviet superiority was what had embold-
ened Khrushchev to issue his Berlin ultimatum. When President
Dwight D. Eisenhower nevertheless replied to Khrushchev with a
defiant *No!* the clock started ticking toward the deadline the So-

viet premier had set. His message was clear: *Get out of Berlin or else!*

This began one of the most perilous four years in the history of the world. It was a brush with nuclear Armageddon that would end only with the Cuban missile crisis in 1962. But the ignition point was Berlin.

After World War II, the victors had carved up Germany and its capital city into four zones of occupation. That division had been frozen in time by Cold War tensions, effectively epitomizing the bipolar partition between West and East. Free Berlin—West Berlin—was well within the otherwise "unfree" Soviet sector of Germany. Red-dominated East Germany had been sealed off from the outside world by the infamous Iron Curtain, which was in fact a heavily armed, impenetrable frontier. To attempt to cross that border was to risk near certain death. The single exception as a mode of travel back and forth were the Allied access routes through East Germany to West Berlin: a stretch of autobahn, a single rail-road track, a canal network, and a narrow air corridor. These pas-sageways were defined—and guaranteed—by the so-called Four Power Agreement of 1945.

But since the war, four million out of seventeen million East Germans had escaped to the West through Berlin, and four thou-sand a week were still doing so. These escapees comprised the best educated and most capable people in East Germany, or the Ger-man Democratic Republic. West Berlin was a capitalist boom-town, while East Berlin was still practically a bombed-out ruin. This stark contrast between the two urban halves belied all Red propaganda and served as a magnet drawing hordes of the disen-chanted from all across Eastern Europe. The communists simply had to shut the escape hatch down. But that meant expelling the Allies from Berlin and cutting off their access to the beleaguered city, even at the cost of war.

. . .

IN WIESBADEN, GOING to and from school and hanging around the "exchange," as the base shopping and entertainment area was called, we "brats" could hear the ticking of Khrushchev's clock. We saw the upswing in the olive-drab truck traffic—ordnance half-tracks shuttling between armories and supply depots. Overhead, with the screeching air war buildup, we traced lumbering C-54 cargo planes making way for incoming F-100 Thunderbirds, and even a wing of B-47 bombers belonging to the Strategic Air Command. We heard the anxious pitch of nervous flight crew laughter in the base snack bar. It was now that I informed myself about relative tank deployments arrayed along a front that felt closer than ever. Just across the Taunus mountain range, visible in the distance, many tens of thousands of Red Army tanks stared down a few thousand of ours. That only meant, of course, that as soon as the Soviets overran the Allied ground defenses, the balloon would go up, to use the phrase I'd learned from the girl on the ship: *Gold Code Launch!*

With a spasm of nuclear assault, the incineration would be general, beginning here, at the base snack bar.

I have no idea how or why my parents permitted it—or did I slip away without permission?—but I went to Berlin in the thick of that late-1950s crisis. Without having the vocabulary to define it as such, I saw for myself, in the devastation in East Berlin as measured against the sumptuousness of West Berlin, the epitome of the moral dichotomy that had long defined my faith. East versus West; the City of Man versus the City of God; slavery versus freedom; communism versus democracy; evil versus good; sin versus grace. I did not fully understand the religious meaning of this political bifurcation then, but I do now.

At Wiesbaden High School, I signed up for the Teenage Automobile Club of Hesse, which was organized around attending sports car races and rallies. I might have joined for the black satin bomber jacket, with the letters TACH emblazoned on the back, but the weekend trips to Nürburgring, Sachsenring, and other German racetracks were the real draw. It turned out, though, that the big-deal German Grand Prix that year was scheduled for West Berlin—probably because the West German government, now housed in Bonn, wanted to make a political point. Astonishingly, I and five of my car-crazy buddies traveled to Berlin to attend the race.

At Berlin's famous AVUS racetrack, the sports car drivers wore goggles but no helmets. They drove Porsche Spyders, Maseratis, Mercedes-Benz Gullwings. Their engines shot flames out of the exhaust pipes, especially when gunning up and around the great banked turn at the end of the mile-long straightaway. Overshadowing the track was the distinctive Eiffel Tower–like Berliner Funkturm, a girdered radio tower. Lining the track were tiered wooden grandstands and flimsy straw bales, which pretended to protect close-in spectators from the hairpin hazard. I saw all of this, standing in the crush of the sunlit infield, cheek by jowl with my fellow TACH members.

I had purloined my parents' 8 mm home movie camera, and once the race began, I did my best to follow the storming cars through the eyepiece, especially once the flashing automobiles entered the swooping concrete slope of the high turn, reaching perhaps sixty feet above the level ground. We had positioned ourselves in line with that structural marvel, the heart of the race action. With the bank's outside more elevated than its inside, the soaring crescent seemed to invite acceleration, even as the cars, upon mounting the sloping wall, bunched together. With the camera whirring at my ear, I did my best to track the knot of racers through the zoom lens. Around and around they went. Each time they screamed out of the straightaway into the pitched bank, I was ready.

Suddenly, in the fourth or fifth lap, one car cut away to go higher than all the others, a daring pass at the top of the bank that was so thrilling I moved my eyes to the side of the camera eyepiece to watch the spectacle unimpeded. Unconsciously, I kept the film rolling for some moments. Well above the pack, the breakaway driver was riding alone at the upper edge of the great curving shell. Then it happened. The sleek gray sports car hurtled up and off the lip of the high banked turn. Flight! The car soared, then began to tumble. I saw the driver being thrown into the air. His flying, flailing form collided with a flagpole as he arced skyward, knocking the pole down before falling out of sight.

No one goes to a sports car race hoping to see a driver die— I later heard race car fans chide themselves with this—but if no driver ever died, no fan would ever go. For me, until that moment the thing had been less complicated. The race and all its hoopla had been a simple festival of my wish for a happy lark in Europe— an adventure whose joys might outweigh the sense of nuclear foreboding I'd felt since meeting that girl on the SS *America*.

But no. That fatality at AVUS hit me like a bolt from the blue— though it was a bolt I'd somehow known to expect. I stood there staring. I had lowered the camera to my side, forgetting it. I was certain that the driver hitting that pole, then disappearing, had been killed. For long moments, the crowd remained still and silent, even as the race cars continued to roar out and off into the straightaway. One of my friends clasped my upper arm. "Wow! Did you get that?" he asked. At first, I did not know what he meant. Then I realized he was talking about the camera. At some point, I had stopped filming. I had no idea when, or what I'd actually recorded. I did not reply. He let go of my arm and fell back into the silence. At last, a whispered buzz of confirmation passed through the throng—*"Tot . . . tot"*—a brusque German word pronounced "tote" and meaning "dead." I heard the definitive statement as if I knew its meaning. Well, I did.

Words from my other language passed through my mind: *De profundis clamavi ad te*, the grief-stricken plea from the depths of the abyss. I had regarded those midmorning funerals at St. Mary's Church in Virginia as an initiation into the enigma of mortality, but in fact I had never witnessed an actual death before. That I was at a distance from this one took nothing away from the shock of what I'd seen. A man in the throes of life—"life to the full": What else is the exhilaration of such speed and power?—had had his life snapped off in an instant, like the flagpole that broke as if it were a toothpick.

In remembering that gruesome but extreme detail while writing this, I wondered if I had imagined the entire event. Didn't drivers wear seatbelts? With research, I found that indeed the Grand Prix tragedy occurred as I recalled it. It had been seared in my memory, no matter what the 8 mm film had caught. The wrecked car was a Porsche RSK Spyder, and the deceased driver was a Frenchman named Jean Behra. Flung from the car, he hit a flagpole. In my research, I discovered no mention of the flagpole actually breaking, but I read that after that race, the great banking AVUS curve was no longer used on the Grand Prix circuit because it was too dangerous.

It came back to me that my club mate had asked if I'd gotten the man's death on film. I may have, but in the moment I wasn't sure. To my surprise, I hoped not. I grasped at once—viscerally—that to have captured that instant of death on film would have been wrong, disrespecting the sacred gravity of the event, akin to pornography. I could not have explained that to my friend. When I then found it utterly impossible to discuss the tragedy with him or the others—our exchanges consisted of nothing much beyond

"Jeez, man, jeez!"—I learned something about the limits of shallow friendship.

IN THE DEATH of one can be glimpsed the deaths of all. Having such a monumental sense of mortality as an overriding point of reference may be what accounted for the experience I had in the hours that followed the race, when I found myself listlessly tagging along as our little clique of Yankee teenagers set out to do the town in Flashpoint Berlin. Altogether, the death at AVUS, followed by a day's exploration of the savagely divided city, burned that weekend into me, lodging it as a cornerstone of identity, with crucial, if oblique, implications for the religious mystery I am plumbing here.

Hundreds of Allied air raids during World War II had left most of Berlin in rubble. What the bombs did not destroy, Soviet artillery finished, and fires did the rest. At war's end, the few buildings that remained standing with roofs intact were mostly uninhabitable. If the walls of thousands of living rooms and bedrooms were still upright, wallpaper exposed, they were open to the sky. Berlin in 1945 was a vast charnel house.

Thirteen years after the end of the war, the stink of ash was still in the air, faint but discernible, even in the western sector of the city, which had become a glitzy showcase of recovery. We lads began our exploration there, with a hooting trek down the Kurfürstendamm, West Berlin's garishly rehabilitated boulevard. Shining with shops, hotels, outdoor cafés, restaurants, and wide sidewalks fit for strolling, it had the glamour of Fifth Avenue—but the Ku'damm was all brand-new. In that central area of the western sector, only Kaiser Wilhelm Memorial Church, deliberately left standing as a hulking half ruin to commemorate the catastrophe, offered any hint of what had befallen the city. Blackened, unroofed, and rough edged, with the half-shorn belfry having the eerie aspect of a giant extracted tooth, the destroyed church stood as a silent rebuke to the surrounding conspicuous prosperity, as if this city, West as well as East, deserved a permanent devastation.

In those days, three years before Khrushchev solved the GDR's escape-hatch problem with the erection of the infamous Berlin Wall, there was ready access between East and West Berlin, even if the checkpoints were festooned with large warning signs: ACH-TUNG! YOU ARE NOW LEAVING THE BRITISH SECTOR! The check-points, with movable barriers and flanking tanks, were intimidating, but it was simpler, in any case, to cross into the Soviet sector by riding on the S-Bahn, a decrepit elevated train that rattled from one side of the city to the other without the fuss of identification and currency checks, and that was how we went. From the train's vantage above the streets, we had our first glimpse of the grid of East Berlin's vast empty spaces, stretching off into the distance, a staggering contrast to what we were leaving behind in the West.

The largest note of immediate difference was the utter absence, in the East, of trees, and only then did I realize that the many trees I'd seen in the West had all been young. What trees had survived the bombs and shells of the war had been cut down for fuel in the war's savage aftermath.

We left the elevated train at Stalinallee, a wide, mile-long bou-levard lined with block after block of monumental buildings, eight or ten stories high. A huge memorial to valiant Soviet soldiers stood at one end, and a mammoth statue of Joseph Stalin stood at the other. The tourist brochure identified the looming buildings as housing for workers and offices for bureaucrats, but the imper-sonal uniformity of the structures made them seem like set-piece backdrops for the socialist parades the place seemed made for.

May Day parades, I thought. And then that phrase took over my mind as a cry for help: *Mayday! Mayday!* The international distress signal, originating in the French *M'aidez!* (Help me!).

My friends and I walked along the mostly vacant sidewalks, silently taking in the scene. Previously a raucous group, we were all at once subdued. I found myself taking up the rear again, aware of a strange feeling of dislocation, set apart from my surroundings but also from my friends. The traffic on the street was sparse, and for once my car-loving pals encountered automobiles they could not identify—the crummy, small products of a backward East German car industry. Stalinallee was meant to impress, but a dreary hopelessness was what landed with weight. The façades of the structures lining the boulevard were uniformly covered with beige and pale blue porcelain tiles, but in many places the tiles had come loose and fallen away. Patches of rough cinder block defaced every building. Even these recent constructions seemed to be sliding into ruin.

But it was the intersections of the boulevard that most invited brooding, because from each set of corners could be seen all that lay behind the movie-set falsehood of what was meant to be a showplace avenue. Stretching out to the right and left, all along the perpendicular streets, was a wasteland of unrepaired ruins, piled rubble, and boarded-up buildings. Even though I had sensed something fake in the frenzy of West Berlin's forced opulence, the desperation of East Berlin's vacancy hit me as a revelation.

The Cold War, with its us-against-them absolutes, was only the latest manifestation of the bipolar structure of the Western imagination that had been put in place a long time ago. European impositions on native peoples, wherever the caravels marked with crosses took conquistadors four hundred years before, had depended on a claim of white supremacy over nonwhite natives everywhere. Before that, in the Middle Ages, the holy wars that had pitted Christendom against Muslim "infidels" far away had enabled Europe to discover what it was by defining what it was not—a positive-negative energy that crackles to this day in the anti-Islamic War on Terror.

But in addition to Muslims, there were "infidels" near at hand, too—Jews, in opposition to whom the Church, from the Gospels forward, had found its primordial identity. A civilizational dualism that began with the Church against the Synagogue continues to be supported by an as yet unreformed triumphalist theology: That is what I see. *Us against them.*

Even while I was in Berlin, the Catholic Church, chastened by what had just been laid bare in Germany, was preparing to turn away from that primordial anti-Jewish theology. But that turn would not actually be brought to fulfillment, and that failure, too, is my subject here.

I see now that the present Catholic Church, with its pope, bishops, and priests—as the living legacy of Christendom—still bears a heavy burden of responsibility for the bipolarity that, in my youth, armed itself with nuclear weapons deployed to defend what we called the Free World. If necessary, we would defend the Free World by destroying the world itself.

Stalinallee might as well have been called Hitler Strasse, for to me and my kind, the Soviets and the Nazis were two sides of the same coin. A stark illustration of the us-against-them moral absolute with which I'd been raised, even if I did not understand it, was right in front of me, but with a difference. When we Catholics smugly proclaimed *No Salvation Outside the Church*, it was not thought that those we were excommunicating could do us any real harm. Protestants might reply with condescension—but what was that? Yet here in Berlin, those we'd damned had put us on notice that they could damn us in return. Indeed, they intended to.

Khrushchev may not have been the demonic Stalin, but with

his *"Get out!"* ultimatum to the West, he had made clear that the communist determination to dominate the world was still alive. In East Berlin, I saw the Soviet threat for what it was—the will to make the whole world into a version of Stalinallee. What was the Free World to do in response if not oppose—and oppose absolutely?

The Roman Catholic Church of that era, my Church, was a rampart of such opposition to that threat, and I should have wholly identified myself with it. I recalled the pamphlet I had worked on in the print shop at St. Anselm's Priory School, *The Pope Speaks,* with its broadside against communism. Pope Pius XII had long been the tribune of resistance to Moscow, helping to arm the West with a readiness to sacrifice everything in opposition to the godless Reds. But now I felt a faint stirring of objection. Our infallible vicar of Christ was the promulgator in chief of the supreme doctrine of the age, enshrined in the rubric "Better Dead Than Red."

Really? What I saw on the Cold War front line, instead of stirring martial ardor, made me wonder. Glimpsing in the barrens of East Berlin the inhuman system enshrined by the Soviets behind the Iron Curtain, I understood for the first time that this was an enemy with little to lose, fully capable of pulling the pin on the postwar stalemate; capable, with an all-out nuclear war, of bringing the pillars of the earth down upon themselves. But were we different?

I wanted out of Berlin as quickly as I could go.

THE SIX-STRONG TEENAGE Automobile Club of Hesse went to and from the divided city on the special U.S. Army Duty Train originating once a day in Frankfurt. An American-controlled train driven by a steam locomotive, the Duty Train bore a large American flag on the side of the first car. Most of the passengers were uniformed U.S. military personnel. Like them, dependents were required to carry travel orders, which we TACH members had obtained courtesy of somebody's father—not mine. Our uniform was the club jacket. Luckily, we lads had a compartment to ourselves.

Our train home, under the authority of a U.S. Army control crew, pulled out of the West Berlin train station in the early evening, which meant traveling through East Germany at night, a repeat of the night trip we'd made on the way in. Now I understood that the communists did not want citizens of the Free World to lay eyes on the daylight bleakness of their realm. In any case, Duty Train passengers were forbidden, while passing through East Germany, to raise the blinds on the windows of the train compartments. Not even the darkness was to be seen. But this time, heading west and having been staggered by the sight of desolate East Berlin, I was dying to see what the subjugated countryside of the imprisoned nation looked like. But orders were orders. As the train rumbled through the darkness, I dozed off.

I snapped awake as the hissing train slowed, then stopped with a loud screeching of brakes. We were at Marienborn, on the East German side of the border. The procedure had been explained to us before. The U.S. control officers—the American train commander, the American train conductor, and their American interpreter—would dismount to present the passengers' travel documents to the Soviet border guards. The Reds would examine the documents, comparing travel orders with identifications, looking for discrepancies. The Soviets would routinely demand to board the train in order to search it. Just as routinely, in the absence of any paperwork inconsistency, the American train commander would deny permission. We waited in our snug, velvet-upholstered compartment in silence. I was next to the blinded window.

But what was out there? Desolation like I'd seen along Stalinallee? Unable to bridle my curiosity, I lifted the window shade, barely an inch. I bent to its edge, and what I saw startled me. There, under harshly illuminating klieg lights, was a formation of tanks—four of them, no six—lined up so that the muzzles of their cannons were pointed directly at the train. The American officers, flanked by a pair of very tall American military policemen, were eye to eye with four Russian officers, red stars prominent on their caps. Without thinking, I picked up the home movie camera from beside me on the seat. I put the lens—only the lens—between the shade and the window glass, and I pressed the button. The camera whirred.

Only seconds later, the door to our compartment slid open with a bang. A very large American MP stormed in, with his side-arm drawn. His blue shoulder patch was emblazoned with a flaming sword. He pointed his free hand at me. "You have the shade up?" he demanded. "Didn't you get the order?"

"Sir, I—"

"A camera! That is a camera! Jesus!"

Before I could say anything further, a second man pressed into the compartment, this one in the dark brown uniform of the Soviets I'd seen outside. He was carrying a machine gun.

The MP turned to him. "I'm handling this!" He said something else, perhaps in Russian. He repeated it fiercely, and the Russian backed away. The MP lunged at me, grabbed my camera, turned toward the Russian, and held it for him to see. With a quick snap of the latch, he opened the camera and efficiently pulled out the reel of film, which he then let fly. The celluloid tape unspooled and spilled out into the compartment.

The MP was doing this so that the Russian would see it. The forbidden film was exposed, ruined—which was the point. The Russian stepped back fully into the corridor. I would never know what I'd captured previously on film, whether it included the Porsche Spyder driver's death or not.

The train commander, an American with captain's bars, pushed into the compartment. He was holding a roster board. The MP pointed at me. "It was him." He handed the movie camera to the captain, who said sharply, "Which one are you?"

"Carroll."

He looked at the list. "General Carroll? Dependent?"

"Yes, sir."

"Do you think your father got to where he is by acting like an asshole?"

"No, sir."

He threw the camera at me. I caught it, but barely.

"I'd write you up," he said with contempt, "but at your old man's altitude, my nose bleeds."

"Yes, sir."

The captain turned and left the compartment. The MP followed him, but leaned back to say, "Some damn fool like you is going to start World War Three."

PART FIVE

✠

The Church Against Itself[1]

Now begins my council.

—Pope John XXIII[2]

✛

CHAPTER 14

Pope John and Me

Madam, this Pope was a real Christian. How could that be? And how could it happen that a true Christian would sit on St. Peter's chair?
—A Roman chambermaid to Hannah Arendt[1]

The year 1958 was the year of Berlin, but it was also the year of Pope John XXIII, whose arrival on the world scene would have intensely personal meaning for me. My whole life followed from what I saw in him, and the present crisis in Roman Catholicism follows from what the Church has refused to see.

It was an unlikely turn in the story of a brooding high school kid, but somehow this new pope addressed the mounting complications of my quiet turmoil. There I was, enthralled with my father's Air Force but beginning to fear that its core mission was in some way wicked. I was striving to be an all-American boy, with a girlfriend and a football letter sweater, but I could not shake the innate religiosity—my Imagined Friend—that I carried now like an embarrassing secret. And running along beneath all of this was the as yet unadmitted qualm I felt about worshipping—much less ever proclaiming—a God of doom.

Perhaps mine was only the common loneliness of adolescence,

but I was primed to layer it over with words I found in the New Testament. I was in the world, but not of it.[2]

Pope John XXIII was a man of wit, and perhaps irreverence. Seeing a crucifix displayed as jewelry on a woman's ample bosom, he declared, "What a Calvary!"[3] Yet he was no buffoon. That he smoked cigarettes and would continue to, surprising as that was, seemed far less shocking than the simple fact that he was a nice person. There was a depth to his goodness. It seems strange to recall this, but the man's evident kindliness came as a large relief, as if we Catholics had been longing for such a person in the Chair of Peter all along. Why should warmheartedness be surprising in a pope?

And something quite pointed struck me about Pope John at once. His kindness was not excluding. He was said to arrive in Rome with the motto "We were all made in God's image . . . and thus, we are all Godly alike," a statement addressed to everyone. John made it clear in what he said and how he said it that his benign goodwill extended to all people everywhere. His predecessor, Pope Pius XII, had embodied the narrow preoccupation that Catholics, on the defensive since the Reformation, had with themselves. Pius was a kind of living personification of the *Nulla Salus* dismissal of those outside the flock. It wasn't unusual to read in the Catholic press after, say, a plane crash in which fifty people died, a headline declaring PLANE CRASH IN MISSOURI; ELEVEN CATHOLICS KILLED. As if only they were made in God's image.

But the stingy focus on our own kind could have historic implications. Pius, whose death in 1958 made way for John's election, had been pope during World War II, and in the war's aftermath we Catholics emphasized his staunch opposition to the Nazis. When I later understood more fully that his record of resistance was based on a narrow defense of Church prerogatives—he spoke up boldly for the rights of German churchmen and for the exemptions of Catholic institutions from Nazi intrusions; the few Jews he expressed open concern for were baptized converts to Catholicism—I understood all the better why John's arrival had, in itself, pointed to a change. It would not be surprising when I learned that Pope John, as the apostolic delegate to Turkey and Greece during the war—he was Archbishop Roncalli then—had actively opposed the Holocaust as it unfolded by supplying fake baptismal certificates to perhaps thousands of Jews, enabling their escape. His empathetic concern was not limited by boundaries of belief or institutional membership.

Pope John was born Angelo Roncalli, and as that name seems to suggest, he was a jolly fellow, a rotund man with the air of a self-accepting peasant. The contrast between him and his sternly patrician predecessor could not have been more striking. The consistory that elected Roncalli had been deadlocked. After eleven ballots, the cardinal-electors chose this elderly nonentity—age seventy-seven, the patriarch of the ornate but insignificant Church of Venice—to keep the Chair of Peter warm for the few years it would take one or another of the proper candidates for the papacy to consolidate support and take over.

Pope John would, instead, launch a vast theological recasting of the Catholic imagination, but the first impression he made on my family was more personal. He began his time as pope by leaving the confines of Vatican City—the first pope to do so since 1870—and visiting without fanfare a hospital in Rome that specialized in the treatment of children with polio.

My brother's polio had long been our family's defining experience. Franklin Roosevelt had been worshipped by my parents less for his resounding defense of people like them than for the affliction of his legs and his refusal to be cowed by the disability. And so it was with Pope John: From that hospital visit on, they felt an unbreakable personal tie to him. My mother pinned to the wall of the large, well-appointed kitchen in Wiesbaden a magazine photo of the luminous pontiff surrounded by smiling children in hospital garb, and we could not help imagining our Joe as one of them. Pope John was a pope for us. But our family was only a microcosmic instance of a global phenomenon. This man's instinctive empathy was a religious revelation and a political turning point.

In line with the Catholic religious imagination, such goodness told us something about God. If medieval popes claimed the title "vicar of Christ" as an exercise of power, for us it only meant that the pope, in himself, could reveal something essential about the Holy One. The papal office was taken to be a kind of sacrament. The unsmiling Pius XII was the perfect pope for the deity of doomsday. Even as a child, I understood that a God who could condemn to an eternal afterlife of misery an innocent like an unbaptized baby—or like my playmate, Peter, living in the house next door—was not a God who could be, as the Catholic catechism put it, "all loving."

No, love could have nothing to do with such a God, and even Catholics would be foolish to put their trust in Him. The forgiveness of Jesus, mediated by a priest, was our rescue from a God who would send you to hell in a flash, and, as I've already noted, we Catholics took that lesson to heart. And, yes, it has calcified in clericalism. So Pius XII, with his stern visage and self-punishing abstemiousness, was the pope for such a God.

But Pope John XXIII was something else, and even I, far from Rome and theologically uninitiated, grasped it at once—and with relief. Pope John made palpable the quiet assurance of the acceptance in which I was still secretly enfolded in the presence of my Imagined Friend, even if in Wiesbaden, among my schoolmates, He was unreferred to. Perhaps Jesus was, after all, what I'd first taken Him to be.

. . .

INSTEAD OF MERELY serving as a stand-in pope, John famously shocked the world by calling for an *aggiornamento*—an updating—of Roman Catholicism. Who had ever dared suggest that the one, holy, catholic, and apostolic Church was behind the times? But the new pope's prophetic gift was to see below the surface of the apparent triumph of mid-twentieth-century Catholicism: Seminaries and convents around the world were overflowing with recruits; missionary priests and nuns in Africa and Latin America were moving into the postcolonial vacuum; the Cold War struggle with communism had validated Catholic politics with Asian figures like the Diem family in Vietnam, European leaders like Konrad Adenauer in Germany and Charles de Gaulle in France, and even, soon enough, John F. Kennedy in Protestant America. Yet as Catholics heard of the pope's *aggiornamento* summons, they viscerally understood. They welcomed it when he quickly called for a Vatican council, a reform-pushing meeting of the world's Catholic bishops. "I want to throw open the windows of the Church," he said, "so that we can see out and the people can see in."[4]

Pope John's Second Vatican Council advanced numerous startling reforms of liturgy and theology, but it was, more broadly, evidence of an already unfolding shift in deeper Catholic awareness. That was immediately apparent in the magnanimity of Pope John, and was soon to explicitly change the way in which we experienced God in daily life.

Before Pope John, for example, relatively few Catholics received Communion at Mass because most were burdened, even after confessing sins to a priest, by that unshakable sense of unworthiness of which I was Exhibit A. The fact of our sinfulness had been drilled into us, and, yes, the weight of "concupiscence" kept almost all but the elderly bent over. Communion time at Mass, therefore, was a scrum of people climbing over one another in pews, as some went forward to the rail to receive the Body of Christ, while most remained hunched on their knees, heads sheepishly bowed.

Within a couple of years of Pope John's election, and without any fanfare from pulpits or great theological pronouncements, that had almost universally changed. At Communion time, congregations began to stand as one, with almost every person filing out of the pew in orderly procession to approach the altar rail, me included. The reasoning seemed simple: If you're hungry, come to the table and eat. God's love, like Pope John's goodwill, was available to all.

Doom was not a feature of Pope John's standing in the Church, and no one could imagine him consigning anyone to the eternal lake of fire. If Pope John would not do that, how could God?

There would be wide news coverage of the proceedings of the liberalizing council, but the embodiment of change was the empathetic pope himself. Soon enough, sermon fixations on hell disappeared, and—amazing grace—so did the overriding Catholic fear of damnation.

We did not see it yet, but this was an opening to a new relationship between the people and the priest, whose function as the gatekeeper of heaven and hell should have become obsolete. It was an opening that would not be taken, however, and Pope John would barely be remembered as having offered it. Nevertheless, those wallet cards—"In case of an accident, please call a priest"—simply vanished. We stopped imagining death as the moment of radical dependence on clergy. Instead of trusting priests, we began to trust God.

. . .

I AM DESCRIBING the inscape of my journey into manhood, the twists and turns that led finally, almost despite myself, to an open embrace of religion. In Wiesbaden, I was supposedly being initiated into the cult of Cold War military valor—the glamour of jet planes, the snappy salutes, the polished ankle boots, the razor-sharp creases on khakis. Yet even as I carried myself as gung ho, I felt that secret ambivalence.

I was surrounded by Air Force brats who channeled their palpable fear of the coming catastrophic war into the anticipated romance of fighter pilot heroism. Classmates of mine would be heading off, after graduation, to the new U.S. Air Force Academy in Colorado Springs, and they expected I would be among them. As a general's son, I would be a shoo-in for admission to the school. We flyboys would be airborne knights of the Free World Crusade, members of the elite defending the virtues of democracy against—as I, too, referred to it—"atheistic communism." Nikita Khrushchev's strident threats of war continued unabated, and I would be one of those standing against them.

The Catholic Church's role—and therefore mine?—as a bastion of opposition to Soviet communism was embodied in the figure of Cardinal Francis Spellman, archbishop of New York. Because of his fame as America's preeminent Catholic, I was primed to think well of him, and I shared my family's excitement when he honored us with a visit to our home at Christmastime in 1958. He was in Wiesbaden in his role as head of the so-called Military Ordinariate—apostolic vicar of the U.S. military—which made him the bishop for all Catholics in the U.S. armed services. This was his annual Christmas trek to visit the troops. My father was the senior Catholic serving with the American forces in Europe, which is what brought Spellman to our house. The cardinal was the godfather of America's mounting resistance to the Soviet Union, and I should have liked him only for that.

Pope Pius XII had excommunicated every communist in the world with a stroke of his pen[5]—something he never did to Nazis, including Hitler, a baptized Catholic on the rolls of the Church until the day he died. Spellman had famously been a papal favorite, and he had been Pius's attack dog when it came to commies. Spellman had been a stalwart defender of the Red-baiting Senator Joseph McCarthy, and, though I did not know it—who'd actually heard of Vietnam?—Spellman was even then, at the time of his visit to Wiesbaden, the chief sponsor of South Vietnam's president, Ngo Dinh Diem, a Catholic fascist. Diem and his brothers' Inquisition-style oppressions of their country's Buddhist majority would soon ignite the internecine conflict that drew the United States into Vietnam's catastrophic civil war—a war that Spellman would notoriously defend by saying "My country right or wrong!"[6] After Pius XII died, Spellman honored him in New York with a statue at the entrance of St. Patrick's Cathedral, while not disguising his contempt for Pius's successor, Angelo Roncalli: "He's no Pope," as I would later learn Spellman said of Pope John. "He should be selling bananas."[7]

When the cardinal arrived at our house on Biebricher Allee—a turn-of-the-century mansion on Wiesbaden's most prominent hill—my mother had me and my brothers lined up at the door to greet him. The cardinal had a fawning priest at each elbow, and his smile seemed forced. A short and portly man like the new pope, Spellman exuded none of the "banana seller's" easy self-acceptance. In the formal vestibule of our house, the cardinal held his hand out in a fey manner that made it clear we were expected to kiss his ring, but we were prepared for that. Indeed, all five of us brothers had been rehearsed. We said, in turn, "Welcome to our house, Your Eminence," then bowed and kissed his ring. When it came to Kevin, the youngest, with a six-year-old's brio, he blurted, "Hi, Your Enema!"

My brother Brian was old enough to know the word and snorted, clapping Kevin on the head. *Enema!*

The priests beside Spellman glowered. Dennis, Joe, and I were on the verge of laughing. Dad looked displeased. Before Spellman could react, though, our mother put a fond hand on Kevin's shoulder, smiled broadly at the cardinal, and said with astounding equanimity, "Oh, Your Eminence, after that, we'll be friends for life. Don't you think?"

Spellman was relieved. "Yes, Mrs. Carroll. Yes, we will."

"Then you have to call me Mary."

My mind goes back across the years to that moment in the Rosary Portico, when I mortified my mother with my question to the Franciscan monk about the hair on his chin instead of on his head. That time, she had been flummoxed, and only the monk's good humor had put her at ease. Now, with the stakes infinitely higher, the good humor was hers to bestow. That she was the one to rescue the encounter spoke volumes about the woman she had become in the intervening years. I wasn't the only one who had changed. My mother, the immigrant's daughter, was now a general's wife.

Our parents had gathered a few friends and dignitaries in the house, a stilted reception for the cardinal. I kept my distance but watched carefully. My readiness to think well of Spellman was undercut by his clerical posturing. He reminded me of Father George, the St. Mary's priest who had rushed me toward the minor seminary, and I allowed myself to feel a surprisingly frank dislike. My judgment was as visceral as it was uninformed: The man was fake in everything but his self-importance. Years later, especially in relation to Vietnam, I would realize how right I had been.

As the cardinal prepared to leave, my father raised a finger toward me. Without knowing why, my heart sank. I approached my parents, who were flanking His Eminence. Spellman eyed me and said, "Jimmy, as a son of the Air Force, you'd be one of mine.

If it's God's will, I'd be happy to ordain you." I flashed a look at my mother: She could not temper her happy smile. My father, no doubt sensing my reaction, put a hand on my arm. "As His Eminence says, if it's God's will."

"Yes, sir," I said—but I was in freefall. A few minutes later, my father took me aside to explain. "No one's rushing things here," he said. "The cardinal jumped the gun. We simply said you'd have the makings of a good priest." I could feel myself blushing. Without remotely knowing how to explain myself, I said, "I doubt if that's true, Dad." He replied by gently squeezing my arm.[8]

IN MY SENIOR year of high school in Wiesbaden, I flunked chemistry—an embarrassing detail that has relevance here. I had been one of those convinced early on that I had no aptitude for math or science, but that does not account for my receiving an F in a course that was anything but demanding. The failed grade in science in effect put an end to the prospect of my going to the Air Force Academy, even as a general's son.

Now, of course, I recognize what I was up to with that chemistry course failure. If I could not yet clearly see ahead to the road I would take, at least I could see the road I would *not* take. There was, as it were, an automatic-pilot quality to the momentum set for the likes of me by militant Cold War fervor, and that dynamic would take me into Air Force ROTC (Reserve Officers' Training Corps) when, a year later, I wound up as a student at Georgetown University in Washington. At Georgetown, I would be a crack cadet, but my heart wouldn't be in it, and in looking back I see that Pope John XXIII was why.

From Wiesbaden, I had quietly paid close attention to the impression Pope John was making in Rome. Eventually, I would get the full picture of his distinction. He stopped his car as it passed the city's synagogue one Saturday and informally greeted the Jewish congregants who were milling about after the service. He promptly ordered the anti-Jewish adjective "perfidious" deleted from the Catholic liturgy. He met with a noted Jewish historian who'd accused the Church of complicity in Nazi anti-Semitism, and he affirmed the man's work.[9] In calling the Second Vatican Council, Pope John instructed organizers to put the Church's relationship with the Jewish people high on the agenda—a clear result of his intimate experience of the Church's failure to forthrightly defend the Jews during the Holocaust. In receiving a Jewish delegation at the Vatican, he came down from his elevated platform to greet them, saying, "I am Joseph, your brother," a reference to the biblical Joseph greeting his long-lost brothers.

In hindsight, one of the most surprising things about Pope John's council was that its slew of documents and declarations never mentioned communism, which, for most of a century, had been the heart of Catholic moral concern and condemnation. This deserves emphasis: The Second Vatican Council, meeting between 1962 and 1965, *never mentioned communism.*

That Roman Catholic deflection of the pivotal subject was an effective opening to the era-defining détente of Ostpolitik. It was foreshadowed, perhaps, when Pope John held a meeting at the Vatican with Nikita Khrushchev's son-in-law, a Soviet official with whom the pontiff made a public show of friendliness.

John's great encyclical "Pacem in Terris" (Peace on Earth), written near the end of his life—it was published in April of 1963, and he died in June—reflected what he'd learned from the Cuban missile crisis the previous October. He called into question the entire structure of Cold War nuclear deterrence.[10] That was a moral challenge to the United States as much as to the Soviet Union. When the Cuban missile crisis had brought the world to the edge of cataclysm, John had intervened behind the scenes with both Washington and Moscow, treating them as moral and political equals. I had instinctively welcomed his openness to people of other faiths, including the faith of my boyhood friend from Alexandria, but openness to the Kremlin? Where would that leave the radically bipolar structure—"Better Dead Than Red"—of America's political imagination? And mine?

It would take me years to know fully of Pope John's upending significance in multiple realms, but I had intuitively grasped his essential meaning early on. He was a revolutionary figure, and with his help a little revolution was stirring in me—and it would grow.

With Pope John, I realized that my ambivalence about my "vocation" had relatively little to do with the usual problems—the vows of poverty, chastity, and obedience, the strictures of the clerical life, including the loss, even, of girls. It had everything to do with the cloud that had hung over my idea of God since childhood.

Yes, Jesus had been the first "great and simple image" to which my heart had opened—the freely wounded Jesus in whom I sensed the compassion (the "suffering with") that changed the meaning of my brother's polio—making Him my trusted friend. But I was troubled by the God who'd required—"God's will"—both my brother and "His only begotten Son" to undergo such suffering. Indeed, this had become ever more clear to me: I simply could not accept that the God whom I would be obliged to preach as a priest was a God of doom who requires human anguish as the price of redemption or of righting the balance of justice. However implicit, this was the through-line of my angst.

And for me—especially in those war-threatened years in Germany, close to those trip-wire brigades of Soviet tanks—the blade of that problem cut even deeper. The dreaded theological doom of the Last Things had bled inexorably into the political doom of a coming nuclear apocalypse, which, according to America's Cold War doctrine—Spellman's doctrine—could somehow fulfill the will of God. No. *No to that!* I wanted nothing to do with such transcendent doom.

But Pope John, whose first visit as pope was to those polio sufferers, put me back in touch with the other God, the God whom I had seen joining the bereaved in grief at those funeral Masses when I was an altar boy. I understood that the God whom my Imagined Friend, Jesus, preached—"God is love, and he who abides in love, abides in God"[11]—could finally be my God. The cloud began to lift.

AND THEN THE most amazing thing happened. Because of my father's VIP status, and perhaps with a nudge from Cardinal Spellman, our family was granted the extraordinary privilege of a private audience with His Holiness at the Apostolic Palace in Vatican City. No one in my family could have known how that prospect concentrated my anticipation. I have written of the experience before, how the power of the peasant pope's personal presence ambushed me, changed me, conscripted me.[12]

In his private library, a room whose walls I remember as heavy with leather-bound books and red woven tapestries, my parents and brothers and I were lined up by a clerical factotum to await the entrance of, well, the vicar of Christ. When Pope John appeared, I was struck first by how truly short he was—and by the red velvet shoes, of course. His white robes shimmered in the shaft of morning light that cut through a nearby window.

Upon seeing us, Pope John threw up his hands and laughed with delight. Then, with a few robust sentences, as the translator explained, he saluted my parents for their large Catholic family.

Beginning with my mother, he moved along the line, greeting

each of us personally. Whatever visceral repugnance I'd felt in the presence of Cardinal Spellman, I felt the opposite here, with the "banana seller." He was himself the distilled essence of charisma, laughing, stroking, embracing everyone with his happy eyes. Yes, I was starstruck. The small old man was my first global celebrity, and that alone might have accounted for my inner effervescence. But that was not all, nor was it what mattered.

When Pope John came to me, he reached up to my shoulders and pulled me down, so that his mouth was close to my ear. I felt the stubble of his whiskers against my cheek. I smelled the aroma of his aftershave. He whispered to me. My impression was that I alone, of my brothers, was given this intimacy. I remember feeling *I know this man.*

Fulfilling the promise of his inclusive motto, Pope John would break every papal precedent to address his encyclical "Pacem in Terris" to all people everywhere—not just "us" but also "them." His large heart was an opening not just to good feelings but to change in the way people related to one another—no matter their class, politics, nationality, belief, or even gender. "There is neither Jew nor Greek; there is neither slave nor free . . ." These are words I would find soon enough in my New Testament, in a letter from St. Paul to the Galatians. ". . . there is neither male nor female . . ." And it is only now, in looking back at that moment with Pope John's peasant hands pressing my shoulders, that I understand what the feeling was: ". . . for you are all one in Christ Jesus."[13] Jesus, my Imagined Friend, my dear companion at my side all those years: Here He is. *Here He is.*

I have no idea what Pope John actually said to me; the words whispered in my ear could have been Latin or Italian. But I felt addressed. Yes, as with the nuns a decade before, I felt singled out, but for once being singled out was not the point. Perhaps that was why an unprecedented outrush of unguarded positive energy sprang from my very center. Unknowingly, I was giving embodiment to nothing less than the Catholic imagination, the readiness—no, the longing—to take an experience of the flesh as an epiphany of the spirit. My inbred ambivalence was simply gone. Whatever Pope John asked of me with that whisper, I said yes.

For years afterward, I would look back on this brief encounter as the instant of my recruitment to the Church, and even now, in the quicksand of regret, anger, and sorrow, I remember that moment as the pure-joy beginning of the rest of my life.

✦

CHAPTER 15

Clericalism and Male Supremacy

Women are gaining an increasing awareness of their natural dignity.
Far from being content with a purely passive role or allowing
themselves to be regarded as a kind of instrument, they are
demanding both in domestic and in public life the rights and
duties which belong to them as human persons.

—Pope John XXIII, "Pacem in Terris"

I regarded the coming of Pope Francis in 2013 as proof that I had been right to shape my Catholic hope around the reforms set moving by Pope John XXIII when I was young. Yes, John's recasting of the Church's religious imagination had been stymied by his successor popes and the bishops they appointed, but I sensed, with many others, that Francis would rescue John's purpose and put the Church back on the path of renewal. I fear now that I was wrong.

One bellwether is the place of women. When Pope John's successors—Paul VI, John Paul II, and Benedict XVI[1]—adamantly refused to alter anything having to do with the patriarchal and deeply misogynistic structure of Catholic power, and when they shored up a broad Catholic suspicion of every erotic impulse, the Church sacrificed the ongoing project of a humanely reformed Catholicism. Even under Francis, the us-against-them bipolarity that John XXIII stood against remains firmly in place, and it is still epitomized by men against women.

The historic character of the opportunity offered by Pope John, and squandered by his successors, is emphasized in recalling that John clearly saw the controlling centrality of attitudes toward woman across the whole culture. In his 1963 encyclical "Pacem in Terris," already referred to in connection with its questioning of nuclear orthodoxy and its ecumenical appeal, John lifted up what he called the three great "signs of the times." He praised labor and the demand for workers' rights; he welcomed the end of colonialism; and he offered an extraordinary affirmation of the women's movement, which had been launched decades earlier but was just then being renewed (as, for example, by Betty Friedan's milestone book *The Feminine Mystique*, published in 1963).

Pope John praised women for "demanding both in domestic and in public life the rights and duties which belong to them as human persons."[2] It is no coincidence that 1963 was also the year in which the birth control pill, the oral contraceptive developed by a Catholic doctor,[3] was approved for use in the United States by the Food and Drug Administration. John could not have been ignorant of the fact that chief among the rights women saw as belonging to them was ready access to birth control.

And what did Pope John do about that? In an all-but-forgotten move entirely unlike anything undertaken by any pope before or since, up to and including Francis, John established just then what he called the Papal Commission on Population, the Family, and Birth-rate. Composed of six members, four of whom were laypeople, the commission, referred to less formally as the Papal Birth Control Commission, was charged with reexamining the Catholic Church's teaching on artificial contraception.

The general assumption among Catholics at that time was that the condemnation of birth control had been the Church's "constant teaching," a kind of eleventh commandment. But that was not so. The issue had rarely arisen in the Church's deep past, since methods of contraception had become more or less reliable only in the modern era, depending, for example, on the nineteenth-century "vulcanization" process that had made rubber suitable for use in condoms and diaphragms. The first official Catholic condemnation of "artificial contraception" (as opposed to supposedly "natural" techniques keyed to the female menstrual cycle) dated only to 1930, when Pope Pius XI promulgated the encyclical "Casti Connubii" (Of Chaste Wedlock). Not incidentally, the encyclical explicitly instructed wives to obey their husbands.

That pronouncement was broadly taken to be an exercise of papal infallibility, which claimed divine authority in "matters of faith and morals."[4] As a result, a new structure of Catholic identity took hold, based more than ever on sexual renunciation. Papal power—and, by extension, the power of the entire clerical hierarchy—was now tied in unprecedented ways to the most intimate moral choices that Catholic men and women could make. The modern condemnation of birth control supercharged the laity-domineering authority of the clergy—from the pontiff in Rome to the parish priest in the confessional.

In 1930, the same year as "Casti Connubii" was promulgated, the worldwide Anglican Communion had, by contrast, formally left the use of contraception up to the consciences of couples, and other Protestant denominations would follow suit. Soon enough, the stand-alone papal condemnation of birth control became a marker of Catholic selfhood, ranking right up there with devotion to the Blessed Virgin Mary. Indeed, Mary's lifelong virginity—and what was presumed to be her husband's superhuman sexual abstinence—took on new salience as Catholic couples grappled in bed as much with doctrinal prohibition as with each other. Catholic men and women found themselves threatened with hellfire if they practiced "unnatural" birth control, and by the mid-twentieth century the now exceptional Catholic birth rates showed that the faithful had largely accepted this teaching.

The reaction to Pope John's initiative in establishing the Papal Birth Control Commission was electric, inside and outside the Catholic world. Everyone understood that there could be no such formal Vatican reconsideration of a doctrine if changing that doctrine was altogether out of the question. Tied in the knot of this one issue—as feminists from Margaret Sanger to Betty Friedan had long made clear—were numerous other threads, from the meaning of sexuality itself to the morality of erotic pleasure to the autonomy of women. For Catholics, a bolt from the blue had struck.

Only weeks later, on June 3, 1963, at age eighty-one and after less than five years in the Chair of Peter, Pope John XXIII died of stomach cancer.

WHAT THWARTED POPE John's reform was clericalism, the vesting of power in an all-male and celibate clergy. A foreseen change in the place of women in the Church—foreseen in the nascent initiative John had taken in the direction of, yes, women's liberation—was what most powerfully ignited the clerical resistance.

To return to this book's central assertion, clericalism is both the root cause and the ongoing enabler of the present Catholic catastrophe. Clericalism epitomizes a woman-insulting patriarchy that cuts deeper into culture than other forms of male dominance because clericalism claims nothing less than divine authority for itself. Indeed, clericalism, by calling each of its officeholders "father," burdens the image of God as Father. That was an image Jesus used, of course, but He addressed God as "Abba," an Aramaic word that carries the intimate meaning of "daddy," rather than invoking the overbearing superego figure of paternal dominance. The Father-God of Jesus was nothing like the Father-God of Catholic clericalism.

It is important to emphasize again, therefore, that clericalism's origins lie not in the Gospels but in the attitudes and organizational charts of the late Roman Empire, with the further calcification of clerical power coming, as we have seen, during the feudal Middle Ages, the time of liege lords and divine-right monarchs. In Christianity's beginnings, something very different was at play.

The first reference to the Jesus movement in a non-biblical source comes from the Roman Jewish historian Flavius Josephus, writing around the same time the Gospels were taking form. Josephus described the followers of Jesus simply as "those that loved Him at the first and did not let go of their affection for Him."[5] There was no priesthood—it evolved gradually—and the movement was egalitarian. Christians worshipped and broke bread in one another's homes.

It was under the emperor Constantine, in the fourth century, that Christianity effectively became Rome's imperial religion and took on the organizational trappings of the empire itself. The diocese, originally a Roman governing unit, became the form of local Church administration. The basilica, originally a monumental hall where the emperor sat in majesty, became the house of God. Gatherings of bishops, called councils, defined a single set of beliefs as orthodox and everything else as heresy. A diverse and decentralized church was transformed into "the Church"—centralized and hierarchical, with the bishop of Rome reigning as a monarch.

This univocal character was reinforced not long after Constantine by Augustine's theology of sexuality—derived, as we have seen, from the eccentric way he read the Adam and Eve story in Genesis. Augustine's painting the original act of disobedience as a sexual sin led to the blaming of the woman for the fatal seduction—

and thus for all human suffering down the generations. This amounted to a major revision of the egalitarian assumptions and practices of the early Christian movement, which had been defined by that Pauline mantra "There is neither male nor female."[6] Now the Church became an institution whose maleness and misogyny were part of, and inseparable from, its structure.

The conceptual underpinnings of clericalism can be laid out simply: Women are subservient to men. Laypeople are subservient to priests, who are defined as having been made "ontologically" superior—a change in their very status as human beings—by the sacrament of Holy Orders. Removed by celibacy from competing bonds of family and other obligations, priests are slotted into a clerical hierarchy whose form replicates that of the medieval social order. The pyramid is all.

Should we be surprised that men invited to think of themselves on such a scale of power—even as an alter Christus—might get lost in a wilderness of self-centeredness? Or that they might find it hard to break from the feudal order that provides them with preferment and community, not to mention an elevated status the non-ordained will never enjoy? Clericalism is self-fulfilling and self-sustaining. It thrives on secrecy, and it looks after itself.

The popes who succeeded John XXIII were in clericalism's grip, which is why the reforms of his council didn't have a chance.

✝

CHAPTER 16

Contraception and Corruption

Birth control is the first important step woman must take toward the
goal of her freedom. It is the first step she must take to be man's equal.
It is the first step they must both take toward human emancipation.

—Margaret Sanger, 1918[1]

There has been, on average, one ecumenical council every
century across nearly two thousand years, convocations summoned for the purpose of Church administration, theological reckoning, or renewal of discipline. Popes were more or less supreme
in the magisterium, or teaching authority, of the Latin Church beginning in the eleventh century, when Pope Gregory VII (1073–85)
wrested control of the appointment of bishops from competing
princes—the already noted Gregorian reform. But councils served
to amplify papal authority, and at times to check it.

Pope John XXIII's Second Vatican Council, or Vatican II, met
in the great nave of St. Peter's Basilica in Rome in four sessions in
the autumns of the years 1962 to 1965, with committees doing
extensive work between sessions. Made up of about 2,400 bishops,
with about 500 *periti*, or theological experts, the council issued
sixteen distinct statements (four "constitutions," nine "decrees,"
and three "declarations"). Together they launched what could
have been the much-needed completion of the reform begun dur-

ing the Reformation, sparked by Martin Luther in 1517. But Vatican II's promise as an overdue historic reckoning with Catholic imperfections still remains unfulfilled.

It is true, nevertheless, that as a result of John's council, the culture of Catholicism has been altered in important ways. The Church that had, across the millennium since the Crusades, peddled the idea of a "just war" became a true "peace Church," notably standing against American militarism, beginning with "Pacem in Terris" but continuing with Pope Paul VI's Vietnam-era cry of "Never again war!"[2] That shift laid the groundwork for my own most consequential transformation—from ambivalent general's son to committed peacenik.

Vatican II would advance numerous other reforms of liturgy and theology, ranging from the jettisoning of the Latin Mass to the post-Holocaust affirmation of the integrity of Judaism. Inside the Church, Catholics would reclaim the Eucharist as the heart of the faith, a positive development already noted, and that change, too, impacted my life in ways impossible to describe.

Decisively, the council defined the Church as "the people of God," with the clerical hierarchy located within the community as servants rather than above it as rulers. This transformation, even if it did not occur in practice, was powerfully symbolized by the liturgical reform that brought the altar down from its high platform at the far end of the church and into the midst of the congregation, where the priest and the people could stand face-to-face.

But, despite what I and most other Catholics settled for in the years after the council, those changes were far from enough. Vatican II raised basic Church questions of ethos, meaning, honesty, and justice, setting in motion a profound institutional examination of conscience. But all too soon, those questions were laid aside, and the greatest moral conundrums have since gone unaddressed.

The terrible weight of that failure has fallen, most notably now, on thousands of minors who have been readily abused, not once but twice—first by predator priests, then by bishop enablers—all because the Catholic Church did not accomplish the full moral reckoning that was begun in the 1960s.

At first, Pope Francis, with his elevation to the papacy in 2013, seemed to embody the retrieval of the council's promise, the long-awaited correction to the reactionary rollback mounted against Pope John XXIII's initiatives by Francis's three predecessor popes. Above all, Francis's firm repudiation of judgmentalism—his famous "Who am I to judge?" in reference to homosexuals—seemed to resuscitate Pope John's magnanimity. But the preference of mercy over judgmentalism proved not to be enough when the iron grip of clericalism showed itself in Francis's own responses to the dysfunction of abusive priests and enabling bishops. That personal failure of the pope from Argentina lays bare, at last, the deep institutional failure of Vatican II.

THE PREVIOUS CHURCH council had been the First Vatican Council, or Vatican I (1869–70), which notably responded to the loss of the papacy's temporal power to Italian nationalists—the "papal states" had comprised various territories in much of the Italian peninsula from the eighth century until 1870—by making the pope's spiritual power absolute. The doctrine of papal infallibility was formally defined only then, and it specifies that the Roman pontiff cannot be in error when speaking authoritatively about "matters of faith and morals," the phrase we noted earlier. When the pope makes pronouncements *ex Cathedra*, or "from the Chair [of St. Peter]"—he does so with the "divine assistance" that was promised to St. Peter.[3] To err may be human, but regarding the key questions of the Catholic faith, it is not papal.

Because of the expansiveness of that doctrine's claim regarding the pope's teaching authority, the assumption after 1870 was that the Church would never need another ecumenical council. From then on, the pope would rule alone.

But that is not how Pope John XXIII saw it. At Vatican I, little notice had been taken of the contradiction in its promulgation of papal infallibility: How do we know that the pope is the Church's sole and preeminent teacher? A council said so.

For all of Pope John's intuitive grasp of the Catholic Church's then unseen and unspoken problems, his response to what he did see drew on an apparently bottomless well of positive energy — the same joyful spirit I'd experienced for myself in his presence. Indeed, so thoroughly affirmative was his spirit that his opening remarks to the council — aptly titled "Gaudet Mater Ecclesia" (Mother Church Rejoices), from his first three words — were a denunciation of denunciation itself, a resounding critique of those to whom, as he put it, "the modern world is nothing but betrayal and ruin . . . prophets of doom who are forever forecasting calamity."

John's vision summoned his council, his Church, and all who heard him to something very unlike doom: "Today, rather, Providence is guiding us toward a new order of human relationships, which, thanks to human effort and yet far surpassing human hopes, will bring us to the realization of still higher and undreamed of experiences."[4] His positive élan went on to infuse the deliberations and conclusions of Vatican II, and that in itself defined what could have been the council's truest revolution.

A prophet can act without foreseeing the consequences of his actions, and surely that was true of Pope John. After all, he delivered his resoundingly fresh council-opening statement in Latin, the Church's stoutest symbol of exemption from the limits of time. Yet within weeks, the council fathers moved away from Latin, having immediately joined the core question — *Does the Church change?*—by taking up as a first order of business the underlying issue of language. When the bishops in St. Peter's Basilica over-ruled the Latin-defending conservatives and voted to mandate the universal use of the vernacular in the Catholic liturgy, Pope John said, "Now begins my council."[5]

The attempts at reform went deep, implicitly recasting the Church's worldview to accommodate, at last, the key insight of evolution: Change is not just inevitable but natural. Church politics might have changed, moving from medieval monarchy to a democratic ecclesial structure, with power centered as much in the laity as in the hierarchy. Exclusive claims for the Roman Catholic Church as the only way to God began to give way to notions of the Church as a "pilgrim people," forever on the way to truth, not sole custodians of it. Above all, it began to be grasped that "God" can only be encountered, and therefore thought about, indirectly, which should have resulted in a new theological and doctrinal modesty. And, finally, the Church's relationship to the Scriptures began to shift, with the Word of God preferred to pieties of novenas and rosaries, and with Jesus, the man of peace, love, and forgiveness, preferred to Catholicism's plethora of saints. Jesus was meant to be returned to the center of faith previously occupied by the stern, condemning Judge.

Alas, as has become clear across the years, this magnificent start begun by Pope John's council was not actually brought to completion within any of these frames of reference. Each of the transformations just outlined was either stalled or reversed. A dozen reasons could be offered as to why that was so, and one must always beware the infamous single-factor analysis. Yet a single undermining factor overwhelmingly presents itself, one with potent relevance to Catholicism's twenty-first-century crisis of clericalism—indeed, one revealed in its full dimensions by that crisis. And that factor is sex.

. . .

WE HAVE SEEN that Pope Francis's arrival has marked a return to Catholic reform in important ways. His emphasis on mercy counters the fearmongering God who stokes the eternal lake of fire, condemns nonbelievers, and even deprives unbaptized babies of His presence in heaven. Francis firmly advances the full dismantling of that old dread that had Catholics turning to the priest, especially the confessor-priest, as the gatekeeper of the afterlife. That spiritual power of the ordained over the laity, rooted in a twisted notion of who God is—and exacerbated by the cult of secrecy of the confessional, where the priest could "absolve" you—was essential to the unhealthy dominance of the clergy, which bore the poison fruit of clergy abuse. We have seen this.

Pope Francis, in line with Pope John XXIII, does, in fact, represent a rejection of that doom-laden clerical power. As the title of one of his books puts it, *The Name of God Is Mercy*.[6] And mercy is not a mere abstraction to Francis, who showed as much early in the Covid-19 pandemic. In March 2020, with Italians in lockdown and Catholic churches shuttered, the Sacrament of Penance was mostly unavailable to the faithful, which posed a widespread crisis of conscience. It was a predicament Pope Francis directly addressed during his morning Mass on March 20: "But many people today would tell me, 'Father, where can I find a priest, a confessor, because I can't leave the house? And I want to make peace with the Lord. I want Him to embrace me. I want the Father's embrace.'" The pope responded to this plea by replying, "If you cannot find a priest to confess to, speak directly with God, your Father, and tell Him the truth. Say, 'Lord, I did this, this, this. Forgive me.'" Francis emphasized, "You can draw near to God's forgiveness without having a priest at hand. Think about it. This is the moment."[7]

Indeed, Pope Francis might have added, the moment to finally lay to rest the priest as gatekeeper of eternity. But priest-promoted fear of hell, centered in the Confessional, was only one of the three legs of clericalism, and Francis has stoutly protected the other two, each of which has to do with sex. They are, of course, Catholicism's all-male priesthood and the almost universal requirement of celibacy for ordination,[8] both of which, in turn, stand on the denigration of women that traces back, as we have seen, to St. Augustine's reading of the Adam and Eve story in Genesis.

Which returns us to the centrality of the place of women and the failure of the Church to recast it.

In 1963, the council fathers had been poised to reconsider the Church's teaching on birth control when Pope John died. They had already been preparing the document that would be called the "Pastoral Constitution on the Church in the Modern World," and it was slated to include sections on "married life" and "responsible parenthood." Cardinals and bishops openly asked in the council discussions of contraception if traditional notions of what was "natural" still held, given contemporary insights in science and philosophy. Was human nature static, or was it, too, subject to the dynamic change showing up in everything from personal consciousness to biological evolution? And, yes, evolution was a paradigmatic touchstone.

The council fathers explicitly returned to the Adam and Eve narrative to ask if, perhaps, the Church had gotten it wrong, not only in reading the story literally, but also in misconstruing its meaning by emphasizing sex for procreation over sex for pleasure and love. St. Augustine again.

John XXIII was succeeded in 1963 by Giovanni Montini, who had been the right-hand man of the change-averse Pius XII. As Pope Paul VI, Montini took John's place in presiding over the Second Vatican Council, but he presided very differently.

Paul VI is remembered as "Pope Hamlet," riven by indecision and fear.[9] For our purposes, the thing to note is that in 1964 he made an extraordinary—indeed, unprecedented—intervention in council proceedings, abruptly forbidding the bishops to discuss birth control any further. The subject was, as the papal order put it, "removed from the competence of the Council." One of the four chairmen of the council, a leading European cardinal, immediately stood to object, daring to say, "I beg you, my brother bishops, let us avoid a new 'Galileo affair.' One is enough for the Church."[10] (The Galileo affair, of course, was the Church's refusal to recognize the truth of the pioneering astronomer's observations and conclusions, which drove a wedge between science and religion ever after.)

Paul VI was right to fear change on the matter of birth control, because that mechanism of reproduction threatened to overturn assumptions about everything from papal authority to sexual morality to the ways in which men and women relate to one another—and, for that matter, to the Church's post-Galileo tension with science itself. Birth control, as feminists understood, is connected to everything—but to nothing more than female sexual autonomy, which is essential, of course, to personal autonomy. Church control over birth control is essential to the dominance of women by men, a dominance that was put in place by a certain reading of the story of Adam and Eve. Birth control goes deep into the psychology of the faith.

FORBIDDING THE COUNCIL to discuss the subject of birth control did not solve Pope Paul's problem. What was he to do with the time bomb he'd inherited—Pope John XXIII's Papal Birth Control Commission? Simple. Defuse it.

Paul attempted to do so by expanding the commission membership from six to seventy-two, including only five women. The massively watered-down group was composed almost entirely of priests and theologians, with an executive body made up of nine bishops and seven cardinals. That should have finished any thought of change, but it did not.

The commission met, took its responsibility seriously, and submitted a report to Paul in 1966. Astoundingly, with only six members in dissent, the pope's commission, not restricting its permissive attitude to the newly invented birth control pill, found that there was nothing "intrinsically evil" about artificial contraception as such. The commission's conclusion was simple and clear: The question of the use of the various forms of birth control should be left to the conscience of the couple.[11]

The report was supposed to be secret, but it was leaked and widely published. The Catholic world understood at once that the tectonic plates under Church teaching had shifted—not an earthquake, but a long-overdue repair of a fault line.

Still, an earthquake came. Two years later, in 1968, Pope Paul VI issued an encyclical on the question, "Humanae Vitae" (Of Human Life), which blatantly rejected the commission's finding and recommendation. The encyclical's full and complete condemnation of artificial birth control (not including the "natural" rhythm method) drew protests from priests and theologians around the world, but those dissenters were stoutly ignored by the hierarchy, and soon enough, especially as they left the Church in droves, the objectors went silent.

As a Catholic writer, I've periodically raised my voice against "Humanae Vitae" across fifty years, but I was wrong in my longtime underestimating of its damage. I was like most Catholics in thinking that the encyclical, especially in light of what the pope's own commission was known to have concluded, was a desperate last-ditch effort to hold the line against birth control, and the prohibition wouldn't last. The issue, I thought, was more about the pope's authority—upholding that 1930 papal encyclical "Casti Connubii"—than it was about sex.

In my brief time as a priest, I declined to affirm the teaching, but that did not matter much in the practice of pastoral ministry, since Catholic couples were already more than ready to ignore the Church's rule on their own. The radical drop in the Catholic birth rate across the next few years was a clear demonstration of the rejecting vox populi, even if, after that initial round of dissent, Catholics remained quiet on the subject. Polls (not to mention the birth rate) soon showed that Catholic couples practiced contraception at the same rate as everyone else.

A modus vivendi fell into place. Few saw this quiet strategy of ignoring the law as a signal of broad Catholic corruption, but that's what it was. Popes and bishops pretended to teach the prohibition. Priests pretended to enforce it in Confession. Catholic men and women pretended to obey it. Across two generations, with bishops chosen by Rome for their willingness, above all, to play this game, a structure of dishonesty was erected. And this was the Catholic Church.

Because the tissue of lies was never acknowledged, the deeper truth was not confronted: The modern magisterium of the Church, after its supposed "updating"—Pope John XXIII's *aggiornamento*— had freshly demonized sexuality and renewed its ancient condemnation of female autonomy. And the guardians of this amorality, responsible to enforce it, were priests. Corruption multiplied.

On many morally complicated, and even contradictory, matters having to do with sex—beginning with birth control but extending to questions like masturbation, sex outside of marriage, and new techniques of reproduction—priests kept the cloak of denial tight around the contradiction between official Church teaching and what they knew to be the actualities of life. The Catholic

Church forbade divorce, but there was this thing called annulment. If that was impossible for technical reasons . . . well, you could get divorced and go on with your practice of the faith by going to Communion where the priest didn't know you. Often acting out of an empathetic pastoral impulse, kindly priests may have simply wanted to help penitents negotiate the labyrinth of Catholic sexual neurosis. What was said in Confession stayed in Confession—but that, too, could be a problem.

Priests also were afflicted with that neurosis, and when, at the mercy of their own sexual restlessness, they failed in their vows, even if it was only, say, to masturbate—which, in the Augustinian economy of salvation, merited hellfire every bit as much as the rape of a child—they could be imprisoned by a sense of hypocrisy about which they felt forbidden to speak. This was the cul-de-sac of denial in which legions of otherwise good priests were trapped.

WHICH BRINGS US full circle: It was in that cloak of denial, sanctified by its tie to the sacrament of Confession, that opportunistic sexual predators could find refuge. Abusive priests could avoid being called to account by exploiting their fellow priests' ambivalence about impossible norms, confusion that left many feeling conflicted and ashamed. Predators could depend on their colleagues to feel morally compromised simply by being ensnared in such a secret web of deceit. The predators' colleagues, as much as their superiors in the episcopate, could be counted on to look the other way, and mostly—as grand jury investigations of priestly sexual abuse have well established—they did.

The priest *did this.* That is the decisive recognition that has slowly but surely come over the Church. The abuse of minors occurs in many settings, yes, but such violation by a priest exists in a different order and, as I have said before, not simply because of its prevalence globally. This must be emphasized again: For Catholics, priests are the living sacrament of Christ's presence, delegated above all to consecrate the bread and wine that define the soul of the faith. Now this symbol of Christ has come to stand for something profoundly wicked.

Even as I write that sentence, I think of the good men on whom I have depended for priestly ministry over the years and how they may well regard my conclusion as a friend's betrayal. But the institutional corruption of clericalism transcends that concern, and anguish should be reserved for the victims of priests. The suffering of victims must be the paramount measure of our responses.

✛

CHAPTER 17

The History of History

If the King's English was good enough for Jesus Christ,
it's good enough for the children of Texas.
—attributed to Miriam Ferguson, governor of Texas,
banning Spanish, 1924

Assessing the lewd impulses of priests who take advantage of powerless and vulnerable minors—the so-called pedophile priests—is complicated by another phenomenon that occurred in the years after the Church's structure of dishonesty was erected around birth control in 1968. Less than a year after "Humanae Vitae" was promulgated, the Stonewall protests took place in Greenwich Village, marking the gay community's milestone rising up to say *No more police brutality against gays! No more oppression!*

With that, homosexual rights came to the fore of social change, and many gays and lesbians began openly claiming their identities—for themselves and with others. Gay priests began to acknowledge their orientation, too, if mainly to one another and to trusted friends. Catholics began to understand that the priesthood and religious orders had long been discreetly hospitable to homosexual men and women, who made up significant percentages of these groups. Like their heterosexual colleagues, most gay priests and lesbians were more or less faithfully celibate.

But gay priests carried a special burden exactly because the official moral teaching of the Catholic Church, reflected in its catechism, regarded "homosexual acts" as "intrinsically immoral" and "homosexual tendencies" as "intrinsically disordered."[1] Until the pontificate of Pope Francis, Catholic gays and lesbians were mercilessly denigrated by their own church. Gay priests felt pressured to keep their own identities secret, even while they were expected to publicly uphold the Church's anti-gay teaching. When it turned out that the large majority of victims of abusive priests were boys or adolescent males, the stereotype of the gay priest as abuser was born.

But—and here is the crucial point—it was difficult to rebut that anti-gay slur for the scapegoating it was, precisely because of that cloak of denial around the Church's broader sexual dishonesty. Gay priests, too, were forced to live a lie. In fact, many of them are forced to administer Church brainwashing programs designed to "pray the gay away."[2] The impossible psychological bind such sacred dishonesty results in is an essential part of the corruption of clericalism, and it is tied to the conspiracy of deceit protecting "Humanae Vitae." Only now as I write this, in other words, do I really see how lethal have been the consequences of a Church doctrine that I once blithely presumed to brush aside. In that blitheness, I, too, have been complicit in the disorder.

And in what activity has the Roman Catholic hierarchy claimed to find its moral center—indeed, its moral superiority—across these years? Is it only a coincidence that the same arc of time defining this reinvigorated clerical corruption about sexuality has seen the rise of the fervently political Catholic Church crusade against abortion? It is as if the 1973 *Roe v. Wade* decision by the U.S. Supreme Court threw a lifeline to the morally discredited Catholic hierarchy. Since then, bishops and priests, brooking no compromise, have sent lightning bolts of condemnation at every instance in which a woman might feel compelled to terminate a pregnancy, or in which a politician might support her right to do so. The ethical absolutism of this campaign guaranteed that extremists on both sides of the question—"life" versus "choice"— could cooperate in walling off the complex middle ground in which morally responsible decision making must take place. A plethora of dilemmas choke the question—the ongoing revolution in prenatal biology, for example, which steadily expands the time frame of fetal viability—but in Catholic sexual ethics, there can be no complexities.

The integrity of the Catholic antiabortion doctrine, meanwhile, is shown to be hollow by the Church's ongoing condemnation of birth control, since birth control is the single most effective way to reduce the need for abortions. (In 2018, the U.S. Centers for Disease Control and Prevention registered the smallest number of abortions since *Roe v. Wade*, citing "improved contraceptive access" as the main reason for the decline.)[3] To be genuinely "pro-life" is to be firmly pro-contraception. By its stubborn theological clinging to "Humanae Vitae" and its collusion with right-wing-sponsored legislative initiatives aimed at restricting birth control, whether through insurance mandates or strings attached to foreign aid, the Catholic hierarchy has, in effect, turned Roman Catholicism into an abortionist Church. To repeat: Catholic condemnation of birth control promotes abortion—period. That tells us that something else is going on here besides a genuine concern for life.

What could that be?

BACK TO AUGUSTINE. The demonizing of erotic longing is obviously at the bottom of the sanctification of virginity, which is the ground of the Church requirement of the celibacy of priests. It is not incidental to this consideration to recall that Pope Paul VI, not long after his "intervention" in 1964 forbidding the Vatican II council fathers to discuss contraception, made a second council intervention forbidding those same prelates to discuss priestly celibacy. "I'd rather give my life," he said, "before changing the law on celibacy."[4]

Pope Paul shut the door on any such change with his 1967 declaration "Sacerdotalis Caelibatus" (On the Celibacy of the Priest).[5] But the two interventions—birth control and celibacy—together make the point. The flight from male erotic longing requires not just the isolation of men but the active denigration of women. In their sexuality, they are the source of men's downfall, which is why their sexuality must be firmly under male control. This is a matter of walling off the female not only as an object of male desire—paradigmatically, the whore—but also as the agent of reproduction, the madonna. Sexual morality, according to the Catholic Church, is all about denial of male restlessness and control of female agency. There is simply no place in this schema for a woman's autonomy.

ONE SHOULD BE clear about what followed when the Catholic Church, after its failed Vatican II attempt to redress this grotesque system of sexual injustice, redoubled its determination to rescue and reinforce the anti-sex structure of male supremacy against all that threatened it in an era of feminist liberation. Obviously, this is the context in which to consider the deeper meaning of the Catholic refusal to ordain women to the priesthood. The priestly elite—the "fathers"—occupied the pinnacle of the pyramid of God-sanctioned authority, or power. Women were simply not eligible to exercise such power, even if, as the sad life of today's average harried priest shows, the power is more mythic than real. That many, many Catholics—obviously women, but also men—walked away from the Church on these grounds puts a burden of shame on those of us who found a way to compromise and stay as Catholics, no matter how we justified it to others or to ourselves.

None of this has occurred in a vacuum. Across the globe, women and girls today are overwhelmingly the victims of an unleashed male panic at the collapse of traditional structures of patriarchy. Women and girls by the millions are subject to enslavement and brute violence as norms of restraint erode and systems of respect between men and women collapse. Rape, more than ever, has become not just a technique of control but a weapon of war. The Roman Catholic Church, as a global defender of patriarchy, has become collusive not just in women being kept in "their place"—a place defined by males—but also in their being beaten and murdered if they dare seek a place of their own.

But the issue goes deeper still. Perhaps the single largest transformation that Vatican II proposed to the Catholic imagination was the long-overdue embrace of historical consciousness, a question that is embedded here. Historical consciousness, a full sense of how the past, present, and future flow in one unending stream of time, was not broadly a mark of the midcentury Catholic mind. That problem was made vivid in the very first issue the council confronted in 1962, which was, as we have seen, the move away from Latin as the language of the Mass and other sacraments. Defenders of Latin as the unchangeable heart of Catholic culture said, in effect, *If Latin was good enough for Jesus, it's good enough for us.* Jesus is memorialized as saying Mass in the vestments of a priest at the Last Supper. He is remembered, similarly, as explicitly establishing the other six sacraments himself, more or less in the form they have today. Most notably for this discussion, He is understood as having ordained the twelve Apostles as the Catholic Church's first "priests."[6]

Historical consciousness suggests otherwise. Jesus did not know Latin. He did not wear vestments. If He presided over something at the Last Supper, it was a Seder, not a Mass. The form of the sacraments, including the Eucharist, evolved over time, and that form was not firmly set until the Council of Trent in the sixteenth century. As for the priesthood, the only priests known to Jesus were the Kohanim, the Jewish elite who presided over rituals of animal sacrifice in the Jerusalem Temple. The twelve Apostles were not priests in any sense. And yet the Roman Catholic Church seriously offers as its only justification for refusing to ordain women to the priesthood the historically nonsensical premise that none of the twelve were women. Or, as Pope John Paul II put it in 1994, the Church excludes women because of "the example recorded in the Sacred Scriptures of Christ choosing his Apostles only from among men."[7] Joseph Ratzinger, who succeeded Pope John Paul II as Pope Benedict XVI, said that this teaching was not only definitive but infallible.[8] The otherwise liberal-minded Pope Francis, for his part, has called his predecessors' rejection of women priests "the last word."[9]

This is rank biblical fundamentalism of the sort that post–Vatican II Roman Catholicism repudiates in almost all other matters of theology and doctrine. How is it possible to find instruction on the question of gender in New Testament texts without reference to the privileged place women clearly occupied in the inner circle of Jesus, even according to the male-authored Gospels? As I began to grasp for myself in those first adolescent forays into my little copy of the New Testament, the women alone did not abandon Jesus at Golgotha; it was to women that Jesus first showed himself after the Resurrection; women, therefore, were literally the first to preach the good news. The letters of St. Paul attest to the place of women as empowered leaders of the first Christian communities.[10] As for the twelve, there were no Irish Catholics among them, either, or black Africans. To discriminate by gender is morally identical to discriminating by race.

The scholarship that requires the reading of Scripture according to norms of historical criticism is a settled question in the Church. Settled on all subjects but this one. The rejection of women priests on these grounds is a blatant lie, a further manifestation of profound institutional corruption.

And the betrayal does not end there. As we have seen, Pope John XXIII began the era of Catholic reform in 1963 by lifting up women's liberation as a precious "sign of the times." Yet, according to his successors, ordaining women to the priesthood was so far out of the question that the Catholic Church readily abandoned the central Vatican II project of working toward reunion with other Christian denominations once those denominations presumed to welcome women into the ordained ministry. Pope John's greatest hope for his council was that it would heal this gaping wound of the Reformation—these scandalous Christian divisions—but that purpose turned out to be less important to his successors than protecting male supremacy.

Not content to simply walk away from the ecumenical movement, the Catholic Church used the question of women's ordination to resuscitate the old habit of denominational insult. Ultraconservative Episcopal priests who reject the contemporary Anglican acceptance of women into full equality with men, ratified by ordination, are themselves heartily encouraged by Rome to convert to Catholicism, a crossing-over commonly known as "swimming the Tiber." Once converted, the former Anglicans are welcomed into the Roman Church as priests, even if they are married. So in that way, the rule of mandatory celibacy has indeed been lifted, if only for these self-acknowledged misogynists. That leaves the inferiority of women as the absolutely overriding Catholic moral principle. It is the keystone of clericalism.[11]

The converted Episcopal priests, with their wives, are designated members of the Personal Ordinariate of the Chair of St. Peter. The prelate who established this jurisdiction was the one-time archbishop of Boston, the late Cardinal Bernard Law, the godfather of the priest sexual abuse scandal.

✠

PART SIX

A Priest Forever?

The Lord has sworn and will not change
His mind, "You are a priest forever,
after the order of Melchizedek."

—Psalm 110:4

CHAPTER 18

✠

The Things That Last

So faith, hope, love abide, these three;
but the greatest of these is love.
—1 Corinthians 13:13

Let me return to the story of how, almost despite myself, I made the decision to take the gamble at last—what I had sensed early in life as the radical thrill of the rolled dice on which one's whole life is bet. How I chose to become a Catholic priest.

In the early 1960s, just as I came of age, the nuclear crisis, centered in Berlin, came to another—and ultimate—breaking point.

Having graduated from the American high school in Germany in 1960, I was a student at Georgetown University, thrilled with the life that was opening up in front of me. I had girlfriends, a fast car, and a favorite jazz club; I went to football games; and I was of legal drinking age. I was enthralled with the arrival just then of John F. Kennedy as the president of the United States. The torch of freedom, passed to a new generation, had been passed to me.

I was like many American Catholics in seeing President Kennedy paired with Pope John XXIII as figures of a new and vibrant identity—a kind of faith-infused patriotism. In both men could be heard that call of Pope John's to "the realization of still higher and undreamed of experiences."

My personal encounter with Pope John had remained with me as a mark of my identity, and now it had a match as I stood among the freezing throng on the east side of the U.S. Capitol at the new American president's inauguration in January of 1961. I heard him speak words that landed on me like prayer, words that have stayed with me as a kind of credo to this day: "With a good conscience our only sure reward, with history the final judge of our deeds, let us go forth to lead the land we love, asking His blessing and His help, but knowing that here on earth God's work must truly be our own."[1]

That a glamorously secular man like Kennedy could exhibit such devotion, ironically, gave me the clearance I'd longed for to finally leave behind the narrow notion that devotedness could only be had in a life defined—hemmed in—by the Church. If you'd asked me that year of my arrival at Georgetown, I'd have told you I had turned decisively away from the track pointing toward a priestly "vocation," an ambition that had never been—or so I insisted to myself—truly mine.

But then Flashpoint Berlin flared up again. In June of 1961, President Kennedy and Nikita Khrushchev had a fraught summit meeting in Vienna. The Soviet leader gave the untested young president an ultimatum: Get out of Berlin, or there will be war. A shaken Kennedy returned to the United States and immediately began to prepare for the worst.

I thought I'd come a far distance from that threatened terrain in West Germany, with the hair-trigger phalanx of Red Army tanks just across the Taunus mountain range. Yet the nuclear dread into which I'd been initiated there—that "Woe! Woe! Woe to those who dwell on the earth. . . . And a great star fell from heaven, blazing like a torch"[2]—was approaching a screeching climax in Washington. Coming from East-West-divided Germany, I was surprised to discover that Washington understood itself as the true ground zero of the looming nuclear holocaust. Once the flash point heated up again, I felt that frisson of danger more intensely there than ever.

My father was stationed once more at the Pentagon, but now our family was fully enmeshed in the military, and we lived in a stately house—"quarters"—on Generals' Row at Bolling Air Force Base, three miles down the Potomac from the Capitol. Dad was a full-fledged member of the so-called Air Staff, the generals who would fight the next war. My mother and brothers and I rarely saw him—he was almost always at work—but I was acutely attuned to his status as one of America's nuclear elite. Our next-door neighbor at Bolling was General Curtis LeMay, the famous bomber pilot who'd initiated the air raids against German cities; commanded the air wing that dropped the atomic bombs on Japan; and then overseen the creation of the Strategic Air Command—America's nuclear behemoth. I could never glimpse LeMay, coming or going from his quarters, without a shudder.

Despite the Joe College panache with which I sought to carry myself, my inner feelings were entirely hostage to the public disquiet that was as pervasive in America just then as the air itself: Like air, dread was everywhere and rarely spoken of. As a college kid, I was still an underachieving student, but I'd found an outlet for my brooding idealism as a ROTC cadet—an alternative vocation. I relished the Air Force uniform, the drill, the discipline, the flying lessons, the feeling of being officially tapped at last for America's crusade against the godless Soviet empire. Virtue had never felt so near at hand, so much my own. I threw myself into "rot-see."

At the end of freshman year, I was singled out as the corps's "outstanding cadet" and presented with a stainless-steel model

B-52 bomber. I should have loved that gleaming trophy, but, like glimpses of LeMay, its creator, the thing sometimes made me shudder. My mind would go back to that air show at SAC head-quarters where, as a boy of nine or ten, I stood beside my father, gawking up at the actual B-52 bomber with its eight mammoth engines, its fuselage motto about peace (PEACE IS OUR PROFES-SION), and my father's mournful voice reciting the deterrence dogma: "Only our readiness to obliterate the enemy keeps him from attacking us."[3]

In the summer of 1961, the Berlin crisis peaked. Americans were building bomb shelters, practicing air raid drills, paying new war taxes, and seeing the sudden increase in the number of young men drafted into the military. And when our vigorous and confident president addressed us on TV in July, in what came to be known as the Berlin crisis speech, we sensed in his somber tone a palpable fear. He closed his remarks by asking "in these days and weeks . . . for your goodwill, and your support—and above all, your prayers."[4]

An inchoate emotion that had so long defined me began to make itself unmistakably clear. In some odd way, that era's unmentioned but firmly felt sense of hazard was the precondition of a fresh encounter with Jesus, my Imagined Friend.

Tracking along the Potomac, upriver from Georgetown, is the C&O Canal, with a towpath along which I took to walking alone, often as daylight faded in the late afternoon. On those walks, I found that I was carrying on a one-sided conversation, apparently talking to myself—until I realized: *No, I'm talking to Him.*

Coming into manhood, I was surprised by a new blast of my childhood fervor, yet I trusted it—or, rather, Him. Jesus again. Still. But in an entirely different way. My religion and my feeling for the world's fragility, first discerned in Germany, had become the same thing. I would later learn to think of this as the thin membrane not just between life and death, but also between being and non-being. A sense of that membrane is the ground of faith. I remembered from Latin class the *mysterium tremendum et fascinans*, the mystery that repels and attracts, and realized that I'd made my home in it—the state of being simultaneously repelled and attracted by what, or Who, was both utterly beyond me and as close to me as my breathing. Religion, I sensed, was not an aspect of my life, as I'd always thought. It *was* my life. Talking to myself was talking to God.

ONE NIGHT, AS the crisis reached yet another peak, my father worked late at the Pentagon. His secretary called the house at Bolling to say the general would like to let his driver go home, but he would only do so if I could come later to pick him up. *Sure!* I was thrilled at the prospect of both getting behind the wheel of his Lincoln and having the time alone with him.

I pulled the car into the generals' zone at the River Entrance of the Pentagon and settled in to wait. Finally, near midnight, Dad came out. In the well-lit plaza, the visor of his uniform hat was ablaze with thunderbolts, and the silver stars glistened on his shoulders. He exchanged salutes with several men. Unusually, he got in the car on the passenger's side, saying, "You drive, Jimmy."

He lit his Camel, smoked in silence. I maneuvered the Lincoln across the 14th Street Bridge and into Washington. Finally, he crushed the cigarette in the dashboard ashtray and turned to me. "Son, I'm going to say something to you. I'm only going to say it once, and I don't want you asking me any questions. Okay?"

I waited.

"You read the papers. You know what's happening. I may not

come home one of these nights. I might have to go somewhere else. The whole Air Staff would go. If that happens, I'm going to depend on you to take my place with Mom and the boys."

"What do you mean?" I asked.

"Mom will know. But you should know, too. I'll want you to get everybody in the car. I'll want you to drive south. Get on Route One. Head to Richmond. Go as far as you can before you stop."[5]

And that was it. Having no words, or need for words, neither of us spoke again. I saw the thing clear: My father, wise and powerful, was as much at the mercy of nuclear dread as I was. *The balloon going up.* His admonition made no sense, as even I knew. The nuclear apocalypse would make any such flight to Richmond an act of futility itself. Richmond, too, would be incinerated, or, at best, reduced to a radioactive wasteland.

Escape was not the point. Love was the point. His love for our family, and for me.

A thousand Hiroshimas! he had once said.

Doesn't your dad tell you anything? that girl on the SS *America* had asked me.

My dad was telling me something now. And I heard him. I did not see this at the time—nor, I'm sure, did he. But now I understand that my father was sending me away from his world and all its works.

We were living on the whetted edge of a knife—a knife of our own making. For the first time in my life, I was fully and completely face-to-face with the radical contingency of human existence. No, more than that: I was face-to-face with the ways in which human choices can make that condition even more perilous. However vaguely I grasped the deep meaning of my father's commissioning, I was changed by it forever.[6]

I did know, of course, that my father was simply telling me that he loved us all enough to harbor an irrational hope and, breaching the iron law of national security, to confide it in his son.

What he most told me, though, was that he was afraid, which made my being afraid more absolute than ever. I found myself looking directly into the pit of my own most vivid nightmare—the very world aflame, the eternal lake of fire—brought fully into time. The fear that had troubled my dreams since I was very young.

The coming horror had already been vivid to me. At a favored desk in a window alcove in the building that housed the George-town University library, I had regularly found myself looking out at the D.C. skyline—the Capitol dome, the Washington Monument, the Old Post Office tower, the Smithsonian castle turrets—and seeing it all burst into flames under the ash of a mushroom cloud. I had seen it: the city, the nation, the planet—all at the end of his-tory, the Last Day. For once, my inner and outer worlds were a match. Brooding had defined me.

But after Dad spoke, what I saw, instead of the abyss staring back with accusation—crossing from Berlin, that American MP saying, *Some damn fool like you is going to start World War Three*—was a way forward into my future.

As enthralled as I could be with the "Off we go!" romance of the flyboy Air Force, there was something in it that I did not trust. And upon the glamorous vista, even, of a new American ideal opened up by President Kennedy, there fell a shadow I would not understand for years: *No, God and country are not the same. And no, destroying the world is not the way to save it.*

Everything is contingent—even received notions of morality. Everything is uncertain—even the Catholic faith. Everything is fleeting—including the perception of transience. All life is mortal. Or is it?

The world with which I had simply not been able to come to

terms—embodied in that shining B-52 trophy—was not the world I wanted. This was a feeling that had nothing to do—yet—with the pacifist dissent from war to which I would come later during the Vietnam era. Something larger even than questions of war and peace was at stake. I was simply turning away from the realm of human life that is wholly defined by well-explained reasons, by virtuous principles, and by the assumption that questions can be answered. Some questions cannot be answered. And some experiences can never be explained with reasons. And virtues can be too sure of themselves.

Ever since I was a child, I had seen more than what was before my eyes, and even when I was alone, I had been accompanied by the One whose presence could not be accounted for, which is what made it trustworthy. I'd been unable, finally, to walk away from the betting table, where I would make the wager at last, staking my whole life on the existence of God.

Except for the private vocabulary I shared with my Imagined Friend, Jesus, I had almost no language for any of this. But then, in that fateful period, I sat alone with my father and confided in him the words that finally did occur to me to say. "I want to give myself, Dad, to the things that last. I want to be a priest."

✝

CHAPTER 19

The Bishop of God's Love

The Christian Bible includes sayings that have caused
much pain, both to Jews and to women. Thus I have felt called
to seek forms of interpretation which can counteract such
undesirable side effects of the Holy Scriptures.

—Krister Stendahl[1]

The Catholic religious order I joined, the Paulist Fathers, is a
particularly American institution, and that's what I liked
about it.[2] By a stroke of luck, I was introduced to the Paulists when
I met one of them at Georgetown, a priest who'd come to campus
to interview a candidate for the order, a classmate of mine. The
priest was hip, irreverent, and smart—but not in the overbearing
way of my Jesuit professors. When I told him I'd been thinking
about the priesthood, he laughed and said, "I know the problem."
Then I laughed, too, feeling understood. He reminded me of John
Kennedy.

The Paulists were founded in New York in the mid-nineteenth
century by Isaac Hecker, a convert to Catholicism who'd been associated with Ralph Waldo Emerson, Henry David Thoreau, and
the New England transcendentalists.[3] The Paulists' American
esprit—democratic, liberal, pluralistic—was essential to what appealed to me. But it was also key that the small community of
priests—there were only about 250 of them—took its identity from

its patron, St. Paul the Apostle. I came to regard him as a kind of ideal of faith—robust, passionate, and fiercely devoted to the figure of Jesus. But unlike the original twelve Apostles, Paul had come to the Christian movement after the death of Jesus, whom he encountered only in a mystical vision.

I'd had no such vision myself, of course, but I took the story of Paul's conversion—knocked from a horse on the road to Damascus, blinded by light, the near panicked question, "Lord, what wilt Thou have me to do?"—as an act of imagination akin to my own. The point was not the melodrama of Paul's conversion, but the content of it. Paul, too, saw more than was before his eyes. In speaking to himself, he was speaking to the One, as in T. S. Eliot's "Waste Land" image, who was ever at his side. Unlike the original Apostles, Paul was not so much remembering Jesus as experiencing Him as an ineffable presence. That Jesus was Paul's imagined friend made Paul a friend to me. I quickly felt at home in the company of men who'd taken their name from him.

Yet, given the understanding I have come to lately—judgments reflected in this book—there is something odd in Paul's centrality to my story. A reading of St. Paul that began with St. Augustine underwrote the negative theology against which I've been unknowingly struggling my whole life.

In *The Confessions*, Augustine described his own conversion: He heard the voice of a child urging him, "Pick up and read! Pick up and read!" The command referred to the Bible. Augustine did as the child ordered. "I opened it," he wrote, "and in silence read the first passage on which my eyes lit: 'Put on the Lord Jesus Christ and make no provisions for the desires of the flesh.'" The text Augustine happened upon was from St. Paul's Letter to the Romans—a verse that reads as a passionate denunciation of what Paul called "sexual immorality and debauchery."[4] Augustine continued: "I neither wished nor needed to read further. At once, with the last words of this sentence, it was as if a light of relief from all anxiety flooded into my heart." The "last words" were "the desires of the flesh." After this, Augustine wrote, "all the shadows of doubt were dispelled."[5]

Here is the point: Augustine's conversion to Catholicism, a milestone of Western civilization, boiled down to a repudiation of sexual desire, which from then on was not only Augustine's bête noire but also, in the unconscious structure of its moral pre-occupation, the West's. The man who had prayed "Make me chaste and celibate, Lord, but not yet"[6] had his prayer answered at last, and the Christian rush into a deeply inhuman renunciation of sexuality was begun. Augustine's Manichaean fixation on bipolarity—light versus lust, spirit versus flesh, grace versus works, the City of God versus the City of Man, ultimately male versus female—was the ground of his conversion. It began with St. Paul and, as we have seen, shuttered the Christian imagination ever after. The Roman Catholic dysfunction that is my subject had its igniting incident.

My time of arrival with the Paulists matched exactly, during the Second Vatican Council, with the Catholic Church's long-overdue attempt to emancipate itself from the narrow negativity St. Augustine found in St. Paul. Beginning then, my association with the Paulists emancipated me from that same thing. And, quite oddly, the instrument of that transformation was an intense first encounter with Protestant theology, just at the moment of its transformation, too. None of this was in any way predictable. Here's the story.

I'VE ALREADY DESCRIBED the institutional reach of the Second Vatican Council, including the ways in which it was unfulfilled. But that the council coincided with my time in the seminary was a momentous coincidence for me. It opened in the fall of 1962 with a gathering of the world's Catholic bishops in the vast nave of St. Peter's Basilica.[7] Precisely then, with a couple of dozen other recruits, I began a yearlong "novitiate," a kind of spiritual boot camp, at a remote retreat house in the woods of western New Jersey. By the time I and my newly "professed" classmates completed that year of initiation and arrived at St. Paul's College in Washington, the Paulist Fathers' seminary, the council was already upending what it meant to be Catholic. I would spend the next six years "in formation" at St. Paul's, where the council's "new theology" defined my entire religious education. The transformation that new theology wrought in my heart and mind across those years was complete.

One aspect of the experience stood out. The seminary curriculum immediately reflected, in a quite particular way, the council's promised end of antagonism toward, as they were still called, non-Catholics. The Paulist order would entirely recast its self-understanding around the so-called ecumenical movement, the drive to overcome the divisions among denominations and churches that had marred Christianity since the Reformation.

As it happened, a Rome-based Paulist priest, Father Thomas Stransky, was a member of the council's just-created Vatican Secretariat for Christian Unity, whose agenda was nothing less than reuniting the Christian denominations—Catholic, Orthodox, and Protestant. This was the council's most fervent purpose, a movement from exclusivism to pluralism—the Catholic repudiation, at last, of No Salvation Outside the Church. The main pillar of doom was being dismantled.

Stransky's broad-minded influence at the council would be extensive, and the Paulists, in line with their American liberalism, would be in the forefront of this new so-called ecumenical movement. At St. Paul's College, our seminary faculty followed Stransky's lead in promoting a new openness to Protestant thought. That was the wedge for the enormous theological liberation that followed. The Church was attempting to complete its unfinished business with the sixteenth-century Reformation, when the Christian religion began its reckoning with the modern age.[8]

That reckoning had become a matter, too, of Christianity's accommodating the new philosophical and political breakthroughs associated with the Enlightenment—evolutionary thought in one sphere, historical consciousness in another, and democratic liberalism in yet another. All of this, by overthrowing traditional structures of hierarchy, amounted to an implicit challenge to Roman Catholic clericalism, for which hierarchy's pyramid remained key.

For us seminarians, the intellectual transformation—the changeless Church grounded in ever-changing history; lived experience over static doctrine; new attitudes toward God—was a matter of surprising personal learning, since our seminary promptly embarked on an unprecedented "dialogue" with the Lutheran seminary in Gettysburg, Pennsylvania. Soon enough, we young Catholics were meeting regularly with our Lutheran counterparts, studying Scripture together and also sharing the startling discovery of the faith's American relevance in those heady days of the minister-led civil rights movement. What we Protestants and Catholics had in common as young religious seekers on the politically charged New Frontier weighed far more than the denominational divide that had, only a short time before, seemed absolute. They had Martin Luther, yes, but we all had Martin Luther King, Jr.

It was our Lutheran compatriots who, in those seminars, first brought our attention to the new thinking that was shifting the ground under Lutheran attitudes, especially having to do with our own patron, St. Paul. Here was a way into the deep currents of theology, from St. Augustine forward.

Martin Luther was an Augustinian monk, and as I learned from his co-religionists, Luther brought forward into modernity Augustine's bipolarity—City of God versus City of Man; spirit versus body; the divisiveness of doom. And Luther brought all this forward into me, as we Catholics, too, had unconsciously applied his lens to St. Paul, emphasizing Paul's bipolarity—law versus freedom; sin versus grace; works versus faith. I had no idea that I had been influenced by the thought of Luther. Indeed, Luther was the anonymous godfather of my own brooding scrupulosity, my dread of doom. The Lutheran seminarians opened a door before me.

AND THEN MY new friends ushered me into a place where I encountered yet another man who changed my life—a Protestant! That surprising turn affected my coming of age as a Christian believer.

A simple, clear, and straightforward declaration of scholarly conviction can transform the religious imagination of an era—and countless lives therefore. Almost uniquely, that was the significance of Martin Luther, who, all that time ago, transformed the imaginations of both those who followed him and those who opposed him.

To a far lesser but still pointed degree, that was the significance, too, of the man to whom my young Lutheran colleagues introduced me: Krister Stendahl, a man very much of our own time.[9]

Not well known outside of religious circles, Krister Stendahl (1921–2008) was a Swedish Scripture scholar whose marks, across the second half of the twentieth century, were made at Harvard Divinity School, where he was a professor and dean, and in the Lutheran Church of Sweden, where he was a bishop. That the shift in consciousness embodied in Stendahl's work upended a basic understanding about Martin Luther's ideas compounds the irony that Stendahl is remembered as a towering Lutheran thinker.

If I take what may seem at first to be a detour here, it is because my encounter with this figure enabled, and still epitomizes, the transformation I underwent during my official apprenticeship in Catholic belief.

Luther famously had his Ninety-five Theses—propositions against the selling of indulgences. All Stendahl had was a short speech, delivered in 1961 to a meeting of the American Psychological Association, a summary of which was published in a theological journal as what its editors called "an explosive analysis," under the title "The Apostle Paul and the Introspective Conscience of the West."[10]

I remember the afternoon when one of the Lutheran seminarians in our group first referred to the Stendahl article, because that phrase struck me with such power. I instinctively knew that mine was an "introspective conscience" from my early childhood forward, what I have been describing throughout this book. The introspective conscience frets and overthinks, worries and broods. It is convinced of its unworthiness. The introspective conscience, indeed, had brought me, through all the detours of my adolescence and young adulthood, into the seminary—a word that I was still capable of mispronouncing as "cemetery."

So, yes, mine was an introspective conscience. But was that true of the whole culture—"the West"? After that session of the interfaith seminar, I went back to my room to grapple with the article.

Introspective conscience! The expression spoke to me and for me.

As a young American Catholic, my preoccupation with rescue from the falling dream of doom might have seemed to owe nothing to the Protestant culture against which my people had so resolutely stood. Yet, as I began to understand at St. Paul's College in dialogue with my Lutheran confrères, I was a living recapitulation of Luther's preoccupation with what he called "justification by faith." By that he meant that we are saved not by anything we do— "good works"—but only by the grace of God—"by faith." The German reformer's dread of death and damnation, tied to a sense of radical unworthiness ("The more we wash ourselves," Luther wailed above his washbasin, "the more unclean we become")[11] had its roots in St. Augustine's doctrine of original sin. That idea had reached a peak of its malevolence in the Irish Catholicism in which I was raised. "But I am a worm," as our beloved psalm put it, "and no man."[12]

Indeed, with our bodies, wills, and minds at the mercy of "concupiscence"—unbridled desire—we were all, Protestant and Irish Catholic alike, children of a flesh-hating St. Augustine. Concupiscence, after all, was the very word he had left to us as the definition of the human condition after the Fall of Adam and Eve. I knew nothing of the theology, but I knew the feeling: from my early childhood stirrings of guilt to my adult fears of collusion with a coming nuclear Armageddon. *Some damn fool like me . . .*

As I bore its weight, concupiscence boiled down to the oceanic longing for life just beyond my grasp, which amounted to a rejection of life as it is. Concupiscence was a passion that transcended the erotic, even if the erotic, once I came of age, could seem to form its core. That feeling was what had brought me into the religious life. I felt that Stendahl's phrase "introspective conscience" had been coined for me.

This is how I put the thought earlier in this book: *God wills suffering because humans deserve it. Here is the root of the brooding Catholic conscience that can never shake off a certain dread of doom. I was Exhibit A of this structure of mind, tormented by the overthought compunction that troubled my dreams—that falling dream, falling into hell—from the very beginning of my self-*

awareness. Suffering is redemptive. Suffering is good. Suffering can be infinite in intensity and eternal in time. God wills it!

Stendahl efficiently tracked that dark phenomenon of an "evermore introspective awareness of sin and guilt"[13] to a particular reading of St. Paul through lenses polished by Luther. But those lenses had been ground in the first place by St. Augustine, who found in Paul a reason to whip himself for "the desires of the flesh." Despite all of Augustine's other contributions, we now saw how his anti-human theology had stamped the culture that followed him. Augustine was not only Luther's monastic patron; he was Luther's most important intellectual influence.

I would fully understand such theological provenance only gradually, but even a first brush with Stendahl's revision made me sit up. It was an overdue reckoning with the mistake Christianity had made in fashioning its most potent moral lesson out of the North African bishop's unhappy self-loathing, ratified by his reading, first, of the Adam and Eve story, and then of St. Paul.

Stendahl forthrightly said that Luther's take on St. Paul, in line with Augustine's, was wrong. According to Stendahl, Paul proclaims not a doomsday God before whom all fallen humans are unworthy, but a gracious God whose faithfulness to the promise inherent in the very act of creation weighs infinitely more than any imagined "faith" on the part even of a perfectly repentant human. God's faithfulness is what matters, not the believer's faith.[14] Against St. Augustine, St. Anselm, and now Martin Luther, Stendahl insisted that God never changed His mind about creation, no matter what happened (or did not happen) at the time of the Fall. *No to divine damnation. No to the eternal lake of fire. God, in Jesus Christ, is faithful and true.*

The introspective conscience, chilled in the shadow of an imagined Last Judgment, is an offense against the God whose judgment comes as love, pure and simple.

Stendahl's insight had broad influence across the boundaries of Christian theology in the 1960s and after. That his treatise was first delivered at a convention of psychologists points to the way Stendahl's thought had relevance outside of religion, too. The brooding introspection of depth psychoanalysis—Freud's terrain—flows along these same currents in Western culture. But for me it registered as an intensely personal solution to my oldest problem: the falling dream, the abyss, the intractability of my unworthiness. What prompted me, even as a child, to hurl at heaven that *De Profundis*: "Out of the depths I cried unto Thee, O Lord."

The intellectual resonance of Stendahl's perception included an undermining of another foundational negative-positive bipolarity: Synagogue versus Church. That opposition is traditionally attributed to St. Paul, who is read as the progenitor of Christian contempt for Jews. But it was in a twisted reading of St. Paul that Christians found a "Jewish piety as the black background," in Stendahl's words, "that makes Christian piety the more shining."[15] This Jewish foil of hopelessness against which Christian joy is posited informs an entire religious schema: Moses versus Christ; law versus grace; works versus faith; form versus substance; judgment versus mercy; greed versus generosity; ultimately—the God of the Old Testament versus the God of the New Testament.

The abstractions of that bipolarity were realized, above all, in a history-laden specificity: The structure of religious anti-Judaism, generated here and carried forward in the history of Christendom, came to flower in racial anti-Semitism, which eventually spawned the white supremacy of European explorers, colonizers, and slave traders. This us-against-them infection marked the entire West, but nowhere more so than in Martin Luther's own Germany, as events of the twentieth century would show.

To all of this, with his simple idea of God's absolute love for all, Krister Stendahl said *No!*

. . .

FOR US SEMINARIANS, there was Martin Luther, and, yes, now there was Martin Luther King, Jr.

There were our seminar rooms, and there were the streets, the bifurcated locus of our transformation away from bifurcation. This was a theological and political realization of what I had intuited as the altar boy at those funeral Masses: God's preoccupation is not with sin and its wages, but with suffering and how to end it.

The full meaning of Stendahl's insight would not become clear to me for some time, although for those of us whose problem was more personal than academic, its flash was bright enough to illuminate the shadows cast by a piety that transcended narrow Lutheran references. If faith was not the enemy of works, or grace the enemy of law, or spirit the antagonist of flesh, who knew what other structures of conflict might fall? Was it possible that the entire economy of salvation—a saving God of mercy over against a damning God of judgment—could be revised?

And what would that mean for an encumbered young man like me? Indeed, my intuitive disbelief in what passed as an overriding Catholic orthodoxy was being vindicated.

It was an astonishment to take up such questions at that moment in the company of earnest young Lutherans, who were daring to think critically about their own tradition. They knew more than we did. Had Luther distorted the New Testament's meaning by transferring his enmity against the pope in Rome to St. Paul's tensions with his fellow Jews, changing how Paul was read by everyone? We Catholics, too, had basic questions to ask, especially we "Paulists," for whom Paul was an all-defining patron. Had we also missed something crucial about the so-called apostle to the Gentiles? All at once, even Paul's "conversion" took on different meaning.

January 25 is the feast of the great history-altering event on the road to Damascus, when Paul asked, "Lord, what wilt Thou have me to do?" That day was always the occasion of the Paulist Fathers' greatest celebration, our best party. We, too, were apostles to the Gentiles, even if our "Gentiles" were said to be the religiously indifferent masses of modern America.

The feast of the "conversion" of Paul had such resonance because the assumption was that the real life of the Church began when Paul, its great persecutor, was converted from Judaism to Christianity; when the Jew "Saul" became the Christian "Paul." When, indeed, the "scales fell from his eyes," the image I appropriated earlier.

But what if the name change from Saul to Paul was only a matter of translation, not transformation—an alteration of "Saul" into "Paul" by the author of the biblical narrative that tells the story, the Acts of the Apostles? What if that alteration, in fact, only rendered the Hebrew name "Saul" into the Latin "Paul" to reflect the geographical change as Saul-Paul made his way from Palestine to Rome?

What if the unblinded Paul, that is, far from seeing an unbridgeable theological opposition between a new status and a former one—between faith and works, between grace and law—saw instead only resolvable tensions between the people of Israel and those Gentiles who, in Jesus Christ, sought adoption into that chosen people? What if the conflict reflected in Paul's letters—and there is conflict—was not between Israel and an outside force, but within Israel; not between the Church and the Synagogue, but inside the hearts and minds of the Jesus people who were struggling to understand exactly what their faith implied?

Historical criticism helped us seminarians understand just then that in Paul's lifetime, "the Church" had not yet come into existence. (Paul died in about the year 65.) The Jesus movement was, at most, a nascent sect within Judaism. If Paul was knocked from his horse, it was for having seen the new *Jewish* meaning of the life and death of Jesus. There was no question of Paul's embracing a new religious identity—of having a "conversion." Nor was there any question of God's having broken His promise to Israel, passing it over to the Church.

All of that anti-Israel denigrating came later (after the traumas of the Roman destruction of the Temple in 70 and the Roman leveling of Jerusalem in 135). Centuries later still, the anti-Israel denigration was squared by Martin Luther, who had his own culture-determined reasons for deploring the Jewishness of Paul. Luther's hatred of Jews would be the deformed gene in the DNA of Germany, as it developed into a modern nation.

We young Paulists confronted these themes in theology, while outside our seminary walls an unfinished reckoning with World War II was being advanced by such phenomena as *The Diary of a Young Girl* by Anne Frank, *Night* by Elie Wiesel, and *The Deputy* by Rolf Hochhuth. Hochhuth's play, a hit on Broadway in 1963, landed on Catholics with particular force because of its demythologizing of Pope Pius XII's supposedly heroic stance against the Nazis. Then, too, the trial of Adolf Eichmann in Jerusalem, reported on the evening news in 1961, had ignited a whole new discussion of what befell the Jews in Europe. In that context, it became clear that the Second Vatican Council, just under way, was nothing if not a Roman Catholic attempt to confront the meaning for theology of abject Christian failures during the Holocaust. History and theology: The Catholic conscience was stirring.

AT THE MOST obvious level, such a Catholic reckoning was centrally a matter of doing away with the supersessionist denigration of the living religion of the Jewish people—the idea that the Church had replaced Israel as God's chosen people. That change came in the form of Vatican II's solemn declaration "Nostra Aetate," a Latin phrase meaning "In Our Time," the statement's first words. That declaration was not what it might have been as a full Christian reckoning with ancient anti-Judaism and modern anti-Semitism, yet it stands as a historic marker for the good.

Famous as the Church's formal renunciation of the "Christ-killer" slander—the idea that the Jewish people as a whole bear the guilt for the murder of Jesus—the declaration is equally important for its assertion that the covenant God made with Israel, far from being renounced, or "superseded," remains in force. "The Jews remain very dear to God," the council fathers declared, "since God does not take back the gifts He bestowed or the choice He made."[16] This simple statement undercuts the either-or bipolarity between a Synagogue regarded as outmoded and an ever vital Church. To dismantle that structure of theology was to dismantle the equivalent structure of the religious imagination that put the consuming fire of the Old Testament God in opposition to the loving Father of the New Testament.

That structure pitted "God the mortal enemy" against "God the great friend," with Jesus taken to be the saving arbiter between them. Yet the negative-positive charge of that dualism threatened doom no matter what Jesus was taken to have done. That is shown by the history, in the nations bracketing the North Atlantic, of anti-Semitism and white supremacy. The former was explicitly promulgated in Jesus's name, while the latter more subtly drew its energy from the black-and-white bipolarity of the Synagogue versus the Church. Christian Europe learned to define itself positively by defining someone else negatively, an opposition that was at first religious but then became racial. At last we could measure fully the destructive character of the "introspective conscience of the West." Not to mention mine.

One of the authors of the transforming "Nostra Aetate" at the Second Vatican Council was the young Paulist Father Thomas Stransky, who by the time of my ordination to the priesthood in 1969 was the president of the Paulist Fathers. Stransky was our intimate leader and our personal prophet. This liberal reformer's elevation by the community to its highest office was a signal of how deeply into our consciousness the upright beams of this transformation had been driven. In those years, the Paulists changed their understanding of their patron (opposed not to Judaism, but to the imperium, or legal establishment, of Rome, which killed him), their understanding of their mission (from "convert makers" to "ecumenists"), and their understanding of the Church itself (not "militant" but "pilgrim").

Indeed, the idea of God changed. Abandoning the notion of an Old Testament God of doom in tension with a New Testament God of love—recovering the Jewish roots of the faith—we could say with resolute new energy that there is One God (*Shema!*), whose benign attitude is constant. "And God saw every thing that He had made," as Genesis says, "and, behold, it was very good."[17] No longer did we need to plead with Jesus to change God's mind from damning us to saving us. It was our minds that Jesus came to change, not God's. No longer, therefore, were we at the mercy of the apocalyptic dread of the Last Things and their doomsday Divinity. All at once, the good news was truly good, and it seemed real: *The One God is the God of love. God is love.* Period, full stop.

The impact of such a large religious transformation on institutional Christianity was one thing, but its effect on the consciences of individual Christians—for example, mine—was something else.

Jesus had been my intimate friend through the labyrinthine ways of a long journey to mature belief, but He had always served as a kind of protector, keeping me safe from the dark will of His

Father. Now I saw what it meant when He said, "I and the Father are one."[18] Jesus was the friend who showed me that friendship defines the heart of the cosmos. Not only that Jesus is love, but that God is, too.

KRISTER STENDAHL PLANTED a seed that, along with many other seeds, sprouted into shoots and blossoms. And then a remarkable thing happened. When I was a Catholic priest, trying to proclaim this good news, I encountered Stendahl personally for the first time. It was 1969. The Vietnam War was flaring, and antiwar protests were warranted but extreme. I was the newly ordained Catholic chaplain at Boston University, and Krister was dean of Harvard Divinity School, across the Charles River in Cambridge. That he was a well-known figure of humane calm in that tumultuous time was no surprise to me. (That year, he was the lone dean to bravely oppose Harvard University's unleashing of police against student antiwar demonstrators.)

I went out of my way to hear Stendahl preach at Harvard, and it was the most natural thing in the world to take him as a model of how to balance faith and politics. He had a striking physical appearance. He was very tall and quite lean. Because of a lifelong arthritic condition in his spine, his head was fused unmovingly to his neck, giving him a rigid posture that seemed to underscore a Nordic sternness. But he was anything but dour, as his broad smile always emphasized. He had a deep-throated laugh, which broke from his unbending form like an unexpected shaft of sunlight dispelling gloom.

Later, after I left the priesthood to become a writer (a decision my once introverted conscience would never have let me make), accidental circumstances brought me and Krister together as friends. Over many years, we lunched regularly in Cambridge, shared an informal discussion group in Boston, welcomed each other into our homes. In successive years for a decade, we walked together in war-torn Jerusalem, where he initiated me into interfaith peace work with Israelis and Palestinians. He was a first reader of much of what I wrote. I often adjusted my schedule to hear him lecture or preach. I remained a Catholic, but he was my bishop.

In his eighties, Krister grew ill. As he approached death, I asked for his blessing. He gave it, pressing my head with his hands.

I was privileged to sit with him in his last hours, and his dear family welcomed me into their circle of grief. At their request, I offered remarks at his Harvard memorial.

I saw up close how the spirit of affirmation that had informed Krister Stendahl's revolutionary theological insight reached, in fact, to the very core of his personality. When that affirmation was, again and again, on offer to me, I knew very well why it was so familiar, so bracing, and so precious. When I dared, for example, to write a long history of Christian anti-Semitism—a work that could offend turf-conscious scholars as much as religious authorities—Krister gave me his personal imprimatur, which served as a kind of bulletproofing.[19] It was only with Krister Stendahl, my unlikely mentor and dear friend, that I could finally and fully appreciate that I had been right to make my life choices—that wager—in response to the Imagined Friend of my childhood, since my connection to Jesus went deeper into my soul, even, than my membership in the Roman Catholic Church. Krister epitomized the transformation that saved my faith.

But now, as I recall Krister Stendahl's role as both a theological mentor and intimate friend, I am in touch with yet another savage disappointment in my own Catholic tradition. I referred earlier to the way the Roman Church abandoned Pope John XXIII's dream of an interfaith reconciliation, and abandoned it largely over the issue of women's ordination. In the years immediately after the

Second Vatican Council, astonishing progress had been made toward theological resolutions of disputes between Protestants and Catholics over essential matters like the place of the papacy, and even the meaning of the sacraments, especially the Eucharist.[20] After twenty years of high-level theological interchange—and nearly universal interfaith cooperation at the parish level across the Christian world—hardly any significant obstacles remained to prevent some kind of formal reconciliation between Roman Catholicism and the High Church denominations. Those decidedly included the Lutheran and Anglican churches, in particular.

But when those and other Protestant denominations admitted women to full equality in the ministry, the Vatican shut down all moves toward institutional amity. Indeed, extensive structures of interfaith dialogue—an early form of which had put me in the room with Lutheran seminarians—all but disappeared. Catholic parishes mostly opted out of even such routine forms of cooperation as jointly sponsored soup kitchens and holiday pageants. Rome alone.

No Salvation Outside the Church had been eliminated as Catholic doctrine by Vatican II, but a kind of *Nulla Salus* practice reasserted itself, especially as Cardinal Joseph Ratzinger, both as "God's Rottweiler"[21] under Pope John Paul II and as Pope Benedict XVI himself, brought back an old Catholic triumphalism. Where once Catholic priests and nuns had routinely formed partnerships with clergy of other traditions—both in the streets, working for social justice, and in sanctuaries, sharing common religious observances—now such routine ecumenical activity largely dried up. If senior levels of theological interchange were continued at all, it was in a firmly pro forma fashion.

A rigorous Catholic determination to forbid non-Catholics of all stripes to receive Communion at Mass reasserted itself.[22] To so use the Sacrament as a means of border protection in this way, of course, grotesquely betrays the Jesus who broke bread with everyone. "Come to me, all you who are weary and burdened, and I will give you rest," Jesus said,[23] which translates as *My food is for the hungry, not the well fed.* The insult inflicted by Catholicism's closed-door Communion policy is blatant at weddings and funerals, when Catholic priests, with routine explicitness, forbid non-Catholics in attendance to come forward to share in the sacred meal.

As a believer whose faith took shape at those Requiem Masses of my childhood, I am, perhaps, overly sensitive to this exclusion, especially at funerals, when the bereaved are most vulnerable to it. The cruelty of this Catholic policy, coldly administered by parish priests, is breathtaking. The heartless totality with which Pope John XXIII's ecumenical vision was jettisoned in this and every realm suggests that something even more basic than an allergy to women's ordination has been at work, which brings us back to clericalism.

THE REFORMATION, AFTER all, boiled down to a conflict over the power of the priest. To translate the Scripture into the vernacular, as Martin Luther and other Reformers did, was to remove the clergy's monopoly on the sacred heart of the faith. Likewise, to introduce democratic structures into Church governance, elevating the role of the laity—a Protestant move that, in fact, generated democracy itself—was to overturn the hierarchy of being, according to which every ordained person occupied a place of superiority to the non-ordained, with bishops and popes on top. The Catholic Church has done everything it can to preserve this system, including, when necessary, protecting the rapists of children.

We have seen how Roman Catholic prelates, including those who otherwise accept the intellectual framework of historical consciousness, defy that consciousness by invoking the all-male Apostles in order to keep women subservient. Historical consciousness knows both that the Apostles were not the only leaders of the Jesus people and that they were not ordained "priests" in any case.

Similarly, Catholic powers wield something called "apostolic succession"—the ahistorical fantasy that the sacramental consecration of Catholic bishops can be mechanistically tracked all the way back to the Apostles—as a bludgeon against non-Catholic priests and ministers. To be outside of this succession—the sequential link broken for Anglicans, for example, during the time of King Henry VIII—means that no Protestant ordinations are "valid." That means, in turn, that the sacraments over which Protestant priests and ministers preside, however sincerely, are sham rituals. Protestant bishops are fakes.

An appreciation of Krister Stendahl—bishop, dean, and prophet of the ecumenical movement—makes clear the insult of this schema. The Vatican's rejection of women and its shutting down of meaningful interfaith dialogue both attempt to protect the excluding power of Rome's priests, bishops, and popes. The priestly sexual abuse scandal has laid bare the deep corruption of Catholic clericalism, and here is another manifestation of it.

✠

CHAPTER 20

Respect and Obedience

Do you promise respect and obedience to me and my successors?
—Catholic rite of ordination, bishop to candidate

I've referred passingly to the transformations that occurred between my arrival at St. Paul's College, the Paulist seminary, in
1963 and my ordination to the priesthood in 1969. For my whole
generation, of course, those were pivotal years, and they were no
less so for me.

At the root of my story, as the reader knows, was the transcending figure of my father, for whom those same years were pivotal,
too. He came to the peak of his power just then, serving, after a
stint as Air Force Inspector General, as founding director of the
Defense Intelligence Agency from 1962, when he was tapped by
John F. Kennedy, to 1969, when his career abruptly ended. Those
years undid him. As head of the DIA, Dad was responsible for supervising Pentagon intelligence during the Cold War's most dangerous phase.

And then there was Vietnam. That misbegotten war was, above
all, a failure of American intelligence—my father's bailiwick.

Even from the distance that opened up between me and Dad, I saw him being broken by the stresses of an impossible situation.

But he was waging another two-front siege of which I knew nothing—hostilities that engulfed him inside the Pentagon. First, he took on his fellow Air Force generals, whom he defied with intelligence assessments that debunked their claims of air war successes in Vietnam. And second, after Richard M. Nixon became president in 1969, my father refused to support the new administration's political manipulations of intelligence about Soviet nuclear capabilities—an unsung act of integrity that destroyed his career. But those conflicts of his were secret.

By the time I was ordained in 1969, the decade's public upheavals had cruelly come between me and Dad. The religious revolution of those years, embodied in Pope John XXIII's Second Vatican Council, was matched by the political revolution of the civil rights and antiwar movements. These new religious and political purposes had filled me with an unexpected passion for the role I could play in the Catholic ministry. But the pleasure my father and mother should have been able to take in my finally becoming a priest was poisoned by my becoming, for them, the wrong kind of priest.

While in the seminary, I joined in the massive war protests that filled the streets of Washington, if always anonymously and on the margins. But, working as an inner-city community organizer, I firmly threw in with Martin Luther King, Jr.'s Poor People's Campaign, a commitment that was only reinforced by Dr. King's assassination in 1968. To my father, King may have been well intentioned, but he was a communist dupe,[1] and my civil rights work alone was enough to infuriate him. Dad was doubly appalled by my association with the Catholic peace movement, with its radical priests and nuns, tentative though my connection was. As the day of my ordination approached, my father was barely speaking to me.[2]

Ironically, of course, it was he who had prepared me to turn away from the Pentagon as the locus of my ideals. He never saw the deeper meaning of what he'd done that night of heightened alarm early in the sixties, but gradually, inexorably, I did. Out of his commissioning—*Head to Richmond. Go as far as you can before you stop*—I had embraced religion at last, but it was the religion I learned from Pope John XXIII, whose "Pacem in Terris" helped me see God as the opposite of war. No war is holy. In the nuclear age, no war is just. God does *not* will it! The inbuilt reluctance I might have felt in reaching such antiwar conclusions was nullified, across the years of my priestly formation, by what even I could see unfolding in Vietnam.

Every human life has its tragic aspect. Mine is this: When my father trusted me enough to confide his nuclear dread, he ignited my rejection of what made that dread inevitable, which he could only experience as rejection of him. I did not see until too late how vastly his tragedy outweighed mine.

Years before, back in Wiesbaden, my parents had happily imagined that I would be ordained to the priesthood by their friend Cardinal Francis Spellman, the archbishop of New York and the vicar apostolic of the U.S. military—the "military ordinary." During my seminary years, though, Spellman emerged as the avatar of America's misbegotten war in Vietnam, and I became secretly appalled at the thought of his ordaining me. I was frankly relieved when he died in 1967. I would not have to kneel before the warmonger-cardinal.

Spellman's successor, as both archbishop of New York and military ordinary, was a much different figure, the benign and modest Terence Cooke. But Cooke followed Spellman's lead as a fervent anticommunist. He defended America's policy of nuclear deterrence and the idea of a moral nuclear war—which Pope John XXIII had called into question. Cooke was firmly associated with the American campaign against the communist enemy in Southeast Asia. And Cooke was Nixon's friend. Vested in his clerical finery, he offered the benediction at Nixon's inauguration in January of 1969.

Learning from the fate of Lyndon Johnson, and aware of the American public's exhausted patience with the war, Nixon had run for president promising peace in Vietnam, but he immediately betrayed that promise. Not long after taking office, he ordered a whole new round of bombing of North Vietnam. Later in his presidency, when launching another bombing operation, he would declare, "The bastards have never been bombed like they're going to be bombed this time."[3] Astonishing the world, Nixon resumed the mass carnage that Johnson had halted the previous spring.

It was exactly then, in February of 1969, that I was ordained a priest by Archbishop Cooke. That he was palpably a nicer man than Spellman somehow made his pro-war fervor worse, especially once it was clear that his friend Nixon's bomb-happy war policy would be even more savage than Johnson's. Like Spellman, Cooke was the Pentagon's avid pastor.

Being ordained by such a figure at that point would have posed a problem for me in any case, but the war was not all of it. Though I was only vaguely aware of this as a source of my unease, the ordination ceremony itself would involve an initiation into the corruption of clericalism, a corruption I already sensed but could not yet name.

. . .

MY ORDINATION TOOK place at the Paulist Fathers' "mother church," the Church of St. Paul the Apostle, on the west side of Midtown Manhattan. The looming granite basilica was notable for having the great vaulted ceiling of its nave painted with the night sky—constellations arranged with astronomical precision to match their positions as they would have been on the night of the conversion of St. Paul.

On that bright winter morning, the mammoth church was crowded with the friends and families of us "ordinands," my twenty-seven classmates and me. But in the sanctuary, arrayed behind the altar, fanning out from the coped and mitered Archbishop Cooke, were some unexpected figures, the source of my quite particular unease.

Because I was, as far as anyone knew, the first son of an active duty Air Force officer to be ordained to the Catholic priesthood,[4] and because the ordaining prelate was the vicar apostolic himself, the ceremony was a big deal for the Catholic military. That's why, to my surprise, a cohort of perhaps a dozen Air Force chaplains were present at the altar that morning. Cooke was their "ordinary," too, and their showing up at my ordination displayed a double-barreled obsequiousness: clergy officers currying church-state favor with both their crimson-robed religious superior and the three-star general high in their military chain of command. Although each chaplain's shoulders were draped with a narrow priestly stole, they were wearing their blue Air Force uniforms, not liturgical vestments. Their getups featured a necktie instead of the Roman collar, and glistening silver rank insignia instead of gold thread. Rigidly at attention, their honor-guard formation gave the sacramental ritual a martial aspect. Presumably, the chaplains had come to bless me, but their presence, as I experienced it, had turned my ordination into a benediction ritual of the war in Vietnam.

As the ceremony started, we ordinands were wearing the white under-robes, called albs, that priests wear at Mass. During the ritual, our vesting would be completed when the archbishop cloaked each of us in a silk chasuble, the capelike outermost liturgical garment. My ordination was supposed to have been a vaunted moment, a signal of my "ontological change," a transformation of my very being, but before, during, and after that sacramental ritual, I was the same stricken fellow: ambivalent, searching, caught.

At the climactic moment, I approached Archbishop Cooke, who was seated on a gilded throne. I knelt before him. An assistant priest stood at his elbow, holding the liturgical book open. The archbishop pressed my head with the soul-changing "imposition of hands," as the ritual gesture is called—the gesture that enacted my permanent elevation to the status of one before whom the angels would hereafter genuflect.

Cooke eyed the text beside him, carefully preparing to utter the exact words, as the rubrics required. After having pressed his hands firmly on my head, he extended them to me. I knew to fold my own hands together and insert them into the receptive slot that his hands made. He closed his hands firmly around mine.

I would only later understand the ancient implication of what we were doing. Beginning with my kneeling before him, a traditional act of homage, and continuing with the placing of my hands between his, we were enacting a feudal ritual dating to the Middle Ages. This was a "commendation" ceremony, according to which a vassal became the "man" of his lord. The ritual peaked with the vassal's oath, swearing fealty to his lordship. This had been the essential ceremony of feudalism, and now it was the rite of clericalism.

Archbishop Cooke, holding my eyes, intoned the governing words: "Do you promise respect and obedience to me and my successors?"

Abstracting from tensions associated with the war, I was desperate to say yes, for I wanted by then, late in the anarchic sixties, nothing more than a trusted authority figure before whom to bow. I wanted to see past the prelate to my Imagined Friend, Jesus. It was He to whom I wanted to pledge respect and obedience. But the constricting feudal ritual said no to that. I was not making an oath to Jesus, or even to God.

In those years of civil rights and antiwar fervor, I had forged a new bond with Jesus, the prophet of justice and peace. But what had He to do with lavish High Church ceremonials? Everywhere I looked just then, I saw bright, shining jewels and silk threads. I saw Church functionaries and tin soldiers. At that moment, my awareness was taken up not by the sandal-shod Galilean, but by the liege lord in the gilded miter and bejeweled cross, the apostolic vicar of the American military—Archbishop Cooke.

A familiar feeling swamped me. As a child in the darkened booth of the confessional, I had lied to the priest by saying I repented my sins for love of God, not for fear of hell. And now—was I to lie again?

I could not yet imagine disobeying the archbishop or his successors—but respect? As military vicar, Cooke was the "blesser in chief" of an evil war. He was institutionally and personally complicit in it.

Respect?

I pushed the qualm aside, and dropping my eyes from his, I answered, "Yes."

The qualm, though, refused to stay aside. As I stood and crossed the sanctuary to take my place on the cold stone floor, lying prostrate in formation with my classmates, I felt awash in guilt.

A solemn vow pledging respect? I had just lied.

Lord, have mercy! Christ, have mercy!

The lifted voices of the large choir, robed in white and arrayed on platforms behind the altar, filled the air in the high vaulted church with the chanted Litany of the Saints. The heavenly prayer soared above our heads, heads that we new priests kept buried in the crooks of our arms. Lying motionless on the floor like corpses laid out on a battlefield, we were enacting a symbolic death — death to the world, the flesh, and the devil.

All ye holy men and women, saints of God, pray for us.

Pray for me! In swearing my oath, I had violated it. It was not the Holy Spirit hovering over me, but the cold shadow of bad faith.

AS A SEMINARIAN, looking ahead to my priesthood, I had dreaded the loneliness of the celibate life, but what I had not imagined was the fulfillment I would find in my pastoral connection with my own little campus ministry flock at Boston University: "Pastor" means "shepherd."

I celebrated their Masses, heard their Confessions, sat with them in the student union coffee shop shooting the breeze. To the students at BU, I tried to relate the story of my oldest friend, Jesus, in ways they would connect with, only to find a new connection of my own. Jesus was, in a way, more "imagined" than ever. I found it the most natural thing in the world to speak of Him as if He were real. To me He was.

Still, the kids taught me how to listen to the Beatles' "Eleanor Rigby" and hear the warning in Father McKenzie's "sermon that no one will hear." They listened patiently when I spoke without a text. They were kind when I lost my train of thought. They trusted me with their secrets, which helped me begin to trust myself. They teased me for being too young to be called "Father," yet my un-precedented paternal feelings were what enabled me to come of age at last. When, back at the rectory late at night, I finally fell on my knees beside my bed, my last thought was always of them.

What intimacy could compare with the bond I had with young-sters who believed in God, so they said, because I did?

After a year of being their priest, I loved those kids. That was all. But then, so it felt, Nixon's Army began to kill them.

In late April of 1970, more than a year after I had come to BU as a freshly ordained priest, President Nixon crossed a red line by extending his savage air war to Cambodia, the theretofore neutral country that bordered Vietnam. Nixon went on television on April 30 to declare, "The time has come for action."

At that point, of course, more than 335,000 U.S. troops were still in Vietnam,[5] and more than 48,000 Americans had already been killed in "action." (Nixon's extension of the war would kill 10,000 more.[6]) "If, when the chips are down," Nixon went on to say that night, "the world's most powerful nation, the United States of America, acts like a pitiful, helpless giant, the forces of totali-tarianism and anarchy will threaten free nations and free institu-tions throughout the world."[7]

But it was the president's speech that set loose anarchy in America. The fantasy that the war would soon end was finished. That's what drove a million U.S. citizens into the streets at once, many of them young people, including legions of college students—none more fervent than my own students at Boston University. I felt the rage as much as they did.

On Nixon's order, tens of thousands of U.S. troops, together with South Vietnamese forces, launched an "incursion" into neu-tral Cambodia (Nixon and his national security advisor, Henry Kissinger, refused to call it an "invasion"), assaulting regions with designations like "Parrot's Beak" and "Fishhook." An air cam-paign, involving bombardment by thousands of U.S. Navy and Air Force sorties (some of them likely flown by classmates of mine from Wiesbaden High School), would continue for nearly three more years. This was yet another savage escalation of the war that

Americans, from across the political spectrum, had expressly voted to end in 1968.

Because the war in Vietnam was thus unnecessarily prolonged for another seven years after that election, our nation fell into a spiritual and moral abyss—a chasm that, even now as I write, has yet to show its bottom. The present American unraveling—however accelerated by economic inequality, anarchic social media, political tribalism, and demagogic leadership—began, I believe, with Nixon's cynical resuscitation of the war in Southeast Asia, a war he had promised to promptly conclude. Given the immediate outrage with which America's young people greeted that news in the first days of May in 1970, it was as if those innocents saw clearly what lay ahead for their nation across the full reach of their lifetimes.

Among those who protested were four students at Kent State University in Ohio: Allison Krause, Jeffrey Miller, Sandra Scheuer, and William Schroeder. Their names live on because they were shot dead by soldiers of the Ohio National Guard, who'd been ordered onto their campus to put down the protest.

When word of those Ohio killings spread at Boston University, hundreds of students—perhaps thousands—spontaneously gathered at the Massachusetts National Guard Armory adjacent to the campus. The armory was a looming brick fortress dominating Commonwealth Avenue, the broad boulevard that ran through the urban university like a spine. The building's martial architecture featured a sham moat, a faux drawbridge, a huge multipaneled oaken door, and castlelike crenellations. I was one of those streaming up the avenue, to take my place opposite the guard headquarters.

Since my ordination, the weight of my father's role at the Pentagon had continued to keep me on the margins of the peace movement that I quietly—if ever more intensely—supported.

Considerable numbers of Catholic priests and nuns, including friends of mine, had stepped bravely into the cauldron of active opposition, up to and including civil disobedience. But the broad antiwar resistance had itself become violent in some quarters, reinforcing my reluctance to actually join the company of lawbreaking protesters. During just that first year of my time at BU, antiwar radicals around the nation had launched over two hundred bombings at draft boards, induction centers, and ROTC buildings. My friends the Catholic pacifists, also targeting such places, did so with disciplined nonviolence, but it had all seemed frighteningly problematic to me.

At BU, I had tempered my sermons, leaving overt war denunciations aside, always aware that the Catholic kids in front of me disproportionately included ROTC cadets. I did not want more-conservative kids feeling unwelcome at the altar. In counseling boys who were confronting the draft, I worked hard to leave to them the momentous decision of whether to go to war. I saw my pastoral role as affirming everyone, as if, in that charged time, I regarded the "for" and "against" arguments over Vietnam as more or less of equal weight.

But all that changed when the students were killed at Kent State.

At the armory on Commonwealth Avenue, the crowd was so large that it spilled from the broad sidewalks out into the street, with the unplanned result that we were blocking automobile traffic, as well as the streetcar tracks of the MBTA Green Line. No one seemed particularly aware of the blockage because our somber gathering felt more like a grief vigil than a demonstration. We stood in silence—without bullhorns, without demands, without speeches of any kind. There was no podium, no soapbox. Silence seemed the only fit response to what had happened. Simply being present at our National Guard Armory in memory of students gunned down by their National Guard in Ohio was enough. Some people were weeping. Others hugged one another. Kent State was us.

Boston police arrived. It was they who had the bullhorns. Orders to disperse were broadcast. The orders were repeated, along with threats of arrest. The crowd stirred. Glances were exchanged. The bullhorn crackled with its demand, its warning, its threat. And then, instead of moving away as ordered, without forethought and without declamation, the crowd simply sat down as one creature. We sat.

We took places on the boulevard pavement, on the streetcar tracks, on the gritty median strip. It was a demonstration, after all, and it was illegal. What I remember most was how readily the students responded to the police order by simply disobeying it. I disobeyed, too, apparently sharing in the spontaneity, but there was nothing ready in me as I slowly sank to the chilly ground.

Disobeying the police order was a minor misdemeanor for sure, but it was still momentous for me. I remember looking up and down the avenue to see not only a massive traffic jam but, on the tracks in both directions, long lines of stalled green trolley cars. *Oh God*, I thought, *this will ripple across the entire MBTA. The whole city will be tied up. The sit-in, spontaneous or not, can't be allowed to go on. How in hell will this end?*

And sure enough, the massive wooden doors of the armory soon swung open slowly. Without fanfare, but with several sharply barked orders, two ranks of U.S. soldiers, dressed in combat gear and carrying rifles, filed out of the massive brick building in disciplined cadence. The rows separated, splitting to march steadily around the gathered students until we were completely encircled by the stoic GIs.

I saw that they were mostly the same age as the BU students. Kids against kids. (The average age of U.S. soldiers fighting in

World War II had been twenty-six; in Vietnam, it was nineteen.) But at Kent State, the guardsmen had been kids with loaded rifles, and all at once the real meaning of the present trauma sank in. At the sight of that ring of soldiers, we of the accidental sit-in felt our silence deepen into something monumental. The GIs eyed us impassively, their rifles ready.

One student stood up and began to climb over others, to get away. Then others followed. Quickly, without waiting for an order to disperse, the seated demonstrators stood up in singles, clumps, and then en masse—including me. Still in silence and avoiding one another's eyes, we moved away from the armory, streaming down the avenue, into the side streets, across the nearby bridge, back to the university dorms, out into the city. The MBTA tracks and the boulevard were quickly clear. At the sight of those combat-ready soldiers, the students, and we few adults, dispersed.

And the next thing anybody knew, all of the students were gone from Boston University itself—just gone. The dorms emptied. Word spread, at first in whispers, that final exams, and even commencement, were cancelled. The BU administration, like those at dozens of colleges across the country, had simply shut the school down. That abruptly, the academic year was over. Along with much else.

THE STUDENTS HAD seemed to commit that simple act of civil disobedience automatically, but to me it was a conscious choice. I was raised to say "Sir!" All my pranks of childhood and adolescence had tested the limits of obedience, but they had prepared me, finally, to make obedience the subject of my solemn vow. For the young people around me, by that point in the war, the act of mass defiance of a Boston cop's dispersal order had been mundane, but for me Commonwealth Avenue at the armory marked a defining line. For a few minutes, I had felt the peace of living at last in the blatant truth of my own condition. *This is who I am.*

It may seem a bit much to have made it defining, that simple moment of dropping to the ground. Martin Luther declared, "Here I stand! I can do no other! God help me."[8] Was my version of that assertion "Here I sit?" I did not know it at the time, but that is exactly what it was. Yet with this difference: Luther was standing alone and would become an icon of individualism. I was throwing in with my community, and soon enough, with them again, I got to my feet.

After that, I would be accused by various authorities of uncritically taking cues from young people, but in the main matters before the American nation at that moment, the young people were exactly right; the authorities were wrong. After the armory doors swung open and the soldiers encircled us, rifles ready, I felt with the kids the other blatant truth of the age: the shock of pure fear as our government's readiness to kill showed itself. Readiness to kill us.

And who's to say it would not have, if some damn fool had triggered that response, either among the youthful and near panicked soldiers, or among our own ranks?

Even as we silently dispersed, obeying the order after all, I was still acting in solidarity with the young. Having sat beside them, and having stood to walk away beside them, I left that defining line behind, but I did so as one who had crossed over into a new place, never to cross back.

YEARS LATER, WHEN people asked me why I left the priesthood, I sometimes replied, half joking, "Three reasons: Poverty. Chastity. Obedience."

I'd had my first hint of those three vows all those years ago when, at age five, I saw the three knots in the white cincture of Brother Upside Down at the Franciscan monastery in Washington. Structuring one's life around the threefold discipline of abnegation was intended, as I learned eventually, to resolve the inevitable tensions humans experience in relation to money, sex, and power. Alas, the ideal had long before yielded to the gritty real, as religious institutions down through the centuries betrayed the initial impulse of self-sacrifice, with the actual lived experience of the vows eventually underwriting communal affluence, sexual repression, and the domineering pyramid of clericalism.

As my own vowed life turned out, it was the vow of obedience, more than the other two, that caused me trouble. A reader of this book won't find that surprising. Once I'd more fully thrown in with the antiwar movement after Kent State and the sit-in at the Commonwealth Avenue armory, disobedience became an actual mode of mine. In joining unlawful demonstrations, I was obviously disobeying my father, an oedipal melodrama. Hell, one of my arrests would be at an Air Force base! Oedipus Wreck!

I could not know it at the time, but inside the Pentagon, the brass had again and again pushed for the use of nuclear weapons against Hanoi, and so I was at last, even if unknowingly, addressing my oldest fear of nuclear Armageddon. The American peace movement, whatever else it did or did not accomplish, stopped escalation to that catastrophic nuclear crossroads in its tracks.

But in those years when the reforms of Vatican II—empowering the laity, reconciling with Protestants, accommodating modern philosophy—were being aggressively rolled back, especially in the aftermath of "Humanae Vitae," the birth control condemnation, I disobeyed the Church, too. I did not make grandstanding claims to some kind of moral superiority, but neither could I teach or preach what I found impossible to believe.

After all, I was undertaking initiatives and upholding ideas that were in line with what the Church of Vatican II had taught me. Every week, for example, having presumed to join the Episcopal chaplain's small congregation with our large Catholic one, I concelebrated Mass with him at BU—our personal end to the scandal of Christian disunity. At Newman House, the Catholic student center over which I presided, I lifted up Pope John XXIII's woman-affirming "sign of the times" by sponsoring the BU women's collective, a resource for feminist organizing of which the archdiocese disapproved. Like legions of Catholic priests, I declined to affirm the Church prohibition of birth control. When asked about it, I explained, with as much respect as I could muster, why the Vatican teaching was mistaken.

What I had only intuited at the bad-faith moment of my ordination by the apostolic vicar for the military had become crystal clear. The American hierarchy's support of the war was doubly outrageous because it defied what the universal Catholic Church was becoming after John XXIII's "Pacem in Terris," Vatican II, and Pope Paul VI's "Never again war!" declamation at the United Nations.

More immediately, the jingoism of numerous U.S. bishops, in the mode of Cardinal Spellman and outweighing the cowed silence of all the other prelates, gave American Selective Service System officials an excuse to reject the conscientious objector claims of Catholic boys—boys of mine. Draft boards would not credit the authority of long-haired priests like me, which was why we campus ministers, especially, were desperate for a firm criticism of the Vietnam War from a major American bishop. It never came.

As a result, I saw young Catholic men faced with the impossible choice of fighting a war they found to be immoral, going to jail, or leaving their beloved country. When I found myself helping draftees escape to Canada, I knew my ministry had become a mockery of my own life.

And, yes, I was impatient. I took as a partner in the BU chaplaincy a radical nun, Sister Gloria Fitzgerald, who joined me at the altar at Mass, doing everything but consecrating the bread and wine. A woman preaching? A woman distributing Communion? A woman put forward as equal in ministry? For those and other provocations, I was repeatedly summoned to the cardinal's office at the chancery or visited by its officials. When I was ordered to forbid Sister Gloria to stand with me to hand out the consecrated Host, I simply left the plates full of sacred bread on the altar and let communicants come forward to help themselves. Sister Gloria and I stood on either side of the altar in mute resistance.

Both I and my bosses recognized the impasse at which we'd arrived: A disobedient priest—a disordered man in Holy Orders—is a figure of the absurd.

But now I know more. My whole story, beginning with those acts of defiance that got me "sent up" at St. Anselm's Priory School, could be taken, as Freud might take it, as the story of a boy looking to be spanked. Was my introspective conscience prompting me to seek chastisement for what felt like my bad faith? Even allowing for such unconscious motivations, I see now that something else—something deeper—was at play. I would take back some of what I said and did back then—I would be less arrogant—but it seems clear to me that, on what mattered most, I was in the right. I did not have the language, either as an adolescent or as a young man, to put the thing into words, but I knew that something was wrong with how I was expected to behave. I knew that something was wrong with, as I would call it now, the culture of clericalism to which I had bound myself. How vastly wrong I did not know.

The problem had been epitomized by that initiating ritual of feudal homage, when I'd put my hands into the hands of the bishop to become his "man." No wonder I had squirmed. The pyramidal power structure of the Church was skewed, and at last I was saying no to it. People on the bottom of that power structure were being crushed. Today we see them with stark clarity as, above all, the vulnerable minors being abused by predator priests. But those young people were also being crushed by the pyramid itself, an unjust construct of domination.

Back then, I had yet to see the thing clear. I only knew enough to disobey, and disobey again—and enough to admit that the clock was ticking on my time as a priest.

I FOUND MY voice as an antiwar priest and writer, mainly for the Catholic press. But I was also a priest to shoot the breeze with, and a priest to turn to with a problem. In a time of the so-called generation gap, I found myself serving as a kind of surrogate parent figure for young people who felt orphaned, and sometimes I could help them turn back to their mothers and fathers at home. And always, there was Jesus, whom I was thrilled to preach. I don't know if I've ever been more happily absorbed than I was then. Still, the clock of my priesthood ticked on.

In January of 1973, nearly three years after Kent State, the last American forces were withdrawn from combat in Vietnam. The American prisoners of war, famously including Navy commander John McCain, were released from captivity. The conflict between North and South Vietnam would drag on for another two years, especially from the air, but the American ground war was over. My kids at BU, like Americans of their generation everywhere, were all at once like freed hostages.

And I saw pretty quickly that my young charges no longer needed me in the way they had. As for myself, I was no longer the man I'd been. I had fully broken with my father and had come to regard the war-friendly hierarchy of the American Catholic Church as completely craven. In print, I said so. Yet the war opened into everything else. The war had been, in an expression of the time, my learning environment.

Momentously, I admitted that I could no longer abide the Church's repressive, anti-female sexual morality, much less instruct people in it.

Chief among my reasons for leaving the priesthood, in other words, was the vow I'd taken to pretend to be someone else: obedience. In fact, in the lives of many priests, the vow of obedience, as a source of restlessness, trumps the vow they take to be celibate, because at issue with sworn chastity is not sex but power. Both vows are at the service of subservience. The Church imposes sexual abstinence on its clergy as a mode of control over their interior lives, since submission in such radical abstinence requires an extraordinary abandonment of the autonomous will. In theory, the abandonment is to God. In practice, the abandonment is, as I said early in this book, to the boss—to, in the ordaining prelate's words, "me and my successors," feudal lords whose purpose is the exercise of total dominance. Once priests yield their will in this way, they are expected to be impresarios of precisely such surrender by the laity. One could say no to this inhuman structure of control without knowing exactly what it was, and I did.

Yet I knew something. In an article published in a Catholic newspaper in 1974, shortly after I left my ministry at Boston University, referring back to that defining homage of my ordination, I would ask, "At what point does the 'respect and obedience' due to bishops slip over into yet another failure of moral nerve?"[9]

In all of this, I had found a new way to feel in sync with Jesus. More than ever, I valued Him above all as that troublemaker, friend to outlaws, enemy of Rome. Jesus, too, made a habit of being called on the carpet, "sent up." But my dissenting on matters of war and peace, and on basic questions of morality, wasn't high school prankishness anymore. The contradiction between my life in "orders" and the disorder of my attitudes and behavior could not be ignored.

When told by my superiors that I had an "authority problem," I did not know what to say, but now I do: *It's not my problem, Monsignor. It's my solution.* If sternly asked now, *How can you say that?* I would answer, *I say it because it's what I think.* Even if, back then, I could not fully explain what had come over me, I knew that the time had come to face the truth of my condition—the new meaning of my faith.

And so the summer after the 1973 U.S. withdrawal from Vietnam, I went, with the support of the Paulist Fathers, on a solitary retreat at a monastery, a place in which to examine my uneasy conscience and to pray for guidance. The cloister was an echo of my story's beginning. It was a monastery in the Holy Land.

✠

CHAPTER 21

Undisbeliever

. . . that willing suspension of disbelief for the moment,
which constitutes poetic faith.

—Samuel Taylor Coleridge, *Biographia Literaria*

Tantur sits on an arid hilltop at the edge of the Judean desert, overlooking Bethlehem, only a few miles from the Old City of Jerusalem. When I was there in 1973, a community of French Benedictine monks maintained the monastery as a kind of theological and spiritual retreat center, receiving people like me—not a tourist, but a cross between a pilgrim and a refugee. From my small room, I could see out through a nearby grove of aged olive trees to the distant rough landscape that, in the Gospels, is called "the wilderness." My first thought, as I took in the view after unpacking my small bag, was of Jesus. If He was out there somewhere, I would find Him. I would imagine Him.

Across the distant hills was the sharp outline of the ancient fortress of Herod the Great, an isolated structure in the raw Judean desert. Herod the Great, Rome's puppet ruler of the Jewish people at the time of Jesus's birth, had sought to kill the infant Jesus by killing every male baby he could find—the infamous "slaughter of the innocents."[1] Years later, Herod's son, known as Herod Antipas, was the mortal antagonist of John the Baptist, the precursor of Jesus and His friend. John the Baptist was known to haunt the desert landscape now spread before me. I imagined him, too.

John the Baptist was an unyielding zealot who defied Herod, hated the Roman occupiers and their Jewish collaborators, and called Israel to repentance. He was the first to recognize Jesus for who He was. I pictured a half-naked John wandering at night, stealing figs and olives, crazy with loneliness, on fire with devotion to the One God of Israel. I imagined Jesus kneeling before that hair-shirted prophet out there somewhere. I imagined Him warned by Herod's murder of John and coming into His awareness of what lay ahead for Him, too. I pictured Jesus, sensing that fate, fleeing at first into Judea's roughest country—out there.

Closer in to my place, just visible on an adjacent hill, was the weary town of Bethlehem, looking nothing like a greeting card. I sat at my room's plain table and opened my copy of the New Testament, looking again for its secrets.

"Do you now believe?" The speaker is Jesus, according to the Gospel of John. "The time will come—in fact, it has come already—when you will be scattered, every man to his home, and will leave me alone." Jesus is describing the utter abandonment He will suffer. But then He adds, "And yet I am not alone, for the Father is with me. I have said this to you that in me you may have peace. In the world, you will have tribulation, but be of good cheer. I have overcome the world."[2]

Strange. What I took Jesus to be saying was that He was alone but had a way to live with being alone. Why? How? Because "the Father" was with Him. There it was. *God.*

If I had a companion in my loneliness by then, it was not "God." Even after all my years of theology—or because of them— I was unclear about what, actually, that word, "God," referred to. In the thick of my seminary training, the Christian world had been upended by the so-called Death of God movement: "Is God Dead?" the cover of *Time* magazine asked on April 8, 1966. In hindsight, the movement is dismissed as a foolish fad of no consequence. But embedded in that media circus were real questions about the shallow ways in which religion speaks of "God" as if He were, well, a "He"; as if He were a "fact" among other facts; as if He were a bearded Ancient One in heaven; as if, indeed, there is a supernatural "place" called heaven; a supernatural "time" called eternity; supernatural solutions to life's problems called "miracles"; an immortal self called the "soul."

The Death of God dispute was asking how rational faith survives a verified evolutionary science which strongly suggests that the lived experience of "nature," versus a religiously affirmed "supernature," is, as far as humans can ever know, all there actually is. In the modern age, the biblical cosmology of a three-tiered universe—heaven, earth, underworld—is gone, along with all that hangs on it. In other words, "God is dead."

Atheists had been debunking the overly literal theology of most religionists for two centuries. Hadn't we seminarians already learned that language about the death of God—as, for example, in Friedrich Nietzsche's works—was concerned less with the Deity than with language itself? "God is dead," Nietzsche wrote in the nineteenth century. "God remains dead. And we have killed him. Yet his shadow still looms."[3]

I'd taken refuge in the idea that the word "God" here is a metaphor for structures of meaning that had lost their rational weightiness once, for example, astronomy demonstrated the earth's insignificance in an evolving and ever-expanding universe. How could such a minor spec of dust floating in a dark and empty vacuum conceivably occupy the center of an omnipotent Creator's purpose? How, for that matter, could one of its randomly fashioned mutants—the human person—represent the moral and intellectual pinnacle of all that exists? We novice theologians, halfway through our seven-year seminary course, had inevitably been engaged by the "God is dead" controversy, but not even we were equipped to take up the important underlying question of secular challenges to sacred traditions in the scientific age.

In my case, that project of critically minded belief had remained unfinished all through the years of my priesthood, and I brought its ongoing anguish with me to the desert, this monastery at Tantur. But if, in those years, the idea of "God" had become newly problematic, the intimacy I felt toward my ever more vividly Imagined Friend had become wholly trustworthy.

If Jesus was not precisely the solution to the problem of what belief means in the modern age, He was the way to see it aslant, a view in which inadequacies of "atheism" and "theism" could both be perceived. To protect both my faith and my critical posture, I adopted the strategy of a "willing suspension of disbelief," the phrase Samuel Taylor Coleridge applied to the magic of literature.[4] Like a reader entering the world of a great novel, I would simply let go of my need to posit all and every value on the basis of facticity alone. Anna Karenina and Atticus Finch can be taken to be real. Indeed, to have their power as inventions, they must be. The literary imagination can instruct the religious imagination because the two are aspects of the one response to experience that sets humans apart from other creatures.

For religion, the suspension of disbelief involves a journey along the *via negativa*, the negative way of thinking that refuses to treat God as readily understandable. All we know for certain about God is that we do not know God. When it comes to God, facticity is beside the point. Extending Coleridge's suspension of disbelief, I came to think of myself as a man of the double negative, an "undisbeliever." That odd word, involving three beats, represents movement from naïve belief to an overcoming of naïveté to a rejection of skepticism. For me, that chosen suspension of disbelief became the key to critical faith—belief that takes for granted that myth is the language of all religion and that evolutionary science, far from undercutting the grandeur of God, expands it.

Yet I also grew into the conviction that a secular critique of Christian faith can be a Christian critique, with believers and non-believers both holding to a more basic faith in meaning, intelligibility, and truth than usually marks the divide between theism and atheism. Indeed, I came to embrace what might be called a religion of secularity: an inclination to regard human existence itself, including thinking and ethical choosing, as having ultimate value—not someday, but today; not in the hereafter, but here. Yet I saw also that the theological and philosophical abstraction that so reduced "God" to a benign but impersonal, ungendered current running through the cosmos, or through history, has proved to be the bane of liberal religion, since it leaves no one to talk to. Or, rather, no One.

So if I had a companion who protected me from the existential loneliness of modernity, it was not "God." It was Jesus Himself, which was reason enough to attend, with that open New Testament of mine, to what He was telling me about the One on whom He depended for such connection—the One He called "Father."

In truth, by the time of my arrival at the monastery in the Holy Land, my question had less to do with the "God" of Jesus than with the Church of Jesus. How were the two connected? And could there be one without the other? I had thought of Jesus so fully in connection to my life in the priesthood for so long that even beginning to contemplate the decision to resign from Holy Orders made my bond with Jesus seem shockingly at risk. My relationship with Him was so tied up with my being a priest that I feared a total loss of faith if I left. Yet that fear, too, revealing a profound denigration of the status of the laity, showed the problem. (To leave the priesthood was to be "reduced" to the lay state.) Hence the retreat to the land where Jesus had trod, the place where—literally and figuratively—He had found Himself. I longed to do the same.

THE WORDS OF the ancient historian Flavius Josephus apply again. He identified the Jesus people as "those that loved Him at the first and did not let go of their affection for Him." But those early followers of Jesus did let go of something essential about Him, if for very human reasons. And that important note of who Jesus was had been missing from my understanding of Him, too. In Israel, the land where Jesus walked, I finally met Jesus—not as I had imagined Him all my life, but as He was. And that recognition opened a way forward, not only in my faith, but in my life.

Here is what happened.

In the years after the death and Resurrection of Jesus, His followers were blindsided by a succession of traumas tied to the violence of what the Romans called "the Jewish War"—the Roman Empire's decades-long (A.D. 66–135), nearly genocidal assault against Jews throughout the Mediterranean. This war is largely unremembered by Christians, yet it was decisive in shaping the Christian Church—from its Scriptures to its basic assumptions about Jesus Himself.

When the Temple in Jerusalem was destroyed by the Romans in the year 70, about forty years after the death of Jesus, all Jews were forced to embrace a new understanding of the Hebrew religion, a necessary reckoning with the loss of Israel's cultic center. The Temple, after all, had braced Jewish belief for a thousand years. Now it was gone. Here is the question with which every Jew was confronted: *What is it to be a Jew without the Temple?*

Most Jews answered by saying that Jewish identity was now to be centered on Torah study—synagogue, kosher practice, Shabbat (the Jewish Sabbath). From now on, the Jewish way of life would be the new Temple. This was the beginning of Jewish religion as it exists today.

But "Jesus Jews" answered differently. For them, Jesus Himself—as remembered and as imagined—was believed to be somehow present as the new Temple. "Jesus answered them, 'Destroy this temple, and in three days I will raise it up.' . . . But He spoke of the Temple of His body."[5] This declaration of Jesus's self-identification with the Temple, tied to its destruction, is read by pious Christians to this day as a divinely inspired prediction by Jesus, made in the year 30 or so, of a future calamity that actually occurred in the year 70. But, of course, as a text written after the Temple destruction (the Gospel of John is dated by scholars to about the year 100), it is not a prophecy of the future but a coping with the recent past—a response to what had already occurred. We Christians forgot that. The simple point of the statement Jesus was imagined as having made when he was still alive in the year 30 or so was that, for those Jesus-believing Jews alive decades later, Jesus was the new Temple—the new center of faith. The Gospel writer, in effect, put words in Jesus's mouth to reflect that.

Across the decades following the Temple destruction, under the pressures of the ongoing Roman wars (it would kill a million or more Jews, approaching the ratio of Jewish dead that Hitler achieved), this post-Temple divide between Jewish factions hardened into a kind of intra-Jewish civil war.[6] That split would culminate in what were, in effect, two new religions: Rabbinic Judaism and the Church. It was just as that divide was opening up, in those precise decades, that the four Gospels were written. (Mark is dated to about 70; Matthew and Luke to between 80 and 90; John, as we just saw, to about 100.) The Gospels are the literature of that intra-Jewish civil war.

That is why the Gospels tell a story of Jesus in brutal conflict less with the Romans, who killed Him in the year 30, than with a group called "the Jews," whose Gospel role as antagonists actually belongs not to the lifetime of Jesus but to the lifetimes of His followers forty to seventy years later. The disparaging phrase "the Jews" appears in the Gospels eighty-seven times, climactically when "the Jews" override the supposedly benign Romans to demand the Crucifixion of Jesus. But the phrase, coming from the pens of Gospel writers who were themselves Jews, actually means "those Jews" who disagreed with "us Jews" about Jesus being the new, post-Temple center of Jewish religion. Indeed, the Gospels were soon read, especially by non-Jews who began to dominate the movement after the Romans obliterated Jerusalem in 135, as if Jesus, at war with "the Jews," was not Himself a Jew.

All of this is to explain one of the great awakenings I underwent during my summer on the desert hill between Jerusalem and Bethlehem—an awakening that would shape the rest of my life.

ACTUALLY, IT WAS in Jerusalem proper—the Old City—that my eyes first opened to something to which they should never have been blind. It was a sweltering summer day when I stood on the parapet above the vast plaza fronting on the so-called Western Wall, the great stone rampart over which the plateau of the Temple Mount looms. Originally the site of that holiest place in Israel's life, the plateau is now dominated by what Muslims call the Noble Sanctuary: the striking Dome of the Rock and the Al-Aqsa Mosque, the second-holiest shrine in Islam. Muslims took over the former site of the Temple of Jerusalem when they conquered the city in 637. The Western Wall was all that was left to Jews of their long-lost but still beloved Temple.

The field of my concentration was centered on the cloaked human figures at the base of the Western Wall—Jewish men who'd come to pray before the sacred stone relic. Their rhythmic bowing struck me, and so did the shawls with which their heads were covered. All at once I imagined my Imagined Friend in their midst— Jesus, a pilgrim up from Galilee, enthralled with the holy majesty of what might have been in His day the greatest religious construction in the world. Approaching the Temple, He would have shown his devotion by wearing some version of the fabric I beheld on the heads of the men there now.

I realized that in all the representations I'd ever seen of Jesus, His head was never covered. Often, in picture Bibles, in stained-glass representations, or on holy cards, Jesus was presented as a man with flowing brown hair, Aryan facial features, the aspect of a northern European. But even in portraits that gave Him the swarthy, dark look of a Semite, his face was never framed by a scarf, veil, or shawl. His head was always bare. Yet from time immemorial, the practice of Jewish males has been to cover their heads, especially when praying—today, one sees the yarmulke, or skullcap. Such garb is a mode of honoring the Divine Presence, which is above, and Jesus, too, would surely have followed this practice.

The simple thought of Jesus as one of those men with a shawl over his head stopped me. It was a picture of his Jewishness, and it stayed with me. If Jesus were in Jerusalem with me that year, he'd have been at home not in the Christian quarter with the displayed rosaries and monk tour guides and men doffing hats as they entered churches, but in the Jewish quarter, where every winding alley leads to the Western Wall and every man is covered. After all my years of academic theology, it should not have come as a surprise that Jesus was a Jew—a firmly committed, we would say "Orthodox," Jew—until the day He died. But I *was* surprised. The sight of covered men at the Western Wall made me see that in this one critical dimension, I had mis-imagined my Imagined Friend.

My mind went naturally back to that boy Peter, who lived next door to me when I was a child. That he was Jewish had troubled me because—*No Salvation Outside the Church*—I was supposed to believe that made him the enemy of Jesus. I had rejected that somehow, putting myself at risk of rejecting God in favor of my friend. But here, at last, was rescue from that dilemma. *The Church had been wrong about my friend, the Jewish Peter, because it was wrong about the Jewish Jesus!*

In that monastery on the edge of the Judean desert, in 1973, I finally came to the climax of the work I had begun under the tutelage of Krister Stendahl nearly a decade before. I had unconsciously internalized the Gospel habit of portraying all of the virtues of Jesus in contrast to the flaws of His Jewish milieu. If Jesus treated women as equals, it was against a fierce Jewish patriarchy. If His message was universal, it violated Jewish tribalism. If He was sincere, the Pharisees were hypocritical. If He was generous, they were greedy. If Jesus was the avatar of my own embrace of "liberation theology," the left-wing movement sparked by Latin American Catholics, I pictured Him as a liberator in resistance to a decidedly Jewish oppressive establishment—the high priests who had seen to His condemnation and murder.

In the Christian memory, and therefore in my imagination until then, it was not just that "the Jews" had caused Jesus's death by forcing the Roman Crucifixion, but that the entire story of Jesus was told as a story against "the Jews." The Parable of the Good Samaritan—the "heathen" who goes to the aid of the robber's victim—could just as readily be called the Parable of the Bad Jews, since those who refuse to help the poor victim are Jews on their way to the Temple. In the Gospels, Jews are everywhere giving Jesus trouble. As the Gospel of John puts it with elegant brevity,

"He came to His own home, and His own people received Him not."[7]

No.

I only came to it now, but that pivotal time across a summer in the profoundly Jewish environs of Jerusalem brought me to realize that the only ones who received Jesus during His lifetime were Jews—"His own people." The God whom Jesus addressed as "Father" was not the philosophical abstraction of the Greeks—whose existence the rational arguments of St. Thomas Aquinas could "prove"—but the intensely personal Lover whose covenant with Israel was betrothal; the Fellow Sojourner who trekked with the banished Hebrews through the wilderness; the Compassionate One who, far from willing the suffering of His people, joined them in it. The God whom Jesus addressed as "Father" was the One God of Abraham, Isaac, and Jacob; the God whom Jesus praised each morning and evening with the proclamation *"Shema, Yisrael!"* Not only was Jesus Jewish; so was His God.

If Christians had not forgotten this essentially Jewish character of Jesus's preaching and piety—forgotten that He was a Jew—the history of the past two thousand years, into the twentieth century, would be very different. This amnesia gave shape to the imagination of the West: religious anti-Judaism eventually spawning racial anti-Semitism and its "strange, secret sharer," white supremacy.[8]

Here is the criminal irony: In preaching the good news that the innocent victim Jesus had brought an end to scapegoating by showing scapegoating for what it was, His followers scapegoated. Under pressures generated by the Roman wars, these members of Jesus's own people scapegoated other members of Jesus's own people. On the landscape and streets across which Jesus walked, I walked, too, realizing that this setting of the Church against the Synagogue, each of which came into being only then, was Christianity's original sin, far more loathsome than anything to do—

pace St. Augustine—with sex. As for consequences, the Church, in misremembering the Jewish Jesus, in effect condemned Him to the boxcars and the camps.

BUT NOW I see something else. The positive-negative bipolarity that pitted Jesus against His own—the Church against the Synagogue, and ultimately the deep culture of Christendom against the Jewish people—set the Christian God of the New Testament, who was all-merciful, against the Jewish God of the Old Testament, who was the damning God I had so feared as a child. St. Anselm, patron of my school, had put this "Jewish God" at the center of doom. From the wrath of that God only Jesus, our fellow Christian, could save us—precisely by trumping the damning God with the loving One. There was an implicit anti-Semitism in the entire economy of salvation into which I was ushered as a child—and from which the Church has yet to declare its full independence. Anselm's formula and Augustine's schema are threads of the rope that is still choking us.

If the Church's original sin was its anti-Judaism, that positive-negative opposition quickly took another form, with males set against females—against and over. The historical criticism that has so recast understanding of Christian origins in recent years—the Gospels, for example, were not written by eyewitnesses—makes plain that women were prominent not only in the inner circle of Jesus's companions, but also in the communities that shaped the first, second, and third generations of faith. We have seen this.

But the deleting of women from the positions of real influence they held depends on an amnesia that extends beyond how and when the Gospels were written to a forgetting of how and when the "divinely inspired" texts of "Scripture" were selected. The four "canonical" Gospels of the New Testament (Matthew, Mark,

Luke, and John) were chosen—a hundred or more years after being written—from among numerous early Christian texts, some of which highlighted the roles of women and were even attributed to women as authors.[9] Those female-friendly texts were suppressed by a conflicted Church establishment whose us-against-them imagination, fevered by war, began by blocking out Jews and ended by blocking out women.

That primal dichotomizing for the sake of male power, ratified by Augustine, is at the heart of Roman Catholicism's contemporary crisis.

Even while New Testament texts were written in the radically dislocating context of the anti-Jewish Roman wars—together with the era's patriarchy and imperial domination that underscored the denigration of "the Jews" and women both—those texts are nevertheless marked with the strong and redeeming notes of what makes the man Jesus unforgettable.

Here is why it is still right that, despite the denigration of "the Jews" and women, the word "Gospel" means "good news." The good news is that from the movement's earliest days on, Jews, non-Jews, women, slaves, public sinners, aristocrats, manual laborers, ethnic foreigners, outcasts, criminals, and peasants all recognized in this itinerant nobody from Galilee signals of the basic revelation, which has become the mantra of this book:

> Not that God, whom Jesus calls Father, causes our suffering or wills it, but that God, in Jesus, joins us in suffering.
> That does not remove our suffering, but it changes suffering's meaning.
> Suffering is not in and of itself redemptive, but because it is universally experienced, suffering is the basis of all human community and of communion with God.
> We are not alone.

As was clear early in this account, that was what I saw, without having language for it, at those funerals when I was an altar boy. I thought I was unusual in presuming to "imagine" my Imagined Friend, but in a version of that very presumption, the Church was born. The Scriptures, that is, are works of remembrance and imagination, of retrieval and invention, and suffering is their subject.

That the story of Jesus, for all its life-affirming power, turns on his death speaks directly not only to the grief His first followers felt at having lost Him, but also to the single most potent fact of the human condition—not only that we humans die, but that we anticipate doing so. In that sense, we humans die twice. That recognition defined my experience at those funerals.

Therefore, mortality—of each person, as well as of the created world—is the core structure of value, an opening into the infinite preciousness of each moment as it becomes present. That is how the meaning of suffering attached to death is changed. The absolute value of this life, fully grasped only in anticipation of its loss, is what gives this life the significance that can alone define salvation. Jesus's proclamation was of transcendence that makes itself felt "now," in this life, not in the "then" of some other life. The past and the future are alike in having resonance only in the present. Or, as Jesus put it with typical succinctness, "For behold! The Kingdom of God is in the midst of you."[10] Here. Now.

The sacredness of history, and of our ongoing human efforts to improve it, follow from this emphasis on an awareness of mortality as the pivot point of human consciousness—what sets us apart from animals. So does the knowledge of the earth's own mortality, and of our obligation, therefore, to treat it as the only heaven we have. The fragile planet's condition today would be vastly different if we had not forgotten that.

All of this is distilled in the core value of Jesus Christ: the absolute preference of love over power. As a result of the double-edged process of memory and imagination, Jesus was soon understood as offering freedom from all oppressions of gender, class, ethnicity, empire, and religion. That is why, in the first generation of Christian belief, the Jesus people greeted one another with that phrase we have noted before: "There is neither Jew nor Gentile, neither slave nor free; nor is there male and female. For you are all one in Christ Jesus."[11]

In Jesus, we know we are not alone—not even at death. So why should a vast population, cutting across all divisions of class, time, and space, not have responded to Him with fevered devotion?

This unforgotten Jesus has survived across the centuries—even centuries torn by contempt for Jews and women—as the standard against whom the Church must measure itself, and to whom, in repentance, it must return. I glimpsed this fuller meaning of Jesus at Tantur nearly fifty years ago, and now, in this recollection, I see it again with crystal clarity.

BUT I SAW something else then, too. In visiting the shrines and holy places in and around Jerusalem—the bubbling spring of the miraculously cured cripple; the "upper room" where the Last Supper occurred; Gethsemane, where a terrified Jesus wept blood; the Stations of the Cross; His birthplace in Bethlehem—I was surprisingly unmoved, finding each site encrusted with myth and legend. Sacred stones worn smooth by the stroking of the credulous meant nothing to me, and the ubiquitous impulse to monetize the Gospel—hawkers in every sanctuary—filled me with sadness.

Nothing dramatized the significance of Jesus's having joined us in the absurd vagaries of history more, though, than the Church of the Holy Sepulcher, the ancient basilica dating to the fifth-century emperor Constantine, which marks both the place where

Jesus died and the place where He was buried—the site of the Resurrection.[12]

Entering the Holy Sepulcher was startling, but not in the way I expected. The ill-lit, shadowy but soaring place was crowded with rudely jostling pilgrims, from whom a communal stench arose to mix with the incense and smoke that already fouled the air. With crosses held high, sacerdotal herders led them along with pokes and swats, and it took me a moment to realize that these drovers were clerics of competing denominations. They were Latin Church Franciscans with their brown robes, sandals, and goatees. They were unfamiliar Orthodox monks of the various Eastern sects—Greek, Armenian, Coptic, Syriac, and Ethiopian. The Orthodox wore an assortment of high hats, severe black robes, shabby cloaks, and scraggly full beards, but they were alike in their shoving impatience. Commercial tour guides, meanwhile, hustled weary tourists in and out of relic alcoves, caverns, and miscellaneous tombs, while kneeling penitents rubbed tears on the polished marble of a wet slab said to be the place where the corpse of Jesus had been prepared for burial.

The walls around us were water stained and crumbling because half a dozen Christian sects had long been unable to cooperate in necessary repairs of the ancient structure. Palestinian Muslims owned the land on which the Christian basilica stood, and Jews of the Israeli state governed it. Christians denigrated one another while claiming to love the place. All for the greater glory of the Son of God, tormented again. While monks and friars shoved one another, Uzi-armed Israeli soldiers looked on, indifferent and blasé, except when eyeing Arabs.

In the center of the basilica rotunda, the knob around which the mob swirled, was a separate roofed structure the size of a cabin, a chapel within the church, and this enclosed the most sacred locus—the tomb of Jesus, the place from which the Savior was raised from the dead. The subdued line there was carefully devout, and I joined it to await my turn to enter the cramped chamber, bowing through the small door. When I finally did, the tomb, alas, was not empty. A foul-smelling monk ambushed me with a demand for money. "Dollar! Please, dollar!" he insisted, and offered me a taper. I fled the place.

Later, I visited another Jerusalem shrine that is said to be the actual tomb of Christ—a competing site. It was a walled garden, clean, uncrowded, and removed from the jostling old city. A rock-hewn crypt was set in the midst of well-tended shrubs and serpentine pathways. Perfect.

The contemplative oasis is called the Garden Tomb and has, for a century and a half, been pronounced by evangelical Anglicans to be the authentic burial place of Jesus. Presumably, those tidy-minded believers had, like me, found the ancient Holy Sepulcher to be a scandal, with its filth, rituals of greed, and warring friars and monks.

So when the Anglicans came upon another ancient burial site, adjacent to a stone hill that might have been Golgotha, they recognized a prettiness more befitting the faith. When I visited, attendants there were polite. Quiet meditation was encouraged. A large stone sat near the crypt entrance, apparently rolled back, and one could just see the Roman soldiers trembling; one could picture a young man robed in white, looking like a gardener; one could envision the weeping woman gasping, "Rabboni!" The page of an illustrated Bible came to mind.

Pretty but false. I fled that place, too.

I returned to the battered basilica, the cockpit of disorder. I saw the place anew. I saw for the first time what it actually meant that Jesus Christ was a human being in the thick of human life, with all its chaos, treason, and ruined dreams—including even the dream of resurrection. The followers of Jesus, after all, lost no time in restoring the bigotries and boundaries that He had overcome—that scapegoating of "the Jews"; that return to male dominance. Glorifications of His rejection of power had themselves become engines of a new power—lethal in different ways, but still lethal.

The Holy Sepulcher, as I saw it now, was a sacrament of Christ's part in our true condition, for it is we who live in the ruins—moral, if not physical. It is we who are the surly monks, sentimental pilgrims, tired soldiers. And it is we who—literally now, with our indifference to the stresses of the climate—are putting the earth on a cross, with no known reason to expect its rebirth.

At the authentic tomb of Jesus, in other words, I saw with power what it meant that the Church had never been innocent, much less the "perfect society" it was claimed to be when I was young.[13] There it all was: mistakes born of forgetfulness, corruptions of power, structures of dishonesty—the Church of Jesus Christ. And that was precisely why I saw at last that there was a permanent place in the Church for one as conflicted—given to smugness, slyly disobedient, passive-aggressive, willfully self-doubting, forever half-ruined—as me. And the reason for that acceptance was simple, the oldest reason: He is here.

I looked around at all the wrongs and all the wants, as in this book I have faced the wrongs and wants of my Church and of my own life. To all this Jesus Christ has come, and come again. Which meant He has come to us as we are, including me. He is the truth at the heart of the lie.

IN THE END, I was led by a trusted Jerusalem guide to a recently uncovered archaeological site two levels below the present Jerusalem street, in a dark cavern lit only by a pair of dangling naked bulbs. Random tools and piles of dirt bracketed a large framed pit, the floor of which was bisected by a broad slab of hewn rock, recently laid bare by the soft brushes of the archaeologists. The rock was two or three feet wide and most of ten feet long.

"It is certain," my guide said, "that this was the threshold stone of one of the ancient city gates—the gate that led to Golgotha. The stone was buried in the rubble of the Roman destruction in the first century—only now uncovered. It is certain that Jesus of Naza-reth stepped on this stone on His way to Golgotha." After a moment, he added, "Certain."[14]

After all the accretions of legend, folklore, piety, wishes, and deception, here was something rock solid, something certain, something Jesus may have touched. For almost two millennia, the stone had been covered, as if preserved—waiting for me.

I recognized that threshold monolith as the defining symbol of my lifelong encounter with Jesus, my oldest friend—my Imagined Friend. Until that moment, I had not fully experienced Him as a man alive on the earth where I live, an actual man with all the particularities that go with actuality. A Jew; a man of a certain height and weight; of a settled temperament and personality; with a look, a voice, a way of being in the world that was only His. And feet. His feet marked with whatever calluses and bruises had come of a life on the road and in the rough.

All these years, Jesus had been my Imagined Friend, but I had taken His discrete and separate individuality utterly for granted— not able in the slightest to conjure it with power. Yet Jesus had not been "imagined" to Himself, and at last that hit me. His feet trod here. His specific feet, one following the other as He stumbled along, about to die.

With no conscious decision to do so, I knelt in the dirt. I brought my face down. I placed my lips on the cold surface of the threshold stone. My threshold, at last. I kissed what the feet of Jesus had perhaps bled upon as He joined us in our suffering. My friend. My friend forever.

✠

PART SEVEN

Chosen Hope

"Hope" is the thing with feathers—
That perches in the soul.

—Emily Dickinson, 1861[1]

CHAPTER 22

✠

A Tiny Opening

*I have always tried to find a crack, just a
tiny opening so that I can pry open that door.*

—Pope Francis[1]

The Catholic Church is a worldwide community of well over a billion people: North and South, rich and poor, intellectually sophisticated and illiterate. It is the only institution that crosses such borders on anything like this scale. As James Joyce wrote in *Finnegans Wake*, "Catholic" means "Here comes everybody."[2] Across the globe, there are more than 200,000 Catholic schools and nearly 40,000 Catholic hospitals and healthcare facilities, mostly in the developing world. The Catholic Church is the largest nongovernmental organization on the planet, with countless women and men caring for the poor, teaching the unlettered, healing the sick, and working to preserve minimal standards of the common good. The Catholic Church of these legions is not going away.

The only question is whether it can resume its place on the path toward positive, fully ecumenical renewal onto which Pope John XXIII and the fathers of the Second Vatican Council attempted to set it.

As the human species flirts with its own self-extinction, whether through weapons of mass destruction or environmental degradation, the world urgently needs this global institution to be rational, historically minded, pluralistically respectful, committed to peace, a tribune of justice, and a champion of the equality of women. That Vatican II occurred at all is enough to validate, if not belief in the Holy Spirit, the hope that this great institution can survive the contemporary moral collapse of its leadership.

That was the hope enkindled by the arrival in 2013 of the pope from Argentina, but since then the ongoing failure of the Catholic hierarchy to reckon with the priestly sexual abuse scandal—indeed, that scandal's worsening—has come close to dashing that hope. It is an irony for the ages that Francis, an apparent prisoner of clericalism, presiding over clericalism's refusal to yield, is the man who offers an almost miraculous invitation to the Church's only possible future. The paradox of the Francis pontificate lies in its setting the "not yet" against the "no longer tolerable," and it presents Catholics who long for the recovery of their Church with a heartbreaking dilemma. It is my dilemma, what prompted me to undertake this long journey into memory, which is also an examination of conscience, a preparation for choice. How might we go forward with this Church?

But any assessment of the moral meaning of twenty-first-century Roman Catholicism must take into account the full measure of the promise Pope Francis has been taken to represent, not just for the Church but for the human future. We would do well to step back from the present desolation of Francis's apparent failures, now eight years into his pontificate, to recall what made those early possibilities so riveting.

. . .

I BRUSHED UP against Jorge Mario Bergoglio not long after he became Pope Francis, as a writer on assignment for a magazine. On the uppermost ledge of the great staircase fronting St. Peter's Basilica, I stood behind a young man who, suffering from an inoperable brain tumor, bowed his head between the pope's pressing hands. I was close enough to touch them both, sharing in the prolonged silence that built into the most potent prayer I'd ever witnessed. I have no reason to believe the man was cured, but what I beheld was surely a kind of healing.[3]

I watched then as the pope, in white garb that was still new enough to shimmer in the noonday light, moved slowly along a row of the infirm, blessing the wheelchair-bound, but also reaching back to whisper to their attendants, a rare encouragement of otherwise unseen caretakers. I experienced firsthand what so many have reported—that the presence of Pope Francis is itself a form of affirmation.

From his immediate eschewing of the red velvet shoes and the papal palace to his prophetic pilgrimage to the politically charged U.S.-Mexican border; from his regaling laughter at his own expense to his cradling and kissing the blistered feet of a Muslim inmate in a Roman prison; from his chastising of rank-conscious prelates to his warm embrace of a gay friend; from his opening up of Cuba to his shutting down of the Catholic mission to convert "the Jews"; from his eloquently silent witness early in the Covid-19 crisis to his salute to its medics and food workers as "the saints next door"[4]—in all this Pope Francis made multitudes think again about religion, power, and possibility. He loves people, and people feel it.

The wide-ranging response to the election of this pope, far transcending all boundaries of religion, marked him as a figure of a profound shift in the very meaning of faith, with implications even for many who have left formal belief behind. Addressing all people as his "companions on the journey," as he did during the pandemic,[5] he has eloquently parsed the connection between expressly religious ideas and the broadly human concerns that define hopes and anxieties everywhere. By publicly measuring what he says, does, and believes against the simple standard of mercy— "God's identity card"[6]—Francis has consistently exceeded the limits of his position. Indeed, the quality of his mercy has emerged as an engine of his own self-surpassing.

The magnanimous example of Francis, in a short time, became a wide-open invitation to a hopeful new way of being human in this beleaguered century. This accounts for the astounding early reach of his message.

Leaving aside for a moment my disappointment in Francis's responses to the clergy sexual abuse scandal and its web of related issues, I'd like to return to what quickened in my breast when he first arrived—a hope I had not dared to fully indulge for decades. Allow me to summarize why Francis came to me, at first, like rescue.

A YEAR AFTER that summer's retreat in the monastery near Jerusalem, I left the priesthood, having served as chaplain at Boston University for only five years. In the decades since, I have been clinging to belief with all my might and against all the odds that confront the sort of secular-minded, skeptical person I became. I found that the new feel for history and science that came so naturally with the times required the rejection—not only by secular people but also by Christians—of many traditional Christian claims, even if that rejection took the form of radical reinterpretation. The key symbols of revelation, including understandings of my Imagined Friend, Jesus Christ, and of the Godhead itself, had to be, well, reimagined. Such reassessment amounted to the full elimination of some traditional beliefs, a less drastic but still momentous recasting of language, and the stout protection of some traditional notions.

Much of this work involved my coming into my identity as an "undisbeliever." But as a secular-minded Christian, I could also see that many among the firmly non-religious have yet to grasp that the explicitly Christian affirmation of a kind of secular faith can drive its intellectual and moral coherence even deeper into human experience than atheism can. It does this by offering language—spoken and enacted, and rooted in the tradition—that dares to express what remains inexpressible. Christian faith is a manifestation not just of the theistic tradition, but also of the secular faith in the absolute value of human experience, past, present, and to come. Against a common prejudice of modernity, belief in God is a mode of absolute belief in the human.

Beginning early in his pontificate, Pope Francis invited a positive turn in the faith of secular-minded Christians by at least implicitly affirming this new, more expansive condition of belief, even while subtly indicating that he was rooted in it himself. I think of his surprisingly simple first words from the balcony of St. Peter's right after his election: *"Fratelli e sorelle, buona sera!"* (Brothers and sisters, good evening); of his carefully crafted speeches and encyclicals that enshrined his appeal. But I also think of his equally eloquent gestures and actions: greeting desperate migrants washed up on Lampadusa, Europe's southernmost island in the Mediterranean Sea; routinely embracing the disfigured; regularly visiting prisoners. Both in what he said and how he said it, he invited believers and nonbelievers alike to understand the religious tradition anew and to see possibilities of spiritual transcendence in ways that were anything but traditional. Francis seemed to understand that if a faith claim can be put forward only on the strength of tradition—because it has been "always believed"—it will fail.

Francis was demonstrating—and inspiring—a kind of self-surpassing, generating new thoughts and possibilities that not even he anticipated. Indeed, he became a magnet of sorts, drawing a diversified array of cultural shavings, cast-off attitudes, and discarded commitments into an unexpected new arrangement. He was the touchstone of widespread, if unacknowledged, longing. That, more than anything, is why the world turned its attention to him at first.

The pope began as a man of science, which scrambled the old assumptions about the clash between methods of belief and rational inquiry. The chemist turned Jesuit could be assumed to understand that the presuppositions of science include the principle of paradigm shift, the overturning through new evidence of the prevailing scientific framework. Maintaining the possibility—or, rather, the necessity—of intellectual overthrow is an ethical mandate of science. Settled ideas are forever on the way to being unsettled.

Religion, on the contrary, has been hostile to such an assumption of ongoing change, defending the ethic of stability, not revolt. Francis represented the arrival of the religious recognition that that must change now. Tenets of religious conviction also must be submitted to the test of experience, which means that open-ended, evidence-based inquiry must define theology's future, as much as any discipline's. Doctrine, too, undergoes the paradigm shift, because all culture does. Science has taught us that intellectual integrity is a matter of morality. There is a morality to belief, too. It is immoral to believe irrationally.

Francis was broadly welcomed, but he also generated fierce opposition, both inside and outside the Church. Conservative Catholics charged him with a "plot to change Catholicism."[7] He has been attacked by proponents of unregulated free-market capitalism and by bigots who despise his appreciation of Islam. Steve Bannon, a former advisor to President Donald Trump, attacked Francis for his criticism of nationalist populism, and Francis drew fire in some circles as the embodiment of anti-Trump conviction.[8]

But inside the Church, the fiercest opposition has come from the defenders of clericalism—the spine of male power and the bulwark against any loosening of the sexual mores that protect it. However much Francis's long life as a Jesuit priest has stamped him with unexamined assumptions of male supremacy, he has shown signs of earnestly seeking to uproot it—even if despite himself. That is why Machiavellian conspiracies within the Vatican itself have sought to unseat him. But all of this has underscored the way in which the Argentinian pope is the icon of a major cultural transition that extends beyond religion. Something crucial in the meaning of human life itself is at stake in the Francis struggles— a reach toward an unprecedented sense of universal commonwealth just as such global solidarity has emerged as essential to human thriving and surviving.

Once, papal power depended on the pope's role as the keeper of the keys of hell. Kings knelt before popes, and paupers slavishly obeyed them, because submission to the vicar of Christ was the only way to eternal salvation. That structure of fear—the prospect of an unending afterlife in a lake of fire—survived until my own time. But dread of damnation is mostly gone. Now, in an age of information overload, political paralysis, unmoored authority, savage inequality, and digital dementia, what humans long for is not salvation but meaning.

America, politically disillusioned and ethically dislocated, is only a local instance of this species-wide crisis of intelligible significance. Francis, having emerged as a unique moral figure on the world stage, seemed to be opening the way into a large and urgent consideration of a deep question Americans and others have been wanting to ask, without knowing how. There is an undefined horizon—let's call it by an old name, "the holy"—toward which human beings still instinctively move, but today such longing for transcendence exists beyond categories of theism and atheism. Francis has somehow gestured toward that horizon with innate eloquence. He has offered less a message that explains than an invitation to explore.

For Francis, an understanding of his role came not from ideology (he is not a "liberal") but from his long and intimate relationship with street urchins, the homeless, the shanty dwellers. In the discarded people of Buenos Aires, he recognized, as he put it, "all the abandoned of the world."[9] Late in 2018, he filled St. Peter's Basilica in Rome with six thousand poor people and condemned the greedy and selfish who "feast on what, in justice, belongs to all."[10] Once you see everything from the point of view of the forgotten, Francis insisted, the whole vista is transformed. Mighty secular assumptions—about "success," "progress," "elites," "merit," the urgent importance of not being a "loser," and, in Francis's phrase, "the ironclad logic of technology"—are all undercut.[11]

Francis holds to the "fundamentals" of tradition, which is why a vast population of the traditionally devout recognized him as one of their own. But he is no fundamentalist. He holds the fundamentals loosely. When, for example, he made a casual observation, to wide consternation, that dogs go to heaven, he implicitly but powerfully invited a demythologizing of heaven itself, subtly suggesting that our dreams of the afterlife live in the realm of metaphor, not fact. Heaven is not a "place." Heaven is an insistence that there is more to life than what we see.

IN MANY WAYS, Francis has already left his mark.

Religious pluralism. Not content to lecture world leaders about militarism and weapons,[12] the pope has sought to disarm religion itself as a source of conflict, beginning with his own. That is the meaning of his insistence—"Who am I to judge?"—on a broadly tolerant Catholic Church; the meaning of his own habit of outreach toward those who believe differently, or not at all. In Francis's view, religion is not a zero-sum enterprise, with the truth of one coming at the expense of the truth of others. Truth may be absolute, but no one grasps the truth absolutely. Therefore, those holding different convictions, making different choices, and confronting different life circumstances have a right to be respected in their differences. There is no rivalry among religions, and no necessary project of proselytizing. "Proselytism," as Francis famously told a journalist, "is solemn nonsense."[13]

The future of the planet. In the summer of 2015, Francis issued his encyclical on climate change, "Laudato Si'."[14] The encyclical stands as his manifesto "On Care for Our Common Home." Grounded in science, it is a prime example of the exercise of rational faith. Its affirmation of this world's absolute value reverses the otherworldliness that often undercuts the commitment of the religiously devout to the protection of the environment. Francis sees God more as the Creator than as the Judge, and creation, therefore, as nothing less than the way the Creator makes Himself present to human consciousness. Divine transcendence is not "out there," beyond, or in a world to come, but here, in this world, where everything is, as Francis says, "a caress of God."[15] This pope's innate feel for that transcendence is precisely what prompts his urgent message: Nothing matters more than rescuing the earth from human squandering.

The fate of the dispossessed. From the very first days of his pontificate, Francis's advocacy on behalf of those desperate refugees washing up on Europe's shores marked the beginning of Europe's effort to deal, however haltingly, with the crisis of displaced persons. In an age defined by hostility to migrants, Francis is their most unabashed friend. Migrants stand in for the world's war victims, slum dwellers, unemployed, young who see no future—all those whom politics and markets have tossed aside. When the Covid-19 crisis dramatized the global scandal of inequality more powerfully than ever, Pope Francis once again threw in with the dispossessed, who were being hurt by the pandemic more than anyone.[16] He denounced the capitalist preference of economic prosperity over the health of masses as "virionic genocide."[17] And when his own fellow bishops protested the Italian government's ongoing prohibition of large gatherings, including for Mass, Francis supported the government, publicly advocating the strict social-distancing requirement in the name of "prudence and obedience."[18] The pope comes so naturally to the defense of those with nothing because he measures everything—from doctrine to economics to social theory—by its actual consequence in the lives of the poor. And he insists that others do so as well.

Experience over doctrine. In Catholicism, the wedge issue has been the question of readmitting divorced and remarried Catholics to the sacrament of Communion, which has sorely divided the hierarchy. Francis has thrown in with liberals who would change the rule. "The Church does not exist to condemn people," Francis says, "but to bring about an encounter with the visceral love of God's mercy."[19] To deny beleaguered people who find conventional commitments impossible the consolations of Communion for the sake of an abstract doctrine is unthinkable. "As a confessor, even when I have found myself before a locked door," Francis explains, "I have always tried to find a crack, just a tiny opening so that I can pry open that door."[20]

In truth, that wedge-issue door opens onto the whole range of questions raised by the sexual revolution, which has been dramatizing the limits of the Church's moral theology for a century. We have seen it: When the Catholic imagination, swayed by St. Augustine, demonized the sexual restlessness built into the human condition, self-denial was put forward as the way to happiness. It was embodied in clerical celibacy, the glorification of virginity, the distrust of bodily experience, and the elevation of sex as a means of reproduction over sex as an expression of love. The cult of sexual renunciation as an ethical standard has collapsed among Catholics not because of assaults launched from a hedonistic "secular" modernity, but because of its inhuman and irrational weight.

The liberal-conservative argument within the Church hierarchy on divorce and remarriage has amounted to an overdue attempt to catch up with the vast population of Catholic laypeople who have already changed their minds on the subject—including many divorced and remarried persons who simply refuse to be excommunicated, no matter what the bishops say.

The pope's critics among his fellow prelates have engaged in intrigue, rumormongering, leaks, and open defiance—a desperate rearguard effort aimed at weakening a pope deemed insufficiently committed to the protection of clerical power.[21] Such critics include some of the Church's most powerful cardinals and bishops, as well as prominent lay figures who loom large in popular culture. Critics such as these worry that a shift in Church discipline on this single question will pave the way—even if Francis and his allies do not quite see it—to a host of other changes regarding matters of sexuality, gender, and indeed the entire Catholic worldview. On this, the conservatives are right.

THE STRUGGLES OF Pope Francis have such resonance because the mythic power of the papacy is rooted not just in religion, but in the Western cultural imagination. The papacy represents the last living vestige of "Christendom" out of which the post-Enlightenment "secular" culture of the West grew. That point deserves emphasis: Secular liberalism is the flower of what it claims to have surpassed. That is why the pope, a surviving symbol of that ancient world, still matters. That the papacy embodies the past is not its problem but its solution, since remembrance is key to meaning. In an era of massive forgetfulness, such historical-mindedness is, ironically, the only way the present can be fully realized. We cannot know where we are if we don't know where we come from. This pope, therefore, has it within his power to protect an inherited structure of ethics even while releasing it from the cruel demands of triumphalist, misogynist institutional morality. In one of the oddest turns in modern history, a humane figure in the papacy has emerged as a kind of potential polestar in relationship to whom a vast population can hope to find its bearings.

Alas, all of this potential may amount to a mere prelude to tragedy. The summary just given of Francis's promise for the human future shows what is at stake in the challenge confronting him in the Church's sexual abuse crisis. It emphasizes the heartbreaking scale of the catastrophe that unfolds as he stubbornly stands with his fellow bishops, sacrificing for their sake the full justice due to victims, women, and future generations of the Church. Alas, Francis's magnanimity seems to extend only to realms apart from the strictures of his own clerical status. Indeed, even as he denounces it, he remains a prisoner of clericalism.

As became clear to me and many others during his tone-deaf visit to Ireland in 2018 and during the 2019 aftershocks of scandal that culminated in the failed "Protection of Minors" meeting in Rome, the pope from Argentina remains blind to what much of the world sees quite clearly. If, owing to his own limits as a Catholic priest, he is unable, finally, to begin a radical transformation of the anti-female, anti-sex clerical culture that has brought ruin to thousands, the precious and prophetic world invitation of Pope Francis will be firmly met by history's *No!* His tiny opening will be slammed shut.

✠

CHAPTER 23

How to Go Forward

We had ten years after the Cold War to build
a new world order, and yet we squandered them.
—Mikhail Gorbachev[1]

The body knows when it's in love, and the body knows when it's ensnared in something awful. My body knew that summer of 2018 when Pope Francis, champion of care for the earth and tribune of justice for the world's poor, showed unmistakable signs of failing his Church in its hour of greatest need in the five hundred years since the Reformation.

Challenged by the disgrace of his ally, the defrocked Cardinal Theodore McCarrick; by accusations of his own complicity in abusive cover-ups; by civil law findings against Catholic dioceses on both sides of the Atlantic; by a further global succession of abuse revelations; and, above all, by the moral wreckage of the Church in Ireland—to all this, Francis responded with silence, denial, and business-as-usual summonings of bishops. Again and again, he circled the wagons around clericalism.

A power structure that is accountable only to itself will always end by abusing the powerless. If exposed, it will ask, paternalistically, to be allowed to repair the damage on its own. These events added up to the igniting incidents of this book.

I felt, as I had not before, the weight of what victims of predator priests must feel. The experience of victims became a touchstone of my perception. And I felt, also freshly, the insult dealt to women by the entire structure of Catholic male supremacy, which colludes with a global epidemic of anti-female violence. This structure is one that Francis shows no sign of dismantling. The experience of women became a touchstone for me, too.

And there I came—only in this writing—to a further recognition, one tied to my own failure in relation to the justice denied to women. It had to do with my last moments in the Catholic priesthood years before.

AFTER THAT SUMMER at the monastery on the arid hill between Bethlehem and Jerusalem, I returned to Boston to conclude my ministry as a priest. In consultation with my Paulist superiors, I aimed to serve out the next academic year at Boston University, fulfilling my priestly obligation to students there. I would not tell anyone of my intention to apply at year's end for a leave of absence and then for a dispensation from my vows. I aimed to leave the priesthood by progressively observing the procedures the Church had set. But before my careful plan could play out, events overtook it, forcing a full-blown confrontation with the source of my discontent.

As noted earlier, my partner at BU was Sister Gloria Fitzgerald, the radical nun who was central to our work for peace and justice. She and I regarded ourselves as co-equal collaborators. At Mass— also as noted—she stood with me at the altar, doing almost everything that I did: proclaiming the Gospel, preaching, distributing

Communion. That "almost" was crucial, of course, since, though her role beside me was unauthorized, it was unthinkable that she should go further to enunciate the words of the Consecration, turning the bread and wine into the Body and Blood of Jesus—my exclusive function as a priest. Our partnership seemed wholly successful, yet she was experiencing a critical dynamic of her own, one of which I was unaware.

Sister Gloria was a feminist, of course, and I knew that her position as my co-chaplain was delicate, since she was institutionally consigned to a role that was inferior to mine—despite our joint determination to act as equal colleagues. The limited character— the inferior character—of her role at the Eucharist, forced upon us both by Church discipline, was the sour note of our collaboration, yet it was one she had fully accepted in signing on to be co-chaplain with me. Well, not fully.

One day in the spring of 1974, a speaking engagement took me out of town for a day. I recruited another priest to take my place presiding at the daily Mass, typically a small gathering held in the third-floor chapel in Newman House, the BU Catholic center. I left Boston and did not think any more about it. But when I returned late that night, there was a note on my door in the rectory where I lived, ordering me to show up at the archdiocesan offices early the next morning. I had no idea why.

The cardinal's assistant, a senior priest, told me that in my absence Sister Gloria had "said the Mass." I was totally taken by surprise. At first, I did not understand what I was being told, but the priest insisted that alarmed eyewitnesses at BU had called the cardinal's office to report on Sister Gloria's sacrilege, even while she was still presiding at the altar.

Gloria said Mass? How could that be? If it was true, I would feel ambushed by Gloria's action, but already I felt a visceral repugnance at what I sensed coming down from the cardinal. The senior priest told me that I was to immediately dismiss Gloria from her job as my co-chaplain—fire her. Knowing nothing of what had actually taken place, I said, "I can't do that." He repeated the command. I was aware that my every word now could have fateful consequences, knowledge that helped me see what mattered most. "I won't do that," I said. The Church was wrong to prohibit women from being priests, and I said so. That trumped the questions of what Gloria had actually done and whether she deserved to be dismissed. "There is a bigger issue here," I said. "A prior question."

The senior priest replied that he had predicted to the cardinal that I would refuse to fire Gloria, in which case, the priest said, the cardinal had instructed him to fire me.

I saw at once that my life as a man in Holy Orders—orders indeed—was over. I took no pleasure in saying a version of the classic line "You can't fire me. I quit."

I went directly to Newman House and found Gloria. My feeling of being let down by her gave way to confusion when, in response to my question, she equivocated about what she had done, insisting that she had only conducted "a prayer service." Without a hint of irony, she said to me, "I couldn't have said a Mass. I'm not a priest." She explained that the designated substitute priest had inexplicably failed to show, and so she stepped in to conduct a prayer service. I sensed her uncertainty and her anguish.

In that fairly freewheeling post–Vatican II time, when liturgies were often more spontaneous, what Gloria did was not as blatant as it would have been, say, in a traditional parish church. After the fact, she may not herself have fully understood what she had done.

The daily Mass at BU, as I habitually conducted it, followed the essential form of the sacrament but was hardly a traditional Eucharist of the sort seen in a church, with a fully vested priest on a high altar and a congregation in pews. At Newman House, we began by sitting in a circle on the carpeted floor for the Scripture reading and a short discussion, before standing around the simple, burlap-covered altar for the Consecration of the bread and wine — pita bread in a basket instead of Hosts in a golden ciborium, and wine in a glass instead of a chalice. Normally, in the casual week-day setting, I eschewed the full set of vestments, wearing only a simple stole. After the Consecration, the Lord's Prayer, the Agnus Dei, and the traditional Communion prayers, we passed the consecrated pita bread from hand to hand, followed by the glass of wine. Informality ruled. So a certain confusion about Gloria's "Mass" was built into our unorthodox tradition. Whatever had taken place in the chapel, it was the farthest thing from the premeditated feminist "action" that archdiocesan officials imagined.

Clarity came as Gloria described to me more fully what she had done. Yes, she had donned some kind of vestment; yes, she had gathered the Mass-goers around the altar and recited the words of Consecration over the bread and wine; and yes, she had recited the other Eucharistic prayers and distributed Communion. She had done, that is, everything I would have done in the New-man House routine of the daily Mass.

Now I got really angry. How had she imagined she could do such a thing without consequences? Not everyone around BU could be expected to agree with what would be taken as a preemptive feminist strike, and it was predictable that someone would drop a dime on her. Indeed, just as I'd been told, an offended, traditionally minded Catholic had called the cardinal's office even while the service was under way.

What Gloria had done, no matter her motivation, had blown up our entire ministry. I was out as chaplain, and soon enough she would be out, too. In fact, having at first equivocated with me, Gloria then equivocated in her explanation to the archdiocesan officials. However haltingly, she denied having "said the Mass," which delayed their response in her case. But I was out immediately.

Hardcore feminist supporters rallied to Gloria, exploiting her for the sensation. It was claimed that she had only conducted "a service of Christian community," not a Mass.[2] By then, Gloria knew that was disingenuous, but the brouhaha had gotten away from her. The archdiocese initiated an ecclesiastical investigation of what she'd actually done. The press got wind of it: THE NUN WHO SAID MASS! That horrified both of us. The Paulist Fathers could no longer protect me from the wrath of the cardinal. He wanted me gone at once.

I ended my time as BU chaplain by gathering students for a farewell party, then cleaning up after everyone had left. Alone, I ran the vacuum cleaner and scrubbed the floors of Newman House. I cleared out my office, then packed my car. At dawn, I drove away from Boston by myself. It would be a while before I formally applied for the necessary dispensations, but that was how I left the priesthood. So much for my carefully orchestrated, discreet departure at year's end. Because the archdiocese was moving against Gloria according to solemn canonical procedures, she was still officially employed at BU when I left the city. The canon law sanctions threatening her—a formal excommunication—were severe, and she soon gave Church officials the confession they wanted. Then she, too, was gone. I never saw her again.

Now I view the entire sorry episode differently. I was quoted in a *New York Times* news story as supporting Gloria and denouncing the Church's prohibition of women in the priesthood—which I firmly did.[3]

But in truth I gave Gloria all too little of what she needed from me, and all too little of what she deserved. She was in an impossible situation, and I had helped put her there. By together pushing the limits of what the Church then allowed a woman to do at the altar—her preaching sermons, her standing beside me throughout the service, her distributing Communion with me—we had jointly moved her to the place where the final anti-female inequality, once accidentally laid bare by a substitute priest not showing up, was simply insufferable. So, in the absence of that priest, this fully committed and beloved campus minister had simply done the natural thing, leading her community in the prayer they had a right to expect. I felt ambushed, yes, but from Gloria's point of view, the ambush she suffered was far more devastating than anything I had a right to complain of. That I did not see at the time how the scale of her hurt grossly outweighed mine only shows how I, too, took for granted the way in which clericalism had perverted our partnership.

I see now that I should not have left Newman House at Boston University so abruptly. No matter what the cardinal wanted, I should have stayed with Gloria, helping to steady her, especially in light of the bad advice she got from others. In the end, I should have taken cues from her about how to respond. And I should have been ready, if she chose, to help mount a massive community protest on her behalf. That would have done nothing to change the Catholic restriction or the archdiocesan response, but it would have worthily honored Gloria for the integrity of her intention, and it would have registered a proper public objection to the Church's unjust exclusion of women. Had I learned nothing from our years of civil rights and antiwar protest? Gloria is long deceased. If she wasn't, I would seek her out and ask her to forgive me.[4]

At the very least, the memory of my failure to properly stand with Gloria tempers the edge of my disdain for Pope Francis's myopia on the matter of the equality of women. Nevertheless, in watching him obfuscate and deny in response to the fresh sexual outrages of clericalism, centered on his visit to Ireland and the disappointing aftermath, I did reach a breaking point. That it was complicated by my own confused history made it no less pointed. Repulsed by the heretofore unperceived scope of priestly betrayal, I faced the fact that I, too, had remained in some way at the mercy of clerical denial. It had to end.

So IT WAS that I embarked, in 2019, on a version of the old Catholic tradition of "fast and abstinence," fasting from the Eucharist and abstaining from the overt practice of my faith for the first time in my life. I understand, in a way I never did before, the stance of the twentieth-century French writer and activist Simone Weil. Born of secular Jews, she had a mystical bent and was drawn to Catholicism, receiving spiritual direction from a priest. But Weil refused to be baptized. She could not bring herself to accept a Church that claimed the right to proclaim *anathema sit,* the ecclesiastical curse of excommunication. To Weil, no one possessed the right to define "the Other" as worthy of damnation. She attended Catholic services but did not receive Communion, a kind of fasting that I recognize now.[5]

Instead of going to Communion, I have been coming to this page. I began by asking what I called "the great question posed by the Catholic sexual abuse scandal." That question was not *How could priests and bishops have done this?* Rather, given the global scale of the clerical crimes against children and the all-but-universal habit of Church disavowal that enabled those crimes, the great questions were *What in Catholic culture gives rise to this grotesquely massive dysfunction? And what else has come of it?*

The virtues of the faith have been obvious to me my whole life long. The world is a far, far better place for those virtues, and I cherish the millions of men and women who, every day and everywhere, bring the faith alive. I cherish their predecessors who, down through the centuries, put in place basic structures of meaning and generosity that flourished in the best achievements of Western civilization, including even some that seemed set against religion. Those believers found it possible to rise above the flaws of theology and tradition to advance the spiritual and corporal works of mercy—and the intellectual project of rational faith. They were imitators of Christ.

But the present hierarchy of the Church is showing itself to be wholly unworthy of those Catholics. The sweep of the hierarchy's betrayals, in scope and depth, is staggeringly new. And to gauge the likelihood of that hierarchy's facing the truth of what it has done and what it has become, consider this: The two contemporary maestros of denial, Pope Paul VI and Pope John Paul II, have, in the very years of the scandal they enabled, been named as saints of the Catholic Church.

As part of the Vatican II generation, I glimpsed it when the Church was offered another way to be. Right-wing Catholics now try to foist the whole sexual abuse crisis off on "the liberal cohort," as they might call us, "of Vatican II priests," as if our liberalism itself was the source of the dysfunction. Proving the point, the pope emeritus, Benedict XVI, supposedly sidelined by his retirement, made a shocking intervention in the spring of 2019. He published in a Bavarian periodical a diatribe that blamed sexual abuse by priests on the moral laxity of the 1960s, the godlessness of contemporary culture, and the existence of homosexual cliques in seminaries—all abuses in the Church that followed in the wake of Vatican II.[6] His complaint offered a barely veiled rebuttal to the pontificate of his successor, which in so many ways sought to rekindle the spirit of Vatican II.

Benedict and his allies are wrong.

It's worth repeating: The Vatican II reform was well and bravely begun. Its liberalism, if that's the word, meant that the positive energy of secular thinking was welcomed, along with an overdue self-criticism. History was embraced as an opening to a deeper appreciation of the tradition. If democracy as such was not adopted in the Church, democratic values such as collegiality, accountability, due process, transparency, and free expression were affirmed, at least in principle. The form of the Mass was itself revised to reflect this new communal ideal, with the language, the altar, and Communion returned to the people. The primacy of conscience was upheld. Most momentously, the Church's relationship with the Jewish people was recast in the single largest revision of Christian theology ever accomplished. That opened the way to the Catholic validation of other religions.

Yet the reform of Vatican II was short-circuited, with tragic consequences. As we have seen, the critical issue turned out to be sex and the related issue of male power. An ancient Catholic malignity resurfaced to halt the dynamic of change. A culture of deceit replaced the nascent way of candor. A cruel insistence on strict doctrinal uniformity was imposed on Catholics, and non-Catholics were once again pushed to the margin of the Roman Catholic Church's concern. The reaction was so consistently and firmly insisted upon across four decades that many Catholics forgot that the humane transformation of their Church had ever seemed possible.

The division between so-called liberals and conservatives took on more significance than it should have—with many of the former sinking into disillusionment and the latter into brittle, scapegoating resentment—precisely because the humane and holy shape of the new Catholic Church was never realized. Liberals and conservatives both might have been surprised out of their mutual antagonism if Pope John XXIII's vision had been allowed to flower. True, at the parish level, celebrations of the renewed liturgy did nourish hope and provide consolation, but at the level of the official Church—the so-called magisterium—something else altogether unfolded. Institutional Roman Catholicism became a bitter, stingy organization.

How bitter and how stingy was not clear until the unexpected arrival of Pope Francis, who embodied in his person the opposite of the hurt that so many Catholics had come to feel. The world-wide relief at the appearance of this figure—his "tiny opening"—was itself the revelation of what had been wanting.

But Francis—yes—has been proving to be incapable of what is needed, despite his own clear diagnosis of the deadly effects of clericalism. Cardinal Blase Cupich of Chicago defended him in late 2018, writing, "Pope Francis is calling for radical reform in the life of the church, for he understands that this crisis is about the abuse of power and a culture of protection and privilege, which have created a climate of secrecy, without accountability for mis-deeds. All of that has to end."[7] But Cupich made that declaration while spearheading preparations for the bishops' 2019 "Protection of Minors" meeting in Rome, from which nothing would come but more empty expressions of shame and regret, with the needed reforms rejected.

The hesitation of Francis, this good and sensible man, in the face of clericalism's death grip on the Church raises the question *What actually could he do?* It's only fair to try to imagine what the conundrum looks like from the storied chair in which Francis sits.

THE MODEL OF potential transformation for this or any pope re-mains the radical revision of post-Holocaust Catholic teaching about Jews, already much noted. The point here is that the formal renunciation of the "Christ killer" slander by a solemn Church council, together with the affirmation of the ongoing integrity of the Jewish religion, reaches far more deeply into Catholic doctrine and tradition than anything having to do with the overthrow of clericalism, women's ordination, married priests, or other questions of sexuality. The habit of Christian anti-Judaism is not fully broken, as uncritical reading of anti-Jewish Gospel texts still show, but its theological justification has been expunged. Under the assertive leadership of a pope, therefore, profound change can occur, and it can occur quickly.

But other broad reforms of Vatican II have been efficiently thwarted because, unlike teaching about Judaism, they have not been pressed from below by an overriding moral demand like the Holocaust. In the absence of such a demand, does the ecclesial power center of the Church so control the levers of change as to be unreformable? Is Francis inevitably stymied? That is suggested by the fate of his predecessor, Pope Benedict XVI. In 2013, he was chased into retirement from the Chair of Peter after brutal conflict with his own Curia, the first papal resignation in more than six hundred years.[8] And Benedict faced nothing like the opposition confronting Francis.

In considering the question of Vatican power struggles, I think back to my coming-of-age adventure in East Berlin, when I saw arrayed along a boulevard named for Joseph Stalin the evidence of the Soviet Union's radical unreformability. Who would have thought then that a leader would come to power in Moscow who would initiate the nonviolent dismantling of the Soviet system by proclaiming glasnost and perestroika? I have long thought that the Catholic Church needs a new Pope John XXIII, but perhaps all it needs is a Mikhail Gorbachev. He showed what can be done, even in the most rigid of command societies.

Francis is challenged by "samurai" clerics who are determined to defeat him, no matter what he does. After all, the Church conservatives know better than most that the opposite of the clericalism they aim to protect at all costs is not some vague elevation of laypeople to a global altar guild, but nothing less than democracy, a robust overthrow of power that would unseat them and their ilk throughout the Church. And that says nothing about other challenges to the status quo that Francis represents, like assumptions about wealth or about Islam. Institutionally, the Curia insiders are fighting to the death.

But how threatening are they, actually? Gorbachev, in a realm of the radically profane, makes the point and shows what is possible. Is the Vatican really a more recalcitrant bureaucracy—more bloody-minded—than the Cold War Kremlin was?

And does the massive rape of children by clergy not itself pose a moral challenge that can be compared to—though not equated with—the Holocaust? The abuse crisis obviously raises the question of sexuality, and for Catholics that always points back to the implication-laden misreading of the Genesis story of Eve and Adam—St. Augustine's dark legacy. For Pope Francis, the wedge issue must be the place of women, an issue famously joined by the Church's insistence on the all-male, celibate priesthood—what I have been calling the pillars of clericalism.

ASSUMING FOR A moment that Francis, in his heart of hearts, was inclined to initiate such change, how could he have done it? Sweeping announcements from on high, a diktat crudely violating the principle of collegiality, would surely have failed. After all, Pope John XXIII's *aggiornamento*—his "updating"—depended on a convocation of all the world's bishops that was years in the making. For various reasons, that cannot be a model now—not least because most of the world's bishops themselves, and the clerical structure they embody, are the problem. What other steps toward amendment could Francis have taken that would have been sufficiently grounded in the will of the people, and gradual enough both to be widely accepted and to withstand the likely conservative pushback under a subsequent papacy?

Let me offer an example of the sort of simple initiative that could have been undertaken—based in a grassroots demand, rooted in precedent, and full of implication for a further reshaping. In fact, even before Francis came onto the scene as pope, the seeds of the necessary transformation had already been planted, and all he actually needed to do was make a demonstrative point of nurturing them.

Francis could have begun the effective abolition of the dysfunctional priesthood by opening up the closed clerical caste to the point of its becoming something new. He could have transformed clericalism, that is, by replacing it with a system of sacramental ministry less rooted in a professed elite—the "clergy"—than in the broad Catholic community, which, as we saw, understood itself in the beginning as a priestly people.[9] This is not as radical as it sounds, for Francis could have significantly reconstituted the form of Church ministry simply by expanding the already re-established diaconate.[10]

AN ANCIENT BUT effectively long-abandoned form of Holy Orders, the Catholic diaconate as a stand-alone office was brought back to the Church in 1967 by Pope Paul VI when he shut the door on married priests. We took note earlier of Paul's encyclical that year, "Sacerdotalis Caelibatus" (On the Celibacy of the Priest), but he also issued the motu proprio "Sacrum Diaconatus Ordinem" (On the Holy Order of the Diaconate), re-establishing the permanent diaconate.[11]

Unlike priests, these Catholic deacons could be married. It seems obvious that Paul was trying to deflect pressure to change the priestly celibacy rule by effectively empowering married men to do, as deacons, everything the priest does except say Mass, hear Confessions, and administer Last Rites. Deacons were expressly commissioned by Paul not only to preach, but to baptize, preside at weddings and funerals, serve as trusted pastoral counselors, and generally be at the service of parishioners. Because it had been more than a thousand years since deacons had been ordained as official ministers in the Church, there was latitude in how their restored service to the Church, not to mention their "ontological status," could be defined. Yet even while they are ordained, and therefore "in Holy Orders" and technically "clerics," deacons, as the contemporary system has developed, do not live as members of the clergy, considered as a caste apart. Unlike priests, they mostly do not depend on the Church for their livelihoods, they are not addressed by a paternal title, and they do not normally wear "clerical garb." While initiated in the religious significance of their roles, they are not the products of a years-long seminary formation. Even as licensed preachers, they make no pretense to being theologians. Unlike priests, they have no place on the pyramid of ecclesiastical power. Married deacons see no conflict between their pastoral role in the Church and their commitments to wives and children. Pope Paul VI, in other words, already introduced into the clerical culture of Catholicism a wedge of substantial change that, if allowed to penetrate further, could transfigure the sacramental ministry of the Church. The priesthood.

Today, there are something like fifty thousand Catholic deacons worldwide,[12] yet the retrieved tradition of the diaconate has yet to fully jell, and its powers can still be adjusted. In 2009, for example, Pope Benedict XVI ordered a clarification of canon law to sharpen the distinction between priests and deacons, protecting the status of the former as being the only ones who are allowed to act "in the person of Christ."[13] Benedict was clearly worried that the purity of the clerical caste system was being polluted, the supernatural status of the priest diluted. But this adjustment, instead of closing the door on further developments in the role of deacons, suggests that such developments are possible, even inevitable. Canon law can be amended again. The reconstituted diaconate is clearly a work in progress. As such, it presented an opening through which Pope Francis could have stepped. The opportunity was handed to him on a golden paten, as it were, in October 2019.

Fifty years ago, Pope Paul VI may have seen the married diaconate only as a way out of the priestly celibacy dilemma, but the retrieval of this ancient form of ordained ministry has turned out to have pointed relevance to a problem Paul could not have foreseen. The twenty-first century's worldwide shortage of priests has turned whole regions of the globe into Eucharistic deserts. The disappearance of the Mass for much of the year for many people in many places violates the proper spiritual claim that the Catholic people have on this central form of worship, and this materialized as a pastoral emergency to which Pope Francis had an urgent obligation to respond.

The crisis was nowhere more pressing than in the Amazon basin, where there are ten thousand Catholics for every priest — compared, for example, with two thousand per priest in the United States. Apparently aiming to confront this challenge, Francis summoned the bishops of the Pan-Amazon region to a special synod, which met in Rome from October 6 to 27, 2019.

At the synod, the bishops, numbering about 180, clamored for a way to make the Eucharist more regularly available. They warned that legions were in danger of being lost to the faith. The bishops settled on the restored diaconate — multitudes of married men already serving in Church ministries — as the key to a way forward. Following the tradition of emergency exceptions — in the absence of a priest, a layperson can validly administer the sacrament of

Baptism when there is danger of death—the Amazon bishops might have proposed allowing today's ordained deacons, under the supervision of bishops, to celebrate the Eucharist where there were no priests available. They might have proposed, that is, that deacons be authorized to say Mass. A vast expansion of the diaconate among the faithful in the region could have readily supplied the Eucharist. Radical as it might have seemed, such a reconstitution of the diaconate would only have built on the reconstitution that had already been under way for more than fifty years.

But, still focused on the diaconate, the bishops proposed something else: simply to ordain as priests the married men—"suitable and esteemed men"—who were already serving as deacons.[14] Since married deacons—family men, holding down jobs in the secular economy and living in the world rather than the rectory—have far more in common with the laity than with the clergy, this solution, too, would have begun the fundamental re-ordering of the structure of clericalism, pointing the way forward to a renewed order of the Church. The bishops voted overwhelmingly to approve this proposal, a possible vindication of Pope Francis's already expressed commitment to tiny openings.

But in February 2020, with the apostolic exhortation "Querida Amazonia" (Beloved Amazon), Pope Francis brushed aside the bishops' diaconate proposal without directly responding to it—an effective, and insulting, no.[15] Still, in the words of one commentator, Francis called for "'a specific ecclesial culture that is distinctively lay,' that gives a greater role for the laity, and especially for women."[16] But Francis, with this deft display of ambivalence, sidestepped the question of how such a culture could possibly come to flower under the system of clerical dominance that he protected. Presented with the most felicitous opportunity for change—one bubbling up from below, rooted in pastoral crisis, and building on steps already taken by his predecessors—Pope Francis left the all-male, celibate priesthood intact, and with it the soul of clericalism.

But there is more. A still-in-progress diaconate, adjusted to bring married men more fully into the life of the Church as sacramental ministers, could also have opened the way toward the solution of an even more urgent problem: ending the unjust exclusion of women from the heart of Church life. And the Amazon bishops pointed to this, too, approving a proposal to study ways of opening up the diaconate to women.[17] Indeed, Pope Francis was already on record as inclining toward such a step, and in 2020 he resuscitated a Vatican commission to study the prospect.[18] Until now, in the contemporary Church, only males have been eligible to be deacons. Yet that presents a further indication of the opportunity that this newly reconstituted form of Holy Orders offers, especially since scholars have found ample evidence that women served in such roles in the early Church. The pope would not have invited a commission—twice—to study a subject that was a priori out of the question. (We saw this before, when John XXIII established a commission to reconsider the Church's teaching on birth control.) Therefore, ordaining women as deacons is on the table. In 2017, the Greek Orthodox Church admitted women to the diaconate, reinforcing the idea of expanded forms of ordained ministry.

All of this suggests how the ground is already shifting under the once rigidly defined institution of Holy Orders—an institution that, as shaped today, is at the malign heart of the Church's current crisis. Francis has had room to act, and even if he has mostly demurred, that broad latitude has become apparent, and the spaciousness of what's possible remains. His successor popes, as pressures for change continue to build, will find trails that have been blazed open in the era of Francis.

Such an indirect strategy for accomplishing a major religious and cultural mutation—changing the priesthood by changing the diaconate—may seem inauthentic precisely for being indirect, but the Church long thought of itself as <u>un</u>changing, and the changes that stick are still the ones that can be experienced as having somehow sprung from the tradition. Think of the stark authority with which Pope Francis, in 2018, announced the new and absolute Roman Catholic prohibition of the death penalty, despite capital punishment's having long been justified not only by moral theology but by explicit biblical texts. In announcing this basic doctrinal change, however, Francis was careful to note that his predecessor popes had themselves disapproved of the death penalty, if not absolutely. He argued, in effect, that his top-down command to revise the Catholic catechism on this question was only an expansion of what his predecessors had already taught.[19]

So it could have been with the expanded diaconate. Francis's open-ended elaboration of the prior authorizations and adjustments of that ordained ministry by the same popes he appealed to in outlawing the death penalty could have been a further instance of how the Church must accommodate unprecedented circumstances, especially when basic questions of morality and meaning are at stake. However much movements toward a married priesthood and the ordination of women will always be opposed by conservatives, such a "de-clericalization" would still barely scratch the surface of the needed transformation of the Catholic imagination—going all the way back to that misogynist and inhuman reading of the story of Adam and Eve. Powerful forces pressing for such transformation are at work, both inside the Church and outside. If they are not brought to completion under Pope Francis, still it has been made starkly clear that the time for Catholic business as usual is long gone.

. . .

WHICH POSES ONE further question. In addition to the self-beleaguered pope, one thinks sympathetically, but with discouragement, of the worldwide network of Catholic priests, good men under enormous pressure. And yet there, too, the disappointment is momentous. Why have priests as a group, confronted by the crimes of their fellow priests and the collapse of the structures of their own lives, been so silent, year after year? They have been silent even as their bishops and popes have continually failed the whole people of God, emphatically including victims of abuse. Why are priests silent now?

In Boston, as the abuse scandal first broke back in 2002, Cardinal Bernard Law was the recalcitrant denier in chief, and the Vatican was steady in its support of him. But then something surprising and noble happened. Fifty-eight priests of the archdiocese, pastors and senior clergy, wrote an open letter to Cardinal Law. It began, "It is with a heavy heart that we write to request your resignation as Archbishop of Boston." The letter concluded, "The priests and people of Boston have lost confidence in you as their spiritual leader."[20] Law resigned immediately. That the Vatican then rewarded him with a prestigious appointment in Rome, which he held until he died in 2017, only suggests how essential the Boston priests' intervention was. If today's priests—organized in diocesan, regional, national, or international groups—forthrightly demanded specific changes related to the malignancy of clericalism (of which they know better than anyone), this unholy order of power would not survive. But the "good priests" are as passive and self-protecting as the bishops.

It may be that the pontificate of the elderly Francis will come and go without the necessary deep reckoning with the violent corruption of the Catholic priesthood, much less the resuscitation of Vatican II reforms. It may be that the ample virtues of Francis—the world-historic invitation he offered early on—will not be institutionalized and that nothing will prevent the Church's clerical cabal from momentarily reasserting its power. Sadly, this is almost certainly the likeliest outcome. The coming of Mikhail Gorbachev, after all, did not prevent the coming of Vladimir Putin.

But I presume to suggest that Catholic clericalism is doomed no matter how endlessly the reactionaries attempt to reinforce it. I think again of the Church of the Holy Sepulcher in Jerusalem, where the warring Christian monks make responsible maintenance of the sacred structure impossible. As a result, the roof beams rot, the walls crumble, the leaking gutters channel rainwater into the sanctuary instead of away. That the Incarnation of Jesus Christ means He made His home in this particular thicket of turpitude does not mean that eventually the ancient basilica will be spared from final collapse.

The Holy Sepulcher is not the Incarnation. Nor is the hierarchy of the Catholic Church the Incarnation. And the origin of that Jerusalem edifice is to the point, since the Holy Sepulcher, originally erected by the emperor Constantine, was modeled on the imperial palace. Indeed, exactly like that scarred edifice in Jerusalem, the Vatican, with its basilica and its proconsul-like episcopate, is the pinnacle of a structure of governance that owes more to emperors than to apostles. With the profound discrediting of that episcopate now firmly under way, this could be the moment, at last, when the Catholic Church is liberated from the Roman imperium that took it captive seventeen hundred years ago.

✝

CHAPTER 24

Hope Is a Choice

Dream dreams, then write them—aye, but live them first.
—Samuel Eliot Morison[1]

I hope we can bring about that overdue liberation of faith from empire. Through this long spiral down into memory and meaning, I see that project as more urgent than ever. Returning to the "great and simple images" in whose presence my heart first opened has restored my sense of what matters most.

When I began, with that jolt of Pope Francis's empty visit to Ireland, the most painfully pressing question had to do with a visceral rejection of my own involvement in the compromised structure of the priesthood, the heart of clericalism. I could no longer go to Mass. Now I see that my Catholic practice—whether one man forgoes consolations of the Eucharist or maintains active identification with the institution—is far from the most pressing issue.

At the most practical level, a reformed, enlightened, hopeful Catholic Church is essential to the thriving—even to the survival—of the human species. The climate crisis makes the point, but so does the increasing threat of nuclear proliferation. My old obsession with nuclear dread remains, and the Church can still be part of the rescue from it. And then, almost equally pressing, there is the plague of global inequality. Urgent change on these questions is a matter of moving small weights from one plate of the scale to the other, so that the balance can shift toward justice and peace. Governments have the major burden of that responsibility, but no nongovernmental organization has more power to influence the outcomes than the Roman Catholic Church.

Pope Francis at his best has made that clear. Socially, religiously, educationally, and politically, the Church can move weights in every corner of the planet, among every population, in every boardroom, palace, seat of power, and union hall. In all such places, the negative weight of reactionary religion of various stripes is being felt, and Catholicism can be the counterweight. That is why its struggle with itself matters so much. Will the Catholic Church go the way of fundamentalist Christianity? Anti-critical? Anti-historical? Anti-rational? Anti-human?

I am painfully aware of the limits of my ability to take on the great questions, but how could I possibly walk away from such a source of far-reaching engagement with the important issues of peace and justice? I am attuned to the way in which the movements and ideologies that have sought to replace religion—to replace Catholicism—have themselves come up short. I am under no illusion that there is some more perfect faith community out there, waiting for me to find it. Yet I am more in touch with the fallibility of institutional Catholicism than ever; more aware than ever of the violence it wreaks in the lives of the vulnerable.

But I also see how I, too, am enmeshed in that structure of mayhem. My condition as a Catholic is comparable to my condition as an American. My nation, with its still dark attachment to white supremacy, male dominance, elite privilege, and militarism, is a threat to the order of the world—more so lately than at any point in my lifetime. Yet there is no question of my not being American. The acute negative energy flowing lately from the United States only makes more pressing the retrieval of its positive legacy as a source of democratic hope. That's why so many of us Americans have chosen to re-embrace our roles as citizens, accepting—however imperfectly—our obligation to help our country move the weights on its scale toward justice and peace.

And so it is with my complicated life as a Catholic.

The complications of Pope Francis make the point. He is immersed—I would say heroically immersed—in a life-and-death struggle with the Church's most reactionary elements. The magnificent invitation he offered to the whole human family in the first flush of his time in the Chair of Peter is now being sorely tested—both inside the Church and outside. For all of the criticisms I have offered in this account, I see Francis's hesitations and deflections less as betrayals than as signs of the pressure he is under—pressure from his enemies, but pressure, too, from his own history. The final significance of his pontificate, a work in progress, is far from settled. Therefore, reform-minded Catholics around the world should rally to this beleaguered pope—not only to support his efforts to resuscitate the reform of Vatican II, but also to help him resolve his own ambivalence about that reform in favor of change.

That ambivalence is perfectly captured in the already-noted contrast between the pope's instinctive refusal to denigrate homosexuals in the priesthood—that famous "Who am I to judge?" statement of 2013—and the insult he offered to gay priests in his 2018 book, *The Strength of a Vocation*, where he says their presence in the clergy "is something that worries me."[2] This tension, no doubt, reflects the pope's experience of the aggressive pushback his initial tolerance drew from conservatives. Liberals should push back, too—in favor of the instinctive openness that first characterized his responses.

The falloff of Catholic laypeople from the normal practice of the faith has been dramatic in recent years—nowhere more so than in Ireland. Where once the Irish routinely made the sign of the cross when passing a church—right-hand fingers brushing forehead, chest, left shoulder, right—now they consciously look the other way. Given the scale of the island nation's trauma, how could it be otherwise?

In the United States, according to a 2018 Pew survey,[3] Catholicism is losing members faster than any other denomination, with 13 percent of Americans now describing themselves as "former Catholics," compared with active Catholics, who clock in at a not considerably larger 20 percent. (When I was a priest nearly fifty years ago, Catholics accounted for more than 30 percent of the American population, and that was before the large influx of Hispanic immigrants.) For every non-Catholic who joins the Church through conversion, there are six Catholics who "lapse." I understand this as well. The decision to walk away from the Church, or even from belief as such, is one made in the deepest recesses of conscience and personal autonomy. I respect such exit choices and have drawn close to making them myself.

But to simply leave the Catholic Church is to leave its worst impulses unchallenged—and its better ones unsupported. When disillusioned liberals depart, Catholic reactionaries are overjoyed. They blithely look forward to a much smaller, more rigidly "orthodox" institution. This shrinkage is the so-called Benedict option—named for the sixth-century founder of monasticism, not for Pope Benedict XVI, although the pope emeritus probably would approve.[4] Catholic conservatives happily look forward to the once world-historic global institution being reduced to a sect of the ideologically pure. That diminishment of Catholicism, cradle of the West, would be a defeat not just for religion but for the whole human family. The Church would become a puritanical remnant, globally irrelevant.

The astounding generosity with which the broader world welcomed the large-hearted esprit of Pope Francis early in his pontificate showed the depth of an ongoing human longing for images of transcendence—for the "tiny opening" he offered. In Francis could be glimpsed the possibility of recovery from the contemporary shattering of multiple structures—not just of authority, but of intelligibility. Francis upheld the common decency that is essential to democratic liberalism, and he renewed the sense that the core virtues of Western culture are worth defending. Francis reminded the world that the human project has always been one of self-surpassing, the very definition of human hope. He made hope seem real again.

But if instead this man turns out to be as gripped by institutional self-interest as any corporate leader, then reasonable expectations of creative solutions to problems as varied as climate change, nuclear proliferation, and mass migration are doubly dashed. That is why the success of Francis, and what he has already promised, is so important. And that success depends overwhelmingly on what Catholics say, think, and do—not only while Francis lives, but also when he is succeeded by the next pope, who can advance Francis's positive purpose or thwart it. Nothing less than the human future is at stake.

That future will arrive, at least in part, in ways determined by the actions of human beings. Against the accumulating weight of evidence that bleak outcomes are unfolding in every sphere, that ground of responsibility remains the key to destiny and lays bare the primal source not of optimism but of hope. For hope is a choice.

✠

A Catholic Manifesto

AN ANTI-CLERICALISM FROM WITHIN

Then I saw heaven opened, and behold, a white horse!
He who sat upon it is called Faithful and True.

—Apocalypse 19:11

So let me directly address Catholics and invite the choice of hope. I want to make the case for another way to respond to the present crisis of faith than by simply walking away. What if multitudes of the faithful, appalled by what the sexual abuse crisis has shown their Church leadership to have become, were able nevertheless to work through anger and disappointment toward cold detachment from the cassock-ridden power structure of the Church, even while choosing to reclaim the Vatican II insistence that that power structure is not the Church? The Church is the people of God, period. The Church is the self-surpassing community that transcends space and time, geography and millennia, past and future.

Recalling that the so-called magisterium is a culture-bound creation of an imperial government with no direct connection to the Gospel—despite its claims to the contrary—Catholics should not yield to clerical despots the final authority over our personal relationship to the Church. I refuse to let a pervert-priest or a complicit bishop rip my faith from me.

I brought up James Joyce earlier and his famous declaration, much repeated by my kind, that Catholic means "Here comes everybody." But referring to the clerical establishment, not to that "everybody," Joyce also said, less sweetly, "I make open war upon it by what I write and say and do."[1] That spirit of resistance is what must energize reform-minded Catholics now—an anti-clericalism from within.

There it is: *an anti-clericalism from within.* That is the stance I choose to take. If there are like-minded anti-clerical priests and even an anti-clerical pope—as one still hopes Francis and his successor could be—then we will make reforming common cause with them. Indeed, now that I think of it, affirming that anti-clericalism from within has been the purpose behind the "writing and saying and doing" of this book.

Joyce was a self-described exile, and that can characterize the position of many former Catholics—people who have sought refuge in another country of the faith or in no faith at all. But exile of this kind is not what I propose. Rather, standing in opposition to the Catholic Church establishment from within the Catholic Church is to be a kind of internal exile—a poignant life on the ecclesial inner margin, that liminal space from which an eye is ever cast toward the center as toward an unforsaken home, still beloved. One imagines the inmates of internal exile as figures in the back of the church—where, in fact, some dissenting priests and many free-spirited nuns can be found as well. Think of us as the Church's conscientious objectors. We are not deserters.

Replacing the diseased model of the Church with something healthy may involve, for a time, keeping one's distance from officially sanctioned Masses. It may mean life on the margins—less in the pews than in the rearmost shadows, or even outside. That remains my stance, as of now.

But such distancing will still involve deliberate performance of the works of mercy that define the Catholic faith: feeding the hungry, caring for the poor, visiting the sick, striving for justice—finding Jesus "in the least of these."[2]

Such chosen forms of faith may involve, for many, unauthorized expressions of prayer and worship—egalitarian, authentic, ecumenical—having nothing to do with diocesan borders, parish boundaries, or the sacrament of Holy Orders. That may be especially true in so-called intentional communities that lift up the leadership of women. These already exist, everywhere. In this connection, I think of my old partner Sister Gloria and what I belatedly learned from her.

No matter who presides at whatever form the altar takes, such adaptations of Eucharistic observance return to the theological essence of the sacrament. Christ is experienced not through the officiant, but through the faith of the whole community. "For where two or three are gathered in my name," Jesus said, "there am I in the midst of them."[3]

IN WHAT WAY, one might ask, can such institutional detachment square with actual Catholic identity? Though I am not proposing a replay of the Protestant Reformation, I do take instruction from the tension that surfaced in past centuries between what was called "Catholic substance" and "Protestant principle." The first refers to the tradition, liturgy, and dogma that developed in the Church across the centuries, while the second refers to the commitment to renew that substance by constantly measuring it against the Gospel and the example of Jesus Christ. The key to a humane Catholic future is to advance both substance and principle. Understanding how Protestants and Catholics alike failed to do that in the past can help us do better in the future.

Nor am I proposing a mere withdrawal by elites as a mode of resistance against unsophisticated "popular" religion. Indeed, popular religion, the true and simple faith of millions that always exists on the margins of magisterial authority, firmly upholds the sacramental imagination that defines the best of Catholicism. It does this through devotions and prayers and rituals that will continue the tradition in many forms, even as the imperial structure of Church governance shrivels.

I envision a range of specific actions of renewal taken by legions of commonsensical believers—from base community organizers, to deacons in priestless parishes, to parents who band together for religious instruction of youngsters, to social activists who take on injustice in the name of Jesus Christ—all insisting on the Catholic character of what they are doing. Such acts of resistance may involve old-fashioned community organizing: congregations sitting-in at their churches or picketing chanceries; strikes by religious women and nuns; priests themselves formed into associations demanding change. It may involve social media campaigns: Why not something like #ChurchResist?

As ever, the Church's principal organizing event will be the communal experience of the Mass, the structure of which—reading the Word, breaking the bread—will remain universal. It will not need to be celebrated by a member of some sacerdotal caste. The gradual ascendance of lay leaders in the Church is in any case becoming a fact of life, driven by shortages of personnel and expertise. And then, in 2020, something else struck, to push such changes forward: the coronavirus pandemic. The worldwide shuttering of churches, necessary social distancing, and live-streaming recourse to "virtual" celebrations of the Mass amounted to an interruption in Church history, which is even now leading to an unprecedented re-imagining of ritual, practice, and belief. The moral impossibility of large gatherings, for example, may lead to the rediscovery of the house-church tradition—bread and wine shared in living rooms and at kitchen tables—that defined the practice of the Church in its first centuries. And who will preside at such Masses? Not the priest, as we know him today. In other words, Catholics, like all people everywhere, are having to re-order their lives and meanings in light of the ongoing challenge of the pandemic and its aftermath. That re-ordering, in the Catholic instance, will surely involve transformations in the way the faithful relate to the clergy and the entire hierarchy of the Church.[4]

Now is the time to make this re-ordering intentional and to accelerate it. The pillars of Catholicism—the Book and the bread, traditional prayers and songs, reflection centered on the wisdom of the saints, an understanding of life as a form of discipleship—will be unshaken. The Vatican itself may take steps, belatedly, to catch up to where the Church goes without it. Fine. But in ways that cannot be predicted, the exiles themselves will become the core, as exiles were the core at the time of Jesus. They will take on responsibility and ownership—and as responsibility and ownership devolve into smaller units, the focus will shift from the earthbound institution to its transcendent meaning. This is already happening in front of our eyes. Tens of millions of moral decisions and personal actions are being informed by the choice to be Catholics on our own terms, untethered from a rotted ancient scaffolding. The choice comes with no asterisk. We will be Catholics, full stop. We do not need anyone's permission. Our "fasting and abstaining" from officially ordered practice, even as it is reinforced by transformations caused by the pandemic, will go on for as long as the Church's rebirth requires, whether we live to see it finished or not. As anti-clerical Catholics, we will simply refuse to accept that the business-as-usual attitudes of most priests and bishops should extend to us.

The future will come at us invisibly, frame by frame, as it always does—comprehensible only when run together and projected retrospectively at some distant moment. But it *is* coming. One hundred years from now, there *will be* a Catholic Church. Count on it. If, down through the ages, it was appropriate for the Church to take on the political structures of the broader culture—imperial Rome, feudal Europe—then why shouldn't Catholicism now absorb the ethos and form of liberal democracy? This may not be inevitable, but it is more than possible.

The Church I foresee will be governed by laypeople, although the verb "govern" may apply less than "serve." There will be leaders who gather communities in worship, and because the tradition is rich, striking chords deep in human history, such sacramental enablers may well be known as "priests." They will include women and married men. They will be ontologically equal to everyone else. They will not owe fealty to a feudal superior.

Catholic schools and universities will continue to submit faith to reason—and vice versa. Catholic hospitals will be a crucial part of the global healthcare infrastructure. Catholic religious orders of men and women, some voluntarily celibate, will continue to protect and enshrine the varieties of contemplative practice and the social Gospel. Jesuits and Dominicans, Benedictines and Franciscans, the Catholic Worker Movement and other communities of liberation theology—all of these will survive in as yet unimagined forms. The Church will be fully alive at the local level, even if the faith is practiced more in those living rooms than in basilicas. And the Church will still have a worldwide reach, with some kind of organizing center, perhaps even in Rome for old times' sake. But that center will be protected from Catholic triumphalism by being openly engaged with other Christian denominations. The ecumenical movement—the Pope John XXIII project of Christian reunion—will be fulfilled.

This Church of the future will have more in common with ancient tradition than the pope-idolizing Catholicism of modernity ever did. Instead of destroying a Catholic's love of the Church, the vantage of internal exile can reinforce it—making the essence of the faith more apparent than ever.

As ALL OF this implies, clericalism will be long dead. The boundary-protecting magisterium will be gone—except in the majesty of old papal museums that preserve as cautionary collections the fossils of domination that prelates once exercised back in the days when the Church lost its way in the thickets of empire. For now, that imperial hangover is what we must recover from. The view as I see it from my place of internal exile shows that the Church, whatever else it may be, is the community of memory, keeping alive the story of Jesus Christ. The Church is an in-the-flesh connection to Him—or it is nothing.

Because of that, even in "the depths," we think of Him continually—an inbred response of which I had a hint way back in the beginning, when I was an altar boy transfixed by the words of the *De Profundis:* "I wait for the Lord, my whole being waits, and in His word I put my hope. I wait for the Lord more than watchmen wait for the morning, more than watchmen wait for the morning."[5] That's me.

I began my story by telling of Jesus my Imagined Friend, ever faithful. His was the cosmic narrative of going into exile—crossing through longing and suffering and waiting and watching—and then coming home. The story was a promise, which is why it's called "good news." I return at the end to where I began. As a boy, in that first monastery, I sensed the radical thrill of the ultimate gamble, a roll of the dice on which one's whole life is bet—a wager on the existence of a loving God. As a young man, I placed that bet because of my Imagined Friend. It is a bet, I see now despite everything, that I have won. Jesus remains really present to me, and through Him, that loving God does, too.

Recalling that first monastery, I think of my mother, who brought me there. This book began with my un-wished-for sense of relief that she is not alive to see the Church's grotesque unraveling, but I understand now that if she had lived to see it, she, too, would recognize in this heartbreak the potential for purification. What remains of the connection to Jesus once the organizational apparatus disappears? That is what I asked myself in the summer before I resigned from the priesthood all those years ago. I asked "out of the depths" back then, and have done so again this year, not presuming in either instance that the old mystery of "death and resurrection" would apply to me. My faith faltered. Perhaps I should have known, should have trusted. After all, the *De Profundis* is one of the psalms collectively called the "Song of Ascents."

I began with my Imagined Jesus, and I end with an imagined Church. In the imagination lies the answer to the question about connection. The imagination, to cite Samuel Taylor Coleridge again, is the "I AM" of God alive in human beings.[6] The Catholic faith is the form that takes in me—that's all.

In the future I foresee, the Church will imitate the Prince of Peace, standing with the dispossessed and against weapons. With Jesus, the Church will accompany suffering to change suffering's meaning. Without platitudes, the Church will offer trustworthy consolation at the time of death. The Church will uphold the hope that humanity will continually surpass itself until it finds its truest home, the opposite of exile, in the fulfillment of a purposeful history, a final recognition of the Creator's blessing never lost. And the Church will be, still, the fellowship—to repeat that earliest definition—of "those that loved Him at the first and did not let go of their affection for Him."

Yet the larger point will be—won't it?—that He did not let go, despite everything, of His affection for us. A friend, faithful and true.

Acknowledgments

✝

My reflections on St. Anselm's theology of atonement owe a debt to Robert Chazen, S. Mark Heim, and Elizabeth A. Johnson. My reflections on St. Augustine owe a debt to Garry Wills, Peter Brown, Paula Fredriksen, and Stephen Greenblatt. Any mistakes in my interpretations belong, of course, to me. I owe a particular debt to Anne Barrett Doyle of BishopAccountability.org. Across these troubled years, she and her colleagues have protected the conscience of Catholicism. Cullen Murphy, editor at large of *The Atlantic*, helped me sharpen the arguments in this book while preparing to excerpt a portion of it for that publication. I have taken up questions considered here in articles for *The New Yorker* and newyorker.com, where my editors were Willing Davidson and Virginia Cannon. I wrote this book while an associate of the Mahindra Humanities Center at Harvard, where Mary Halpenny-Killip provided crucial support. Thanks also to my fellow participants in the Humanities Center Seminar on Art, Culture, and Civic Life, chaired by Kiku Adatto and Michael Sandel. My thanks, as well, to the Harvard librarians.

Profound thanks to William D. Phillips, my friend and publishing guru, for crucial help with this work. I am especially grateful to Tina Bennett, without whose encouragement at an early stage I would not have written this book; and to John Sexton for his generous reading of an early draft. My editor, Kate Medina, helped me bring this project into focus, and her sharp eye was a continuous resource. Her colleague Noa Shapiro provided an unfailing steady hand. Showering this book with attention and support was the tremendous Random House team, especially including Gina Centrello, Andy Ward, Robin Desser, Avideh Bashirrad, Benjamin Dreyer, Rebecca Berlant, Mark Birkey, Sandra Sjursen, Greg Mollica, Vicki Wong, Maria Braeckel, Susan Corcoran, Barbara Fillon, and Leigh Marchant. Thank you all for your skill and diligence.

This book begins with "a snap." The person who most forcefully helped me face its meaning is my son, Patrick, to whom I am forever grateful. My first and most careful reader is my wife, Alexandra Marshall. For her support through the writing of this book, and for her love across the years, I am profoundly thankful. This book is dedicated to the memory of James Parks Morton, dean of the Cathedral of St. John the Divine in New York City. His friendship sustained my faith. And this book is dedicated to the memory of my brother Joe, who died as I was completing it. I loved him more than I could ever say.

Chronology

✠

c. 4 B.C. Jesus of Nazareth is born. He is a Jew.

c. 30 Jesus is murdered by the Romans, although Christian accounts will later blame "the Jews," as if Jesus were not one of them.

30–55 Jesus's followers believe he is "the Christ," the incarnation of the good and loving God at the heart of all creation.

c. 50 In his Letter to the Galatians, St. Paul defines the egalitarian ethos of the Jesus movement: "There is neither Jew nor Greek, there is neither slave nor free, there is neither male nor female, for you are all one in Christ Jesus."

70 The Romans destroy the Temple in Jerusalem, igniting a crisis among Jews, some of whom locate the new Temple in observance of the law, while others find it in Jesus Himself. This increasingly polemical conflict shows up in the Gospels, written just now, as hostility between Jesus and "the Jews."

c. 93 In *Jewish Antiquities*, the Roman Jewish historian Flavius Josephus makes the first non-biblical reference to Christians, describing them as "those that loved [Jesus] at the first and did not let go of their affection for Him."

135 The Romans obliterate Jerusalem, eliminating the Jewish center of the Jesus movement. From now on, Gentiles will dominate the way Jesus is remembered, helping to ignite the Church's anti-Judaism.

312 The Roman emperor Constantine converts to Christianity, and the Catholic Church becomes the empire, with the imperial palace providing the physical form of churches, and the Roman administrative system providing the model for the Church structure of dioceses and bishops.

426 In his book *The City of God*, St. Augustine defines the City of God as the world of spirit, while the City of Man is the world of the flesh. He develops a theology of original sin, which denigrates erotic longing and scapegoats the female (Eve) as the instigator of the Fall. In his *Confessions*, he prays, "Make me chaste and celibate, Lord, but not yet."

1054 The East-West Schism (also called the Great Schism) divides the Roman Catholic Church and the Eastern Orthodox churches.

1073 The start of the Gregorian Reforms, initiated by Pope Gregory VII, which include claims to papal supremacy over civil rulers, the forbidding of simony (the buying or selling of church offices) and other abuses, and the advancing of clerical celibacy.

1089 At the Council of Melfi, Pope Urban II orders the enslavement of women married to priests.

1095 Urban II, crying "God wills it!" calls for the First Crusade.

1098 Anselm, archbishop of Canterbury, publishes *Cur Deus Homo* (*Why God Became a Man*), putting the crucifix, suffering, and the violence of God at the center of the Catholic imagination.

1123 The First Lateran Council makes celibacy mandatory for Roman Catholic priests. Orthodox priests will continue being free to marry.

1198 Pope Innocent III claims for himself and his successors a place "between God and man, lower than God, but higher than man, who judges all and is judged by no one."

1215 The Fourth Lateran Council declares of the Eucharist, "No one can effect this sacrament except a priest who has been properly ordained."

1302 Pope Boniface VIII formally declares, "It is absolutely necessary for salvation that every human creature be subject to the Roman Pontiff."

1517 Martin Luther launches the Protestant Reformation, challenging Church corruption but also ratifying a damning God and justifying Christian contempt for Jews.

1545–63 The Council of Trent, responding to the Reformation, fixes the number of sacraments at seven; defines the Real Presence of Christ in the Eucharist as "transubstantiation," versus the Protestant "consubstantiation"; sanctifies the one-on-one form of Confession; formalizes the doctrine of original sin; and puts in place the seminary system, a key to clericalism.

1870 The First Vatican Council declares that in "matters of faith and morals," the pope is infallible.

1885 Pope Leo XIII publishes the encyclical "Immortale Dei," declaring the Roman Catholic Church to be a "perfect society." Leo later issues the apostolic letter "Testem Benevolente," condemning the heresy "Americanism," which includes nefarious ideas like separation of church and state and freedom of the press.

1930 Pope Pius XI publishes the encyclical "Casti Cannubi," condemning "artificial contraception."

1943 Pope Pius XII publishes the encyclical "Mystici Corporis," defining the Catholic Church as the "Mystical Body of Christ" and reinforcing the claim to perfection. But the encyclical also says non-Catholics can be attached to the Church "by some kind of unconscious desire and longing."

1943   The word "genocide" is coined. The atomic bomb lab at Los Alamos, New Mexico, opens.

1958   Pope John XXIII is elected. He announces plans for the Second Vatican Council.

1961   John F. Kennedy is sworn in as president of the United States. He declares that "here on earth, God's work must truly be our own."

1962   The Second Vatican Council opens. The Cuban Missile Crisis occurs. The author enters the seminary.

1963   *The Deputy*, a play by Rolf Hochhuth, accuses Pope Pius XII of "silence" in the face of the Holocaust. It becomes an international sensation and prompts a major reckoning among Catholics.

1963   Dr. John Rock, inventor of the Pill, publishes *The Time Has Come: A Catholic Doctor's Proposals to End the Battle over Birth Control*. Betty Friedan publishes *The Feminine Mystique*. Pope John appoints a commission to reconsider Church teaching on birth control.

1963   Pope John publishes the encyclical "Pacem in Terris," a resounding criticism of war—and of prevailing nuclear orthodoxy. The encyclical also praises the women's movement as a "sign of the times" and women themselves for "demanding both in domestic and in public life the rights and duties which belong to them as human persons." Weeks later, Pope John dies of stomach cancer.

1964   The Second Vatican Council publishes "Lumen Gentium," which effectively repudiates *No Salvation Outside the Church* and reverses the condemnations of "Americanism." But Pope Paul VI intervenes in the council's deliberations, forbidding the bishops to discuss either priestly celibacy or birth control.

1965   The Second Vatican Council promulgates "Nostra Aetate" (In Our Time), which renounces the "Christ killer" slander against the Jewish people and affirms the ongoing validity of the Jewish religion—a template for profound Catholic change.

1965   Pope Paul, reversing Pope Urban II, goes before the United Nations General Assembly to cry "Never again war! Never again war!"

1965   The Second Vatican Council publishes "Dignitatis Humanae," the declaration on religious liberty that affirms the primacy of conscience. For Catholics, the God of doom begins to give way to the God of love.

1966   The Papal Birth Control Commission submits its findings to Pope Paul, concluding that there is nothing "intrinsically evil" about artificial contraception. Birth control should be left to the conscience of the couple. The pope keeps this conclusion secret.

1967   The *National Catholic Reporter*, a lay-run U.S. Catholic weekly, publishes the commission's findings, revealing that all but six of the members of the Papal Birth Control Commission, including dozens of priests and prelates, voted to change the Church's teaching on birth control.

1967 Pope Paul issues "Sacerdotalis Caelibatus" (On the Celibacy of the Priest). He says, "I'd rather give my life before changing the law on celibacy." He also publishes "Sacrum Diaconatus Ordinem" (On the Holy Order of the Diaconate), establishing the permanent diaconate.

1968 Pope Paul promulgates "Humanae Vitae" (Of Human Life), a resounding condemnation of artificial contraception. Catholic laypeople will ignore the prohibition. Legions of Catholic priests begin an exodus from the priesthood.

1968 Dr. King is assassinated.

1969 Richard Nixon becomes president. The author is ordained to the priesthood.

1970 Nixon invades Cambodia. Protests erupt. Four students are shot dead at Kent State University.

1973 On the same day that peace talks in Paris achieve the agreement to end the U.S. war in Vietnam—January 22—the U.S. Supreme Court hands down its *Roe v. Wade* decision. The Catholic hierarchy launches its anti-abortion crusade but, ironically, advances abortion by continuing to condemn contraception as its moral equivalent.

1974 The author leaves the priesthood.

1978 The Pole Karol Wojtyla is elected Pope John Paul II, the first non-Italian pope since the sixteenth century. He is an avatar of Cold War resistance to communism, but also a figure who knows from his own experience about the sufferings of Jews during the Holocaust.

1979 John Paul II visits Ireland, where he is hailed by millions of people.

1980 John Paul II establishes a "pastoral provision" to allow Anglican clergy who reject the ordination of women to enter the Catholic Church and continue as priests even if they are married.

1989 The Berlin Wall is dismantled nonviolently. John Paul II is widely credited as key to the resolution of the nuclear standoff between Washington and Moscow.

1991 John Paul II condemns the U.S. war against Iraq. The Vatican consistently opposes American war making.

1992 James Porter, a Catholic priest in Fall River, Massachusetts, is charged with sexually abusing a child. Boston's Cardinal Bernard Law condemns *The Boston Globe* for its reporting about the Porter case.

1993 The Archdiocese of Boston secretly pays $40,000 to a man who claims to have been raped as a child in 1972 by Father Paul Shanley. Shanley is allowed to remain a priest in good standing.

1994 John Paul II issues "Ordinatio Sacerdotalis," forbidding the ordination of women to the priesthood because of "the example recorded in the Sacred Scriptures of Christ choosing his Apostles only from among men." Joseph Ratzinger, who will succeed John Paul as Pope Benedict XVI, will declare that this teaching is infallible. In 2016, Pope Francis will call it "the last word."

1996 Cardinal Law writes a letter to Shanley, who is retiring, saying, "Without doubt over all of these years of generous and zealous care, the lives and hearts of many people have been touched by your sharing of the Lord's Spirit."

2000   John Paul II observes the new millennium by repenting of Catholic sins, especially anti-Semitism and violence "in defense of the truth."

2001   Cardinal Joseph Ratzinger sends a secret letter to the world's Catholic bishops, ordering them to report crimes "perpetuated with a minor by a cleric" to the Vatican, not to civil authorities.

2001   Islamic militants drive hijacked airliners into the World Trade Center in New York and the Pentagon in Washington and crash another plane in Pennsylvania, sparking widespread concern about connections between religious intolerance and violence.

2002   *The Boston Globe* begins publishing its Spotlight team reports of predator priests, the basis of the 2015 movie *Spotlight*. A new Catholic lay movement is born in response to the clergy abuse scandal, led by a Boston group calling itself Voice of the Faithful.

2002   Cardinal Law is forced to resign as archbishop of Boston for having protected abusers instead of the abused. John Paul II will name him archpriest of St. Mary Major Basilica in Rome.

2005   Paul Shanley, exposed by the *Globe*, is sentenced to twelve to fifteen years in prison for raping a child, one of dozens of his victims.

2005   Cardinal Ratzinger is elected Pope Benedict XVI. Traveling to his native Germany, he blames Nazi anti-Semitism on "neo-paganism," with no mention of Christian anti-Judaism.

2007   Pope Benedict restores the Latin Mass, which Vatican II had abandoned. It includes a prayer for the conversion of Jews.

2009   The Ryan Report is issued in Ireland, documenting the priestly abuse of thousands of children in orphanages and schools run by the Catholic Church.

2013   The film *Philomena*, starring Judi Dench, tells of the so-called Magdalene laundries, Church-run institutions where women and girls were condemned to lives of coercive servitude.

2013   Cardinal Jorge Mario Bergoglio of Argentina becomes Pope Francis. In answer to a question about homosexuals in the priesthood, he says, "Who am I to judge?" He seems to mark a humane revolution in Catholic attitudes, which is signaled by the fierce pushback he receives from Catholic conservatives.

2015   Pope Francis issues "Laudato Si'," his magnificent and prophetic encyclical on the climate crisis. This manifesto, perhaps the high point of his papacy, was a factor in the unanimous approval by the world's nations of the Paris Agreement on climate change the following year.

2017   At the Bon Secours Mother and Baby Home in Tuam, county Galway, Ireland, remains of hundreds of infant corpses are discovered in mass graves and sewage pits. Many had died of undernourishment and neglect.

2018   Pope Francis visits Ireland, where fewer than half as many greet him as greeted John Paul II in 1979. Ireland's confirmable number of priest abuse victims is reliably put at 18,500. Francis expresses "shame and sorrow" but does not address the underlying causes of the problem. Referring to the Magdalene laundries, he tells reporters he has "never heard of these mothers . . . the laundromat of women."

2018   Before, during, and after the pope's visit to Ireland, a grand jury in Pennsylvania finds that more than a thousand children were abused by more than three hundred priests over the course of seventy years; attorneys general in fifteen other states open investigations into Church crimes and cover-ups. An investigation in Germany reveals that in the years 1946 through 2014, 1,670 clergy assaulted 3,677 children.

2018   A Pew survey shows Catholicism losing members faster than any other denomination, with 13 percent of Americans describing themselves as "former Catholics," compared with the 20 percent of Americans who remain as Catholics. A Gallup poll finds that two-thirds of American Catholics decline to rate as "high" the honesty of Catholic priests.

2019   Cardinal Theodore McCarrick, formerly archbishop of Washington, is found guilty by a Vatican tribunal of abusing a minor and is "reduced to the lay state." Selected Catholic bishops meet at the Vatican to discuss the protection of minors in the Church, leading to the promulgation "Vos Estis Lux Mundi" (You Are the Light of the World). It requires bishops to report allegations of sex crimes to other bishops, but not to civil authorities. It mandates no penalties for offenses, requires no public transparency, and establishes no lay participation in the process of adjudicating clerical abuse or episcopal cover-up.

2020   After receiving a landmark petition from the Catholic bishops of the Amazon region to allow the ordination of married deacons in order to alleviate a severe shortage of priests, Pope Francis issues "Querida Amazonia" (Beloved Amazon), in which he simply turns aside the request: no to married priests.

2020   The coronavirus pandemic forces the shuttering of churches. Pope Francis, standing alone, offers an *urbi et orbi* (to the city and the world) blessing to a vacant St. Peter's Square. Forbidden to gather in large groups, Catholics begin to imagine other ways of practicing the faith.

Notes

✠

Prologue

1. Albert Camus, "Between Yes and No," in *Lyrical and Critical Essays*, ed. Philip Thody, trans. Ellen Conroy Kennedy (New York: Random House, 1968), 17.
2. See James Martin, SJ, "The Case Against Abolishing the Priesthood," *America*, May 17, 2019, https://www.americamagazine.org/faith/2019/05/17/case-against-abolishing-priesthood.
3. "Pope Holds Dramatic Solitary Service for Relief from Coronavirus," Reuters, March 27, 2020, https://www.reuters.com/article/us-health-coronavirus-pope/pope-holds-dramatic-solitary-service-for-relief-from-coronavirus-iduskbn21e34a.

Chapter 1

1. Quoted in Harriet Sherwood, "Pope on Sexual Abuse: 'We Showed No Care for the Little Ones,'" *The Guardian* (U.S. edition), August 20, 2018, https://www.theguardian.com/world/2018/aug/20/pope-on-sex-abuse-we-showed-no-care-for-the-little-ones.
2. James T. Keane, "The Uncertain Future of Catholic Ireland," *America*, February 23, 2018, https://www.americamagazine.org/arts-culture/2018/02/23/uncertain-future-catholic-ireland.
3. Commission to Inquire into Child Abuse, https://www.gov.ie/en/publication/3c76d0-the-report-of-the-commission-to-inquire-into-child-abuse-the-ryan-re/.
4. Erin Blakemore, "How Ireland Turned 'Fallen Women' into Slaves," History, March 12, 2018, updated July 21, 2019, https://www.history.com/news/magdalene-laundry-ireland-asylum-abuse.
5. Niall O'Dowd, "Tuam Babies: 'It Would Be . . . Kinder to Strangle These Children at Birth' Said Doctor," IrishCentral, August 22, 2017, https://www.irishcen

tral.com/news/tuam-babies-it-would-be-kinder-to-strangle-these-illegitimate
-children-at-birth.

6. Katrin Bennhold and Melissa Eddy, "In German Catholic Churches, Child Sex
Abuse Victims Top 3,600, Study Finds," *The New York Times*, September 12,
2018, https://www.nytimes.com/2018/09/12/world/europe/german-church-sex
-abuse-children.html.

7. Commonwealth of Pennsylvania, Office of Attorney General, "Pennsylvania
Diocese Victims Report," n.d., https://www.attorneygeneral.gov/report/.

8. Michelle Boorstein and Gary Gately, "More Than 300 Accused Priests Listed in
Pennsylvania Report on Catholic Church Sex Abuse," *The Washington Post*,
August 14, 2018, https://www.washingtonpost.com/news/acts-of-faith/wp/2018
/08/14/pennsylvania-grand-jury-report-on-sex-abuse-in-catholic-church-will-list
-hundreds-of-accused-predator-priests.

9. Tom Jackman, Michelle Boorstein, and Julie Zauzmer, "The Pennsylvania Report on Clergy Sex Abuse Spawned a Wave of Probes Nationwide. Now What?,"
The Washington Post, November 22, 2018, https://www.washingtonpost.com
/local/public-safety/the-pennsylvania-report-on-clergy-sex-abuse-spawned
-investigations-nationwide-now-what/2018/11/22/101dcce8-e467-11e8-8f5f
-a55347f48762_story.html.

   A raid led by Texas Rangers of the offices of the Archdiocese of Galveston-
Houston, presided over by Cardinal Daniel DiNardo, president of the U.S. Conference of Catholic Bishops, seized an archive of abuse—boxes of sex allegation
files and computers, including the personal computer belonging to DiNardo
himself. Having been put forward by the Church as the face of the new day of
Church accountability and transparency, DiNardo was accused of protecting
a particularly egregious predator priest. Laurie Goodstein, "Investigators Raid
Offices of President of U.S. Catholic Bishops," *The New York Times*, November 28, 2018, https://www.nytimes.com/2018/11/28/us/houston-catholic-church
-raid.html.

   In December, the Illinois attorney general scathingly revealed that the
Church in that state had withheld the names of more than five hundred accused
priests. "Catholic Church in Illinois Withheld Names of At Least 500 Priests
Accused of Abuse, Attorney General Says," Laurie Goodstein and Monica
Davey, *The New York Times*, December 19, 2018, https://www.nytimes.com
/2018/12/19/us/illinois-attorney-general-catholic-church-priest-abuse.html.

10. Jason Horowitz and Elizabeth Dias, "Pope Acknowledges Nuns Were Sexually
Abused by Priests and Bishops," *The New York Times*, February 5, 2019, https://
www.nytimes.com/2019/02/05/world/europe/pope-nuns-sexual-abuse.html.

11. Horowitz and Dias, "Pope Acknowledges Nuns Were Sexually Abused."

12. Associated Press, "Indian Bishop Charged with Repeatedly Raping Nun,"
Yahoo! News, April 9, 2019, https://news.yahoo.com/indian-bishop-charged
-repeatedly-raping-nun-114338550.html. See also Maria Abi-Habib and Suhas-
ini Raj, "Nun's Rape Case Against Bishop Shakes a Catholic Bastion in India,"

The New York Times, February 9, 2019, https://www.nytimes.com/2019/02/09/world/asia/nun-rape-india-bishop.html.

13. Anthony Faiola, Chico Harlan, and Stefano Pitrelli, " 'The Pope Ignored Them': Alleged Abuse of Deaf Children on Two Continents Points to Vatican Failings," *The Washington Post*, February 19, 2019, https://www.washingtonpost.com/world/europe/the-pope-ignored-them-alleged-abuse-of-deaf-children-on-two-continents-points-to-vatican-failings/2019/02/18/07db1bdc-fd60-11e8-a17e-162b712e8fc2_story.html.

In November of 2019, two priests were found guilty of the abuse of deaf children by a court in Argentina. Anthony Faiola, Chico Harlan, and Stefano Pitrelli, "Argentine Court Finds Two Catholic Priests Guilty of Sexually Assaulting Deaf Children; First Convictions in Long-Alleged Abuse," *The Washington Post*, November 25, 2019, https://www.washingtonpost.com/world/the_americas/argentine-court-finds-two-priests-guilty-of-sexually-assaulting-deaf-children-first-convictions-in-long-alleged-abuse/2019/11/25/460af56a-0f8b-11ea-924c-b34d09bbc948_story.html.

14. Elizabeth Dias and Jason Horowitz, "Pope Defrocks Theodore McCarrick, Ex-Cardinal Accused of Sexual Abuse," *The New York Times*, February 19, 2019, https://www.nytimes.com/2019/02/16/us/mccarrick-defrocked-vatican.html.

15. Frederic Martel, *In the Closet of the Vatican: Power, Homosexuality, Hypocrisy*, trans. Shaun Whiteside (London: Bloomsbury, 2019).

16. Chico Harlan, " 'Gay Priests Are in the Crosshairs': As Vatican Abuse Summit Begins, Debate over Homosexuality Is Divisive Undercurrent," *The Washington Post*, February 20, 2019, https://www.washingtonpost.com/world/europe/gay-priests-are-in-the-crosshairs-as-vatican-summit-on-abuse-begins-debate-over-homosexuality-is-divisive-undercurrent/2019/02/20/70635f76-3469-11e9-8375-e3dcf6b68558_story.html.

17. Jason Horowitz and Elisabetta Povoledo, "Vatican's Secret Rules for Catholic Priests Who Have Children," *The New York Times*, February 18, 2019, https://www.nytimes.com/2019/02/18/world/europe/priests-children-vatican-rules-celibacy.html. See also Michael Rezendes, "Children of Catholic Priests Live with Secrets and Sorrow," *The Boston Globe*, August 16, 2017, https://www.bostonglobe.com/metro/2017/08/16/father-father-children-catholic-priests-live-with-secrets-and-sorrow/mvYO5SOxAxZYJBi8XxiaqN/story.html.

18. Angela Giuffrida, "Pope Francis Decries Critics of Church as 'Friends of the Devil,' " *The Guardian* (U.S. edition), February 20, 2019, https://www.theguardian.com/world/2019/feb/20/pope-francis-decries-critics-of-church-as-friends-of-the-devil.

19. Reuters, "Pope Blames Clergy Abuse on 'Satan' as Activists Dismiss His Speech a 'PR Stunt,' " *The Guardian* (U.S. edition), February 25, 2019, https://www.theguardian.com/global/video/2019/feb/25/pope-blames-clergy-abuse-on-satan-as-activists-dismiss-his-speech-a-pr-stunt-video.

20. Livia Albeck-Ripka and Damien Cave, "Cardinal George Pell of Australia Sen-

tenced to Six Years in Prison," *The New York Times*, March 12, 2019, https://www.nytimes.com/2019/03/12/world/australia/george-pell-sentence.html.

21. Livia Albeck-Ripka and Damien Cave, "Cardinal Pell's Acquittal Was as Opaque as His Sexual Abuse Trial," *The New York Times*, April 7, 2020, https://www.nytimes.com/2020/04/07/world/australia/cardinal-george-pell-acquittal.html.

22. "Bishops Accused of Sexual Abuse and Misconduct: A Global Accounting," http://www.bishop-accountability.org/bishops/accused/global_list_of_accused_bishops.htm#PELL.

23. Nicole Winfield, "Pope Requires Sex Abuse Claims Be Reported in Vatican City," AP News, March 29, 2019, https://www.apnews.com/623d479ea7574118891a7c032a7ea201.

24. Pope Francis, "Vos Estis Lux Mundi," Apostolic Letter Issued Motu Proprio by the Supreme Pontiff Francis, May 7, 2019, http://w2.vatican.va/content/francesco/en/motu_proprio/documents/papa-francesco-motu-proprio-20190507_vos-estis-lux-mundi.html.

25. An example of what it means to have bishops investigating bishops came—just as the new policy was being promulgated—with the case of West Virginia's Bishop Michael J. Bransfield, who was accused of years of "predatory and harassing" sexual behavior, as well as financial misconduct. The Vatican launched an investigation, supervised by Archbishop William E. Lori of Baltimore. The investigation found that Bransfield had improperly given cash gifts totaling more than $300,000 to some of his accusers and to many senior Church officials. Before forwarding the report to the Vatican, Lori ordered the names of senior clerics who had received the improper payments redacted. *The Washington Post*, which had brought Bransfield's behavior to light in the first place, then reported that one of the complicit Church officials whose names were removed from the report was Lori himself, who had received annual Bransfield gifts from 2012 to 2017. Robert O'Harrow, Jr., and Shawn Boburg, "Warnings Went Unheeded About West Virginia Bishop as He Doled Out Cash Gifts to Catholic Leaders," *The Washington Post*, July 3, 2019, https://www.washingtonpost.com/investigations/warnings-about-wva-bishop-went-unheeded-as-he-doled-out-cash-gifts-tocatholic-leaders-/2019/07/03/7efa27f4-8d4c-11e9-b162-8f6f41ec3c04_story.html.

26. Chico Harlan, "Vatican Establishes New Rules for Sexual Abuse Complaints and Coverups Involving Bishops and Other Church Leaders," *The Washington Post*, May 9, 2019, https://www.washingtonpost.com/world/vatican-establishes-new-rule-for-sexual-abuse-complaints-and-coverups-involving-bishops/2019/05/09/4571e0b0-71b5-11e9-9331-30bc5836f48e_story.

27. The conflagration rages on. More than a year after "Vos Estis Lux Mundi" was issued, the American Catholic Church reported that clergy sex abuse allegations were quadrupled in 2019, totaling for that one year 4,434—complaints reaching back decades. Michelle Boorstein, "Scandals, Compensation Programs Lead Catholic Clergy Sex Abuse Complaints to Quadruple in 2019,"

The Washington Post, June 26, 2020, https://www.washingtonpost.com/religion/2020/06/26/scandals-compensation-programs-lead-catholic-clergy-sex-abuse-complaints-quadruple-2019. On the first anniversary of "Vos Estis," the Catholic watchdog group BishopAccountability.org published an assessment: "This looks less like progress than business as usual" (http://www.bishop-accountability.org/statements/2020_05_10_Doyle_Assessment_of_Vos_Estis_Lux_Mundi.htm).

28. Catherine Sanz, "Pope's Ignorance of Magdalene Laundries Confounds Survivors," *The Times,* August 28, 2018, https://www.thetimes.co.uk/article/pope-s-ignorance-of-magdalene-laundries-confounds-survivors-p665fc6m5.

29. The American philosopher William James, after beholding the depth of human suffering, described such a snap: "After this, the universe was changed for me altogether. I awoke morning after morning with a horrible dread at the pit of my stomach, and with a sense of insecurity of life that I never knew before." William James, *The Varieties of Religious Experience* (Cambridge, Mass.: Harvard University Press, 1985), 134–35. I was forced to face my version of this harsh transformation during a fierce conversation with my son, Patrick, who, even as I expressed my dismay at Pope Francis, challenged me on my still-clinging attachment to the Catholic tradition of the seal of Confession. In response to Patrick's reaction, I realized he was right, that this cult of the absolute secrecy binding the priestly confessor is not only the symbol of what protects the priest predator, but can also be the mechanism of that protection. Patrick forced me to face the meaning of my "changed universe," of my "snap." That recognition began this book. I will return to the question of the Confessional seal in chapter 7.

Chapter 2

1. James Carroll, "Catholicism After Porter," *The Boston Globe,* September 29, 1992.

2. Steve Marantz, "Law Raps Ex-Priest Coverage," *The Boston Globe,* May 24, 1992, https://archive.boston.com/globe/spotlight/abuse/archives/052492_porter.htm.

3. James Carroll in *The Boston Globe,* January 8, 2002, and February 26, 2002. Years later, I was still at it in the *Globe* with, for example, "No Excuses for Priestly Child Abuse," February 10, 2014.

4. James T. Keane, "The Uncertain Future of Catholic Ireland," *America,* February 23, 2018, https://www.americamagazine.org/arts-culture/2018/02/23/uncertain-future-catholic-ireland.

5. His name is Leo Eric Varadkar. He came out as gay during the 2015 gay marriage referendum.

6. To learn more about the famine, see "Irish Potato Famine," History, October 27, 2017, updated June 7, 2019, https://www.history.com/topics/immigration/irish-potato-famine.

7. Author interview with Anne Barrett Doyle, co-director of BishopAccountability
.org, 2019. See also, for example, "Litany of Catholic Abuse in Ireland," France 24,
https://www.france24.com/en/20180825-litany-catholic-abuse-scandals-ireland.

8. Russell Shorto, "The Irish Affliction," *The New York Times Magazine*, February
9, 2011, https://www.nytimes.com/2011/02/13/magazine/13Irish-t.html. "Ireland is a prime example of what the church is facing, because they made this
island into a concentration camp where they could control everything. And the
control was really all about sex. They told you if you masturbated, it meant you
were impure and had allowed the devil to work on you. Generations of people
were crucified with guilt complexes. Now the game is up."

Part Two

1. Roger Scruton, *Notes from Somewhere: On Settling* (New York: Continuum,
2004), 10.

Chapter 4

1. Matthew 22:14.

Chapter 5

1. "Conversion to Christianity" is the way Paul's Damascus Road experience is
usually referred to, but that is inaccurate. There was no "Christianity" during
Paul's time. He was a faithful Jew throughout his life, as was Jesus. His devotion
to the memory of Jesus unfolded wholly within his identity as a faithful son of
Israel. We will return to Paul in chapter 19.

2. Reuters, "Pope Blames Clergy Abuse on 'Satan' as Activists Dismiss His Speech
a 'PR Stunt,'" *The Guardian* (U.S. edition), February 25, 2019, https://www
.theguardian.com/global/video/2019/feb/25/pope-blames-clergy-abuse-on-satan
-as-activists-dismiss-his-speech-a-pr-stunt-video.

3. James Carroll, "After Pennsylvania, What Pope Francis Should Say in Ireland,"
August 22, 2018, Daily Comment, *The New Yorker*, https://www.newyorker.com
/news/daily-comment/after-pennsylvania-what-pope-francis-should-say-in-ireland.

4. James Carroll, "Who Am I to Judge?," *The New Yorker*, published ahead of print,
December 16, 2013, https://www.newyorker.com/magazine/2013/12/23/who
-am-i-to-judge.

5. James Carroll, "The Renewed Importance of Pope Francis's Encyclical on Climate Change," News Desk, *The New Yorker*, June 2, 2017, https://www.new
yorker.com/news/news-desk/the-renewed-importance-of-pope-franciss
-encyclical-on-climate-change.

6. James Carroll, "Pope Francis Is the Anti-Trump," News Desk, *The New Yorker*,

February 1, 2017, https://www.newyorker.com/news/news-desk/pope-francis-is
-the-anti-trump.

7. Ray Sanchez, "Pope Francis Defends Chilean Bishop Accused of Covering Up
Sex Scandal," CNN, January 19, 2018, https://www.cnn.com/2018/01/19/ameri
cas/pope-francis-chile-defends-bishop/index.html.

8. When addressing Synod 2018 on Young People, the Faith, and Vocational Discernment, Pope Francis said, "Clericalism arises from an elitist and exclusivist vision of vocation, that interprets the ministry received as a power to be exercised
rather than as a free and generous service to be given. This leads us to believe that
we belong to a group that has all the answers and no longer needs to listen or learn
anything. Clericalism is a perversion and is the root of many evils in the Church:
we must humbly ask forgiveness for this and above all create the conditions so
that it is not repeated." "Address By His Holiness Pope Francis at the Opening
of the Synod of Bishops on Young People, the Faith, and Vocational Discernment," October 3, 2018, http://www.vatican.va/content/francesco/en/speeches
/2018/october/documents/papa-francesco_20181003_apertura-sinodo.html.

9. Junno Arocho Esteves, "Clericalism Is Ugly Perversion, Pope Tells Seminarians," *Crux*, November 26, 2018, https://cruxnow.com/vatican/2018/11/26
/clericalism-is-ugly-perversion-pope-tells-seminarians/.

10. Jamie Doward, "Pope 'Obstructed' Sex Abuse Inquiry," *The Guardian* (U.S. edition), April 24, 2005, https://www.theguardian.com/world/2005/apr/24/children
.childprotection. At the end of 2019, Pope Francis did away with the "pontifical
secret" as applied to sexual abuse cases but retained it for other Church matters.
Elise Harris, "'Pontifical Secret' Still Has Role Despite Its Abolition in Sex
Abuse Cases, Expert Says," *Crux*, December 20, 2019, https://cruxnow.com
/vatican/2019/12/pontifical-secret-still-has-role-despite-its-abolition-in-sex-abuse
-cases-expert-says/.

11. NCR Staff, "Catholic Dioceses and Orders That Filed for Bankruptcy and
Other Major Settlements," *National Catholic Reporter*, May 31, 2018, https://
www.ncronline.org/news/accountability/catholic-dioceses-and-orders-filed
-bankruptcy-and-other-major-settlements.

12. Already in 2002, *The Boston Globe* was reporting on priestly sexual abuse cases
in many countries. See Michael Paulson, "World Doesn't Share US View of
Scandal," *The Boston Globe*, April 8, 2002, http://archive.boston.com/globe
/spotlight/abuse/print/040802_world.htm.

13. This quote is attributed to the Greek poet Archilochus, from the seventh century B.C.

14. Esteves, "Clericalism Is Ugly Perversion."

15. Elise Harris, "Pope Says No to Women Priests, Yes to Women in Curial Leadership," Catholic News Agency, June 20, 2018, https://www.catholicnewsagency
.com/news/pope-says-no-to-women-priests-yes-to-women-in-curial-leadership
-78750.

16. Yaron Steinbuch, "Pope Francis Dismisses Proposal to Ordain Married Men in Amazon," *New York Post*, February 12, 2020, https://nypost.com/2020/02/12 /pope-francis-dismisses-proposal-to-ordain-married-men-in-amazon. We will see more of Pope Francis's response to the bishops of the Amazon region in chapter 23.

17. He said this, quoting Pope Paul VI, in a press conference on the return flight from Panama in January 2019. Cindy Wooden, "Affirming Celibacy, Pope Explains Narrow Possibility for Married Priests," Catholic News Service, January 30, 2019, https://www.catholicnews.com/services/englishnews/2019/affirming -celibacy-pope-explains-narrow-possibility-for-married-priests.cfm; http://w2.vati can.va/content/francesco/en/speeches/2019/january/documents/papa-francesco _20190127_panama-volo-ritorno.html.

    In the same exchange with reporters, Francis said "that celibacy 'is a gift to the Church' and that he did not agree with allowing 'optional celibacy.' He said, 'My personal opinion is that optional celibacy is not the way forward. Am I someone who is closed? Maybe, but I don't feel like I could stand before God with this decision.'" Junno Arocho Esteves, "What's in a Name: Vatican Questions Use of Term 'Viri Probati,'" *Crux*, June 18, 2019, https://cruxnow.com/ vatican/2019/06/whats-in-a-name-vatican-questions-use-of-term-viri-probati.

    Exceptions to the Catholic Church's requirement of celibacy for priests include the waiver given to Anglican priests who convert rather than affirm the Anglican ordination of women. Twenty-three Eastern rite, or Uniate, churches in full communion with the Roman Catholic Church have married clergy.

18. Garry Wills, "Changing the Changeless Church," *The New York Review of Books*, November 7, 2019.

19. When speaking to reporters about homosexual men in the Catholic priesthood, Francis said, "If someone is gay and he searches for the Lord and has good will, who am I to judge?" See Rachel Donadio, "On Gay Priests, Pope Francis Asks, 'Who Am I to Judge?,'" *The New York Times*, July 29, 2013, https://www .nytimes.com/2013/07/30/world/europe/pope-francis-gay-priests.html.

20. "Catholic Cardinals Urge End of 'Homosexual Agenda,'" BBC News, February 20, 2019, https://www.bbc.com/news/world-europe-47302817.

21. Agence France-Presse, "Gay People Should Not Join Catholic Clergy, Pope Francis Says," *The Guardian* (U.S. edition), December 1, 2018, https://www .theguardian.com/world/2018/dec/02/gay-people-should-not-join-catholic -clergy-pope-francis-says.

22. In 1517, a Dominican friar named Johann Tetzel raised money for the papacy by selling letters of indulgence that promised the forgiveness of sins and exemption from hell. Martin Luther, a professor at the university in Wittenberg, Germany, proposed a debate on the question of such indulgences by publishing a set of questions called the Ninety-five Theses. That sparked a broad reaction, culminating in the Protestant Reformation.

23. At any given time, according to experts, about half of Catholic priests are faithfully celibate. See A. W. Richard Sipe, *Celibacy in Crisis* (New York: Routledge, 2003), 43–57. See also A. W. Richard Sipe, "The Vatican Has a Right to Be Wrong," Awrsipe.com, n.d., http://www.awrsipe.com/Click_and_Learn/us _bishops_and_sexual_orientation.htm.

24. "Studies suggest that perhaps 30 to 50 percent of priests (especially those under age fifty) are homosexual in orientation, compared with about 5 percent of the population at large." Donald Cozzens, "The Clergy's Buried Truths," *The Boston Globe*, April 28, 2002, http://graphics.boston.com/globe/spotlight/abuse /stories/042802_focus.htm.

25. Matthew 5:48.

26. Thomas Reese, "Abolishing the Priesthood Will Not Save the Catholic Church," *National Catholic Reporter*, May 23, 2019, https://www.ncronline.org/news/ac countability/signs-times/abolishing-priesthood-will-not-save-catholic-church.

Chapter 6

1. Friedrich Nietzsche, *Beyond Good and Evil*, trans. Judith Norman (Cambridge, UK: Cambridge University Press, 2002), 38.

2. 1 Peter 2:9.

3. See Joe Holland, *Roman Catholic Clericalism: Three Historical Stages in the Legislation of a Non-evangelical, Now Dysfunctional, and Sometimes Pathological Institution* (Washington, D.C.: Pacem in Terris Press, 2018), 7–10.

4. The Catholic catechism speaks of "an indelible mark imprinted on the soul for all eternity." This "sacramental character" is imprinted by Baptism on all Catholics and by Holy Orders on priests. *Catechism of the Catholic Church*, part 2, sec. 1, chap. 1, art. 2, para. 1121, https://www.vatican.va/archive/ccc_css/archive /catechism/p2s1c1a2.htm#1121.

5. Code of Canon Law, c. 1583, in *Code of Canon Law: Latin-English Edition* (Washington, D.C.: Canon Law Society of America, 1999), 99.

6. The bishop is quoting Psalm 110:4.

7. Thomas Aquinas, *Summa theologiae*, III, q. 63, arts 1–3. Ontology, speaking generally, refers to the study of the very essence of things, as opposed, for example, to epistemology, which refers to the study of the essence of things as they appear from a certain point of view.

8. Megan Brenan, "U.S. Catholics' Faith in Clergy Is Shaken," Gallup, January 11, 2019, https://news.gallup.com/poll/245858/catholics-faith-clergy-shaken.aspx.

Part Three

1. Pope Boniface VIII, *Unam Sanctam*, Fordham University, Medieval Sourcebook, https://sourcebooks.fordham.edu/source/b8-unam.asp.

Chapter 7

1. James Joyce, *A Portrait of the Artist as a Young Man* (New York: Black and White Classics, 2014), 64.

2. Russell Shorto, "The Irish Affliction," *The New York Times Magazine*, February 9, 2011, https://www.nytimes.com/2011/02/13/magazine/13Irish-t.html.

3. See James Carroll, *An American Requiem: God, My Father, and the War That Came Between Us* (Boston: Houghton Mifflin, 1996).

4. I wrote a book about the significance of Jewish experience for the Catholic faith titled *Constantine's Sword: The Church and the Jews; A History* (Boston: Houghton Mifflin, 2001).

5. Apocalypse 21:8. "But as for the cowardly, the faithless, the polluted, as for murderers, fornicators, sorcerers, idolaters, and all liars, their lot shall be in the lake that burns with fire and sulphur, which is the second death."

6. John 20:21.

7. John 20:22–23.

8. Michael Rezendes, "Church Allowed Abuse by Priests for Years," *The Boston Globe*, January 6, 2002, https://www.bostonglobe.com/news/special-reports/2002 /01/06/church-allowed-abuse-priest-for-years/cSHfGkTIrAT25qKGvBuDNM /story.html#. As I was writing this, the Vatican official in charge of handling the sexual abuse crisis, Father Hermann Geissler, chief of staff for the Congregation for the Doctrine of the Faith, resigned his position after a former nun accused him of having solicited her for sex in the confessional—what canon law calls a "grave delict," or crime. Amy B. Wang, "Vatican Official Who Handled Sexual Abuse Cases Quits After Being Accused of Sexual Abuse," *The Washington Post*, January 29, 2019, https://www.washingtonpost.com/religion/2019 /01/29/vatican-official-who-handled-sex-abuse-cases-quits-after-being-accused -sex-abuse/. Ultimately, in May of 2019, Geissler was acquitted by a Vatican tribunal that refused to take testimony from his accuser. That finding led one of the Church's leading canon lawyers to denounce what he called a "scandalous verdict." Christa Pongratz-Lippitt, "Acquittal of Vatican Official a 'Scandalous Verdict,' Says Canon Lawyer," *The Tablet*, May 21, 2019, https://www.thetablet .co.uk/news/11706/acquittal-of-vatican-official-a-scandalous-verdict-says-canon -lawyer.

9. Sacha Pfeiffer and Thomas Farragher, "Suit Names Archdiocese, N.H. Bishop," *The Boston Globe*, March 24, 2002, http://archive.boston.com/globe/spotlight /abuse/stories/032402_mccormack_spotlight.htm.

10. In 2002, the Vatican reiterated the policy of initiating children at age six or seven in the practice of Confession: "The First Communion of children must always be preceded by sacramental confession and absolution." Congregation for Divine Worship and the Discipline of the Sacrament, "Redemptionis Sacramentum: On Certain Matters to Be Observed or to Be Avoided Regarding the Most Holy Eucharist," para. 87, http://www.vatican.va/roman_curia/congregations

/ccdds/documents/rc_con_ccdds_doc_20040423_redemptionis-sacramentum
_en.html.

Chapter 8

1. Eliot wrote this in a letter to Marguerite Caetani, on the death of her only son. Quoted in Helen Barolini, *Their Other Side: Six American Women and the Lure of Italy* (New York: Fordham University Press, 2006), 210.
2. Psalm 130:1, the Douay-Rheims Bible.
3. *The Complete Letters of Oscar Wilde,* ed. Merlin Holland and Rupert Hart-Davis (New York: Henry Holt, 2000), 683–780.
4. Max Beerbohm, "A Lord of Language," *Vanity Fair,* March 1905.
5. Matthew 27:46. Jesus was quoting Psalm 22:1.
6. "I have come that they may have life, and have it to the full." John 10:10, New International Version.
7. The term "black Irish" was originally used to refer to the dark-haired and dark-complected Irish people said to have descended from survivors washed up when the Spanish Armada sank in the Irish Sea in 1588.
8. The words Jesus spoke when he resigned himself to the monstrous fate God the Father required of Him. Luke 22:42.
9. Matthew 22:14.
10. Acts 9:6, King James Version. Paul surrenders his will after being knocked from his horse.

Chapter 9

1. Matthew 6:6, New English Translation.
2. Genesis 4:1.
3. Luke 2:49, King James Version.

Chapter 10

1. I have grappled with Anselm and Augustine before, but only now see the full reach of their problematic influence. See *Constantine's Sword* (Boston: Houghton Mifflin, 2001), chapters 18 and 28.
2. John 1:14.
3. "Father, if Thou art willing, remove this cup from me; nevertheless, not my will, but Thine be done." Luke 22:42.
4. "That God needs a human sacrifice to reconcile his own creation with himself, that he, the ruler of the world, cannot justify anyone without a blood sacrifice, is as incomprehensible to Jews as it is contrary to the Bible." Pinchas Lapide, quoted in Hans Kung, *Judaism: Between Yesterday and Tomorrow,* trans. John Bowden (New York: Crossroad, 1992), 386.

5. 1 Timothy 2:5–6.
6. Genesis 2:15–18.
7. Genesis 2:23.
8. Genesis 3:6.
9. Anselm, *Cur Deus Homo*, bk. 1, chap. 14, Medieval Sourcebook, Fordham University Center for Medieval Studies, https://sourcebooks.fordham.edu/basis/anselm-curdeus.asp.
10. "Litany of the Most Precious Blood of Jesus Christ," Devotion to the Most Precious Blood of Our Lord Jesus Christ, https://www.preciousbloodinternational.com/prayers_06.html.
11. 1 John 3:16.
12. This violence is shown, for example, in the following passage: "When he opened the sixth seal, I looked, and behold, there was a great earthquake; and the sun became black as sackcloth. The full moon became like blood; and the stars of the sky fell to the earth, as a fig tree sheds its winter fruit when shaken by a gale. The sky vanished like a scroll that is rolled up, and every mountain and island was removed from its place. Then the kings of the earth and the great men and the generals and the rich and the strong and every one, slave and free, hid in the caves and among the rocks of the mountains; calling to the mountains and to the rocks, 'Fall on us and hide us from the face of Him who is seated on the throne, and from the wrath of the Lamb; for the great day of their wrath has come, and who can stand before it?'" Apocalypse 6:12–17.

Chapter 11

1. The Gregorian Reforms, dealing with the discipline and integrity of the Catholic clergy, were initiated by Pope Gregory VII (1073–85). In earlier centuries, there were Church edicts (as, for example, at the Synod of Carthage in 390) that instructed married priests to abstain from sex with their wives. Today, such edicts are put forth by defenders of celibacy to show that this was an ancient discipline, but in fact the reinforcing of anti-sex norms at that time shows that they were being flouted in practice. There is simply no evidence that celibacy was universally required of Catholic clergy during the first millennium.
2. In a papal bull promulgated in 1302, Pope Boniface VIII wrote: "Urged by faith, we are obliged to believe and maintain that the Church is one, holy, catholic, and also apostolic. We believe in her firmly and we confess with simplicity that outside of her there is neither salvation nor the remission of sins." Pope Boniface VIII, "Unam Sanctam," Medieval Sourcebook, Fordham University Center for Medieval Studies, https://sourcebooks.fordham.edu/source/B8-unam.asp. Before Boniface, Pope Innocent III made the same claim at the Fourth Lateran Council in 1215.
3. Pope Innocent III, "Sermon on the Consecration of a Pope," quoted in Brian

Tierney, *The Crisis of Church and State, 1050–1300* (Englewood Cliffs, N.J.: Prentice Hall, 1980), 132.

4. Gratian's *Decretum*, which spawned the decrees of canon law, was published in 1143.

5. This is constitution 1 of the Fourth Lateran Council. See "On the Catholic Faith," in *Decrees of the Ecumenical Councils*, ed. Norman Tanner, SJ, vol. 1 (Washington, D.C.: Georgetown University Press, 1990), 230. The Fourth Lateran Council also formally defined the six other sacraments, including the seal of Confession. Today's Catholics learn about the Lateran notion of "transubstantiation" as if the idea originated in the New Testament, but it is a profoundly time-bound way of understanding how Christ is present to His people, depending on contingent categories like "substance" and "accidents" (the substance of the consecrated Host becomes Christ, while its accidents remain bread), which come from Aristotle. Today's assumption that Catholic "transubstantiation" makes the presence of Christ "real," while Protestant "consubstantiation" makes it "merely symbolic," is an anachronism, depending on philosophical categories that no longer hold.

6. Jesus said, "For where two or three are gathered in my name, there am I in the midst of them." Matthew 18:20.

7. It is not incidental to this entire story that such emphasis on the transcendent sacramental power of the priest—and only the priest—was reasserted by the Vatican in its responses to the discrediting of clericalism that followed the 2002 revelations of priestly sexual abuse of minors. No sooner had questions been raised about a dysfunctional clerical culture as a source of the criminal acts of predators and their protectors than the Roman Catholic Church designated 2004 "The Year of the Eucharist." The point of that ritual observance, with worldwide devotions and sermons, was to emphasize anew not only the centrality of the Mass in Catholic life, but also the unique power of the priest—and only the priest—as the one authorized to celebrate it. As questions continued to be raised by fresh scandals about a dysfunctional clerical culture, the Vatican responded in like manner again, by declaring June 19, 2009, to June 19, 2010, "The Year of the Priest," once more emphasizing the unique power of the ordained cleric. Clearly, in a time of widespread Catholic disillusionment with priests, the Vatican saw the urgency of reinforcing the traditional, and uncriticized, role of the priest—and only the priest—as the holder of Church power. I learned the subliminal significance of these Vatican observances in correspondence with the American Church historian David O'Brien.

8. Here are the promulgations of the First Lateran Council in 1123:

Canon 7: "We absolutely forbid priests, deacons, and subdeacons to associate with concubines and women, or to live with women other than such as the Nicene Council for reasons of necessity permitted, namely, the mother, sister, or aunt, or any such person concerning whom no suspicion could arise."

Canon 21: "We absolutely forbid priests, deacons, subdeacons, and monks to have concubines or to contract marriage. We decree in accordance with the definitions of the sacred canons, that marriages already contracted by such persons must be dissolved, and that the persons be condemned to do penance." First Lateran Council, 1123; *Papal Encyclicals Online:* https://www.papalencyc licals.net/councils/ecum09.htm.

9. Canon 12 of the Council of Melfi reads: "We remove from every sacred order those who, from the subdiaconate, wish to have leisure for their wives, and we decree that they be without office and benefice of the church. But if, warned by the bishop, they fail to correct themselves, we give permission to rulers that they subject their [the priests'] wives to servitude." Here the Latin word *servituti*— derived from *servus*, or "slave"—is translated as "servitude." Robert Somerville with Stephan Kuttner, *Pope Urban II, the* Collectio Britannica, *and the Council of Melfi (1089)* (Oxford, U.K.: Clarendon Press, 1996), 261.

10. Somerville, *Pope Urban II*, 288. Somerville, a distinguished historian at Columbia University, comments that such women were sold "with diocesan bishops as vendors. Melfi, on the other hand, invites princes . . . to perform that degradation" (289).

11. Joe Holland, *The Cruel Eleventh-Century Imposition of Western Clerical Celibacy: A Monastic-Inspired Attack on Catholic Episcopal & Presbyteral Families* (Washington, D.C.: Pacem in Terris Press, 2017).

12. Augustine, *The Confessions*, 4:1.

13. "In those days, I lived with a woman who I had chosen for no special reason but that my restless passion had alighted on her." Augustine, *The Confessions*, 4:4.

14. Augustine, *The Confessions*, 8:23.

15. Augustine, *The Confessions*, 8:7.

16. Stephen Greenblatt, "How St. Augustine Invented Sex," *The New Yorker*, published ahead of print, June 12, 2017, https://www.newyorker.com/magazine /2017/06/19/how-st-augustine-invented-sex.

17. It is not incidental that Augustine's formal justification of coercive force to bring about the submission of heretics licensed Church-sponsored violence then and after. In the ominously titled "The Correction of the Donatists," he wrote, "For many have found advantage (as we have proved and are daily proving by actual experiment) in being first compelled by fear or pain, so that they might afterwards be influenced by teaching." Augustine, "The Correction of the Donatists," in Philip Schaff, ed., *Nicene and Post-Nicene Fathers*, vol. 6 (Peabody, Mass.: Hendrickson, 1994), 641.

18. Genesis 3:7.

19. Genesis 3:7.

20. Augustine, "On Marriage and Concupiscence," 1:5:6.

21. Augustine, "On Marriage and Concupiscence," 2:7:17.

22. Augustine, "On Marriage and Concupiscence," 1:14:16.

23. The four Last Things are death, judgment, heaven, and hell. The study of the Last Things is called eschatology.
24. Galatians 3:28.
25. Genesis 5:2, New Living Translation.
26. Golgotha is the name of the skull-shaped hill outside Jerusalem where Jesus was crucified. The Aramaic word *golgotha* means "skull."
27. Matthew 26:72–74, King James Version.
28. Matthew 26:75, King James Version.
29. John 21:15–17.
30. Greenblatt, "How St. Augustine Invented Sex." See also Stephen Greenblatt, *The Rise and Fall of Adam and Eve* (New York: W. W. Norton, 2018), 607.
31. *Concupiscence*, according to Webster's Unabridged Dictionary, is "a longing of the soul for what will give it delight or for what is agreeable especially to the senses—used chiefly by Scholastic philosophers."

Chapter 12

1. In the mid-fifties, there were about 300,000 U.S. troops stationed in Germany and well over half that many family members, or "dependents." Hubert Zimmermann, "The Improbable Permanence of a Commitment: America's Troop Presence in Europe During the Cold War," MIT Press Journals, https://www.mitpressjournals.org/doi/pdf/10.1162/jcws.2009.11.1.3.
2. "He who fights with monsters should be careful lest he thereby become a monster. And if thou gaze long into an abyss, the abyss will also gaze into thee." Friedrich Nietzsche, *Beyond Good and Evil* (San Bernardino, Calif.: Millennium, 2014), 41.
3. The word "apocalypse" is the first word of the text. It is Greek for an unveiling, or revelation. Hence the book is also called Revelation.
4. Apocalypse 21:1.
5. Apocalypse 19:13.
6. Apocalypse 19:15.
7. Apocalypse 8:13.
8. Apocalypse 8:10.
9. Apocalypse 9:1–2.
10. The much-quoted statement was attributed to an anonymous U.S. Army major by reporter Peter Arnett, writing in 1968 for the Associated Press. The quote has generated much commentary, https://www.bloomberg.com/opinion/articles/2018-02-09/destroying-a-quote-s-history-in-order-to-save-it.
11. The United States had almost 19,000 nukes by 1960, ten times more than Moscow had. Robert S. Norris and Hans N. Kristensen, "Global Nuclear Weapons Inventory, 1945–2010," *Bulletin of the Atomic Scientists* 66, no. 4 (2010): 77–83, https://www.tandfonline.com/doi/pdf/10.2968/066004008.

12. Gerard Manley Hopkins, "God's Grandeur," Poets.org, https://poets.org/poem
/gods-grandeur.
13. John 10:10, New International Version.

Chapter 13

1. Quoted in John Lewis Gaddis, *The Cold War: A New History* (New York: Penguin, 2005), 71.
2. Greg Thielmann, "The Missile Gap Myth and Its Progeny," Arms Control Association, n.d., https://www.armscontrol.org/act/2011-05/missile-gap-myth-its
-progeny.

Part Five

1. I owe this phrase to Rosemary Radford Ruether, *The Church Against Itself* (New York: Herder and Herder, 1967).
2. "Pope John XXIII's New Pentecost," *Time*, January 4, 1963, http://content.time
.com/time/subscriber/article/0,33009,829723-1,00.html.

Chapter 14

1. Hannah Arendt, "The Christian Pope," *The New York Review of Books*, June 17, 1965.
2. John 17:14.
3. Thomas Cahill, *Pope John XXIII: A Life*, Penguin Lives (New York: Viking Press, 2002), 147. As Golgotha is the Aramaic word for skull, Calvary is the Latin for skull, both referring, as we saw, to the shape of the hill on which Jesus was crucified.
4. Pope John XXIII, quoted in James Martin, SJ, "Saint Pope John XXIII," *America*, April 28, 2011, https://www.americamagazine.org/content/all-things/saint-pope
-john-xxiii.
5. Camille M. Cianfarra, "Decree of Vatican Puts a Strict Ban upon Communism; Excommunication Is Declared of Roman Catholics Who Aid Red Doctrine or Activity," *The New York Times*, July 14, 1949, https://www.nytimes.com/1949/07
/14/archives/decree-of-vatican-puts-a-strict-ban-upon-communism-excommuni
cation.html.
6. Marjorie Hyer, "How Our War Blessing Catholic Bishops Got Religion on Nukes," *The Washington Post*, May 1, 1983, https://www.washingtonpost.com
/archive/opinions/1983/05/01/how-our-war-blessing-catholic-bishops-got
-religion-on-nukes/a9ec5e76-d679-4a9f-9806-f220b20c9b5e/.
7. Cardinal Francis Spellman, quoted in John Cooney, *The American Pope: The Life and Times of Francis Cardinal Spellman* (New York: Times Books, 1984), 261.

8. I recounted this incident in my memoir *An American Requiem*, pages 70–73. If here, and in some subsequent passages, I return to events and themes I have written of before—personal and historical—it is because they have urgent new salience in light of "the snap" with which this book begins.

9. This was Jules Isaac, whose 1948 book, *Jésus et Israël*, found roots of Nazi anti-Semitism in the long tradition of what he called Christian "teaching of contempt" for Jews. Jules Isaac, *Jésus et Israël* (Paris: Albin Michel, 1948), published in English as *Jesus and Israel*, trans. Sally Gran (New York: Holt, Rinehart and Winston, 1971).

10. Pope John wrote, "Justice, right reason, and the recognition of man's dignity cry out insistently for a cessation on the arms race. . . . Unless this process of disarmament be thoroughgoing and complete, and reach men's very souls, it is impossible to stop the arms race, or to reduce armaments, or—and this is the main thing—ultimately to abolish them entirely. . . . The stockpiles of armaments which have been built up in various countries must be reduced all round and simultaneously by the parties concerned. Nuclear weapons must be banned. A general agreement must be reached on a suitable disarmament program, with an effective system of mutual control." John XXIII, "Pacem in Terris," Encyclical of Pope John XXIII on Establishing Universal Peace in Truth, Justice, Charity, and Liberty, April 11, 1963, para. 112–13, http://www.vatican.va/content/john-xxiii/en/encyclicals/documents/hf_j-xxiii_enc_11041963_pacem.html.

11. 1 John 4:16.

12. Carroll, *An American Requiem*, 73–79.

13. Galatians 3:28.

Chapter 15

1. I omit Pope John Paul I from the list of Pope John's successors because he reigned as pope for only thirty-three days, beginning August 26, 1978.

2. John XXIII, "Pacem in Terris," Encyclical of Pope John XXIII on Establishing Universal Peace in Truth, Justice, Charity, and Liberty, April 11, 1963, para. 41, http://www.vatican.va/content/john-xxiii/en/encyclicals/documents/hf_j-xxiii_enc_11041963_pacem.html.

3. "The Pill" was developed by a Harvard obstetrician and gynecologist named John Rock, author of *The Time Has Come: A Catholic Doctor's Proposals to End the Battle over Birth Control* (New York: Alfred A. Knopf, 1963). When Rome denounced Rock, his friend Cardinal Richard Cushing, archbishop of Boston, said to him, "My God, Johnny, you've got the whole Vatican pregnant." J. Anthony Lukas, *Common Ground: A Turbulent Decade in the Lives of Three American Families* (New York: Random House, 1986), 389.

4. This is from the Vatican's "Declaration in Defense of the Catholic Doctrine on the Church Against Certain Errors of the Present Day," given in 1973: "Paragraph 3. The Infallibility of the Church's Magisterium: Jesus Christ, from whom

derives the task proper to the pastors of teaching the Gospel to His people and to the entire human family, wished to endow the pastors' Magisterium with a fitting charism of infallibility in matters regarding faith and morals," http://www.vatican.va/roman_curia/congregations/cfaith/documents/rc_con_cfaith_doc_19730705_mysterium-ecclesiae_en.html.

5. Flavius Josephus, *Jewish Antiquities*, trans. Louis H. Feldman, Loeb Classical Library 18.3.3 (Cambridge, Mass.: Harvard University Press, 1981), 63.

6. Galatians 3:28.

Chapter 16

1. Margaret Sanger, "Morality and Birth Control," *Birth Control Review*, February–March 1918, https://www.nyu.edu/projects/sanger/webedition/app/documents/show.php?sangerDoc=213391.xml.

2. Addressing the United Nations General Assembly in October of 1965, Pope Paul VI all but explicitly denounced President Lyndon Johnson's recently launched air war in Vietnam by crying, "Never again war! Never again war!," http://www.vatican.va/content/paul-vi/en/speeches/1965/documents/hf_p-vi_spe_19651004_united-nations.html.

3. First Vatican Council, "Pastor Aeternus," First Dogmatic Constitution on the Church of Christ, 1869–70, chap. 4, from *The Vatican Council and Its Definitions*, trans. Cardinal Henry Edward Manning (New York: D. & J. Sadlier, 1871), http://www.catholicplanet.org/councils/20-Pastor-Aeternus.htm.

4. *Vatican II: The Essential Texts*, edited by Norman Tanner (New York: Doubleday, 2012), 20.

5. "Pope John XXIII's New Pentecost," *Time*, January 4, 1963, http://content.time.com/time/subscriber/article/0,33009,829723-1,00.html. My own reflections on Vatican II draw inspiration from the essay I published as an introduction to *Vatican II: The Essential Texts*, ed. Norman Tanner, SJ (New York: Doubleday, 2012).

6. Pope Francis, *The Name of God Is Mercy* (New York: Random House, 2016).

7. Cindy Wooden, "If You Can't Go to Confession, Take Your Sorrow Directly to God, Pope Says," Catholic News Service, March 20, 2020, https://www.ncronline.org/news/vatican/francis-chronicles/if-you-cant-go-confession-take-your-sorrow-directly-god-pope-says.

8. I say "almost universal" because Latin rite Catholicism does make an exception for married Episcopal priests who convert. In practice, these priests are motivated by their conscientious objection to the Anglican Communion's admission of women to the priesthood. The Catholic discipline of celibacy is trumped by the Catholic disregard for women. We will return to this point in chapter 17.

9. Paul Collins, "Pope Hamlet: Paul VI's Indecisive, Wavering Papacy," *National Catholic Reporter*, October 13, 2018, https://www.ncronline.org/news/people/pope-hamlet-paul-vis-indecisive-wavering-papacy.

10. Cardinal Leon-Joseph Suenens of Belgium, quoted in Alana Harris, "'A Galileo-Crisis Not a Luther Crisis'? English Catholics' Attitudes to Contraception," in Alana Harris, ed., *The Schism of '68: Catholicism, Contraception and 'Humanae Vitae' in Europe, 1945–1975* (London: Palgrave Macmillan, 2018), 74.

11. Robert G. Hoyt, ed., *The Birth Control Debate* (Kansas City, Mo.: National Catholic Reporter, 1968), 15–111.

Chapter 17

1. *Catechism of the Catholic Church*, part 3, sec. 2, chap. 2, art. 6, para. 2357, http://www.vatican.va/archive/ccc_css/archive/catechism/p3s2c2a6.htm.

2. Bernadette C. Barton, *Pray the Gay Away: The Extraordinary Lives of Bible Belt Gays* (New York: NYU Press, 2012).

3. Jessica Ravitz, "Abortion Rates in US Reach a Decade Low, CDC Reports," CNN, November 21, 2018, https://www.cnn.com/2018/11/21/health/abortion-surveillance-cdc-2015-bn/index.html.

4. Nicole Winfield, "Pope Reaffirms Priest Celibacy but Makes Case for Exception," AP News, January 28, 2019, https://apnews.com/160e10c195274958af851 6aa04379457.

5. Paul VI, "Sacerdotalis Caelibatus," Encyclical of Pope Paul VI on the Celibacy of the Priest, June 24, 1967, http://w2.vatican.va/content/paul-vi/en/encyclicals /documents/hf_p-vi_enc_24061967_sacerdotalis.html. A further signal of the Vatican's firm defensiveness on clericalism came that same year, 1967, with the condemnation of an anti-clerical article written by the New York priest Ivan Illich ("The Vanishing Clergyman," *The Critic* 25 [June–July 1967]: 18–27). Illich called for replacing the bureaucratic priesthood with "the sacramental ministry of ordained laymen." As a result of the article, Illich was silenced by Rome—a disciplining that did not stop him from becoming a celebrated social critic and author. See, for example, Ivan Illich, *Deschooling Society* (New York: Harper & Row, 1970).

6. In April 2020, for example, Cardinal Gerhard Müller, former Prefect of the Congregation of the Faith, told an interviewer, "Women cannot become priests because this is excluded by the nature of the Sacrament of Holy Orders. It is just not simply a ministry that one can aspire to. Nor can a man simply say that he has a right to become a priest. One is called to the priesthood, and Jesus called to Him those He wanted. He appointed the twelve disciples as his Apostles. Throughout the history of the Church, this has always been understood as normative and as a truth contained in Revelation, not a habit subject to change," https://www.lifesitenews.com/blogs/women-cannot-become-priests-cdl-mueller -reacts-to-popes-new-commission-to-study-female-ordination.

7. John Paul II, "Ordinatio Sacerdotalis," Apostolic Letter of John Paul II to the Bishops of the Catholic Church on Reserving Priestly Ordination to Men

Alone, May 22, 1994, http://w2.vatican.va/content/john-paul-ii/en/apost_letters
/1994/documents/hf_jp-ii_apl_19940522_ordinatio-sacerdotalis.html.

8. Richard McBrien, "Infallibility on Women's Ordination in Question," Essays in
Theology (blog), *National Catholic Reporter,* June 13, 2011, https://www.ncron
line.org/blogs/essays-theology/infallibility-womens-ordination-question.

9. Joshua J. McElwee, "Pope Francis Confirms Finality of Ban on Ordaining
Women Priests," *National Catholic Reporter,* November 1, 2016, https://www
.ncronline.org/news/vatican/pope-francis-confirms-finality-ban-ordaining
-women.

10. In his Letter to the Romans, Paul identifies a woman named Priscilla, who is
mentioned five times in the New Testament, as "a fellow worker in Christ Jesus"
(Romans 16:3, English Standard Version). He also mentions as fellow mission-
aries women named Julia (Romans 16:15), Phoebe (Romans 16:1–2), and Try-
phena and Tryphosa (Romans 16:12).

11. This relative openness to the ordination of married men, in contrast to adamant
rejection of woman priests, was on display again at the Vatican's 2019 Synod of
Bishops for the Amazon, which looked favorably on ordaining older married
men while avoiding the question of ordaining women. "Results of Amazon
Synod Mixed for the Church, Bad News for Women and LGBTQI People, Says
Gay Catholic Organization," DignityUSA, October 27, 2019, https://www.digni
tyusa.org/news/results-amazon-synod-mixed-church-bad-news-women-and
-lgbtqi-people-says-gay-catholic. We will see more of this in chapter 23.

Chapter 18

1. "Transcript of President John F. Kennedy's Inaugural Address (1961)," Our
Documents, https://www.ourdocuments.gov/doc.php?flash=true&doc=91&page
=transcript.

2. Apocalypse 8:13, 8:10.

3. B-52 devotees proudly claimed that its wingspan was wider than the distance of
the Wright brothers' first flight. As for my own model B-52, a few years later,
during the Vietnam War, I would hurl the gleaming thing into a ravine.

4. John F. Kennedy, "Radio and Television Report to the American People on the
Berlin Crisis, July 25, 1961," John F. Kennedy Presidential Library and Mu-
seum, https://www.jfklibrary.org/asset-viewer/archives/TNC/TNC-258/TNC-258.

5. In recounting this incident in *An American Requiem* (page 83), I recalled it as
occurring in 1960. Now I know it was 1961.

6. In fact, I could never have imagined what my father knew just then: that the
danger of nuclear war had reached its pitch not because of the Soviet Union, but
because men inside the Pentagon—his fellow generals, colleagues down the
hall, led by our neighbor Curtis LeMay and by SAC Commander Thomas
Power—were driving hard to launch a preemptive strike against Moscow. Right
then. The window was closing on our strategic superiority: The Soviets would

soon have the capacity to survive our first nuclear strike and retaliate, but they did not have that capacity yet. The pressure to launch a U.S. nuclear attack would never be this high again. Armageddon would begin with America. See Fred Kaplan, *The Wizards of Armageddon* (New York: Simon & Schuster, 1983), 85.

Chapter 19

1. Quoted in "Krister Stendahl, 1921–2008," Harvard Divinity School, April 16, 2008, https://hds.harvard.edu/news/2011/02/07/krister-stendahl-1921-2008.
2. Late in the nineteenth century, the Paulists were tarred with an association with a heresy called Americanism, which the Vatican condemned in 1895. The heretical ideas included affirmation of the separation of church and state and of the primacy of conscience—the proposition that the Holy Spirit operated in the Church through the whole people, not just through the hierarchy. Jonathan Wright, "When Rome Condemned 'Americanism,'" *Catholic Herald*, July 27, 2017, https://catholicherald.co.uk/magazine/when-rome-condemned-americanism/.
3. Hecker, who founded the Paulist Fathers in 1858, had been a member of the Brook Farm commune in Massachusetts in the early 1840s.
4. Romans 13:13, New International Version.
5. Augustine, *The Confessions*, 8:12.
6. Augustine, *The Confessions*, 8:7.
7. The Second Vatican Council's opening coincided with the Cuban missile crisis. The council fathers' readiness to think with unprecedented boldness about Catholic tradition and doctrine was no doubt reinforced by the sense they shared with the broader world of a terrifying brush with historic disaster. Certainly, the council's spirit of affirmation, reflecting Pope John XXIII's, was a crucial antidote to my own nuclear dread.
8. The Reformation, dated to 1517 and led by figures such as Martin Luther and John Calvin, spawned mass literacy, which sparked a new individualism; introduced a new work ethic essential to capitalism, the growth of cities, and industrialization; midwifed the nation-state and, ultimately, democratic governance; and transformed artistic culture, music, and literature. The Reformation also brought witch trials, the Inquisition, and religious wars, which decimated Europe for centuries.
9. My memories of Krister Stendahl come in part from my essay "Krister Stendahl and the Introverted Conscience of a Friend: A Personal Appreciation," in *Krister Among the Jews and Gentiles*, ed. Paula Fredriksen and Jesper Svartvik (New York: Paulist Press, 2019).
10. Krister Stendahl, "The Apostle Paul and the Introspective Conscience of the West," *Harvard Theological Review* 56, no. 3 (July 1963): 199–215, https://www.cambridge.org/core/journals/harvard-theological-review/article/apostle-paul

-and-the-introspective-conscience-of-the-west/4172993A034F101DAD7998180
9A47F52.

11. Martin Luther, quoted in W. O. Loescher, *Dr. Martin Luther, 1483–1546* (self-pub., Lulu, 2018), 3.

12. Psalm 22:6.

13. Krister Stendahl, "The Apostle Paul and the Introspective Conscience of the West," in *Paul Among Jews and Gentiles* (Philadelphia: Fortress, 1976), 86.

14. God's promise is the overarching theme of biblical faith—from the promise made to Noah, never again to destroy the earth; to the promise made to Abraham, to bring forth his children as the special people of God; to the promise made to Moses, symbolized by the Promised Land; to the promise that, as Christians believe, the Resurrection of Jesus foretells the resurrection of all people. Faced with death, the believer trusts not in an immortal soul or some kind of afterlife, but in God's promise. Not even death can break it.

15. Krister Stendahl, *Meanings* (Philadelphia: Fortress, 2008), 222.

16. Paul VI, "Nostra Aetate," Declaration on the Relation of the Church to Non-Christian Religions Proclaimed by His Holiness Pope Paul VI, October 28, 1965, http://www.vatican.va/archive/hist_councils/ii_vatican_council/documents/vat-ii_decl_19651028_nostra-aetate_en.html. The Second Vatican Council's declaration put an end to so-called replacement theology, with Israel understood as being "replaced" by the Church.

17. Genesis 1:31.

18. John 10:30.

19. James Carroll, *Constantine's Sword: The Church and the Jews; A History* (Boston: Houghton Mifflin, 2001). Krister's comment appeared on the book jacket: "A deeply religious book written at levels of understanding and with clarity of insights rarely—if ever—reached in the telling of this painful story."

20. As noted earlier, the old saw about Protestants believing in "consubstantiation" while Catholics believe in "transubstantiation" is outmoded on both sides, not least because "substantiation" reflects a philosophical paradigm from another age.

21. Zoe Ryan, "'God's Rottweiler' Silenced Many as Head of Doctrinal Congregation," *National Catholic Reporter*, February 27, 2013, https://www.ncronline.org/news/vatican/gods-rottweiler-silenced-many-head-doctrinal-congregation.

22. For example, Cardinal Gerhard Müller, cited earlier regarding women's ordination, told an interviewer in 2020, "There are objective conditions for receiving Holy Communion. One must belong to the Catholic Church through Baptism and the profession of faith and must not have offended against the Commandments of God by the way one lives. It is essential for the *communio* with Christ and the Church that I affirm the doctrine of the Catholic Church," https://www.lifesitenews.com/blogs/women-cannot-become-priests-cdl-mueller-reacts-to-popes-new-commission-to-study-female-ordination.

23. Matthew 11:28, New International Version.

Chapter 20

1. My father took his cues from J. Edgar Hoover, who had evidence that Dr. King's close associate Stanley Levison had been an important member of the Communist Party. David J. Garrow, "The FBI and Martin Luther King," *The Atlantic*, July/August 2002, https://www.theatlantic.com/magazine/archive/2002/07/the-fbi-and-martin-luther-king/302537/.
2. I tell this story in *An American Requiem*, 210–22.
3. Nixon said this in 1972 when launching Operation Linebacker. President Richard Nixon to White House Chief of Staff H. R. Haldeman and Attorney General John Mitchell, April 4, 1972, "Nixon on Bombing Recorded on Tape," *The New York Times*, June 30, 1974, https://www.nytimes.com/1974/06/30/archives/nixon-on-bombing-recorded-in-tape-reason-for-moving.html.
4. This would not have been true of the U.S. Army or Navy, but the Air Force, founded in 1947, was a new service branch.
5. Per Wikipedia, "1970 in the Vietnam War."
6. "Vietnam War Casualties, 1955–1975," Military Factory, https://www.militaryfactory.com/vietnam/casualties.asp.
7. Richard M. Nixon, "Address to the Nation on the Situation in Southeast Asia," April 30, 1970, Miller Center, University of Virginia, https://millercenter.org/the-presidency/presidential-speeches/april-30-1970-address-nation-situation-southeast-asia.
8. PBS.org, "About Martin Luther," viewers' guide for *Martin Luther: The Reluctant Revolutionary*, https://www.pbs.org/empires/martinluther/about_relu.html.
9. James Carroll, "The Philadelphia Ordination," *National Catholic Reporter*, August 6, 1974. For more about this article and the circumstances surrounding it, see chapter 23, note 4.

Chapter 21

1. As described in Matthew 2:16–18.
2. John 16:31–33.
3. Friedrich Nietzsche, *The Gay Science*, trans. Walter Kaufman (New York: Vintage, 1974), 125.
4. Samuel Taylor Coleridge, *Biographia Literaria: Or, Biographical Sketches of My Literary Life and Opinions*, ed. James Engell and W. Jackson Bate (Princeton, N.J.: Princeton University Press, 1985), 308.
5. John 2:19–21. For my deeper consideration of the meaning of Jesus as the New Temple, see, for example, *Christ Actually: The Son of God for the Secular Age* (New York: Viking, 2014), chapter 2.
6. That violent Roman oppression spawned such conflict among Jews was part of the Roman method of controlling subject peoples—internecine conflicts that served the purposes of the imperial overlords. In just such a way, imperial Brit-

ain's oppression spawned civil wars among dominated peoples in Ireland, India, Palestine, and Sudan.

7. John 1:11.

8. Edward W. Said observed that in writing his history of Western prejudice against colonized people, "by an almost inescapable logic, I have found myself writing the history of a strange, secret sharer of Western anti-Semitism." *Orientalism* (New York: Vintage, 1979), 27. In 2017, when white supremacists in Charlottesville, Virginia, chanted "Jews will not replace us," they were unconsciously invoking the ancient trope of "replacement" theology—the doctrine that the Church "replaced" the Synagogue in God's favor. See chapter 19 for more on this topic.

9. By around the year 200, the twenty-seven books that make up the New Testament were beginning to be regarded as "canonical," or "on the list" of sacred texts, but it was not until 367 that Athanasius, bishop of Alexandria, made the canon in some way official. Dozens of "non-canonical" texts were left aside, some of them because they were attributed to women or portrayed women as Church leaders. One example is "The Gospel of Mary," a text probably dating to the second century but not discovered until the late nineteenth century. See Karen King, *The Gospel of Mary of Magdala: Jesus and the First Woman Apostle* (Santa Rosa, Calif.: Polebridge Press, 2003).

10. Luke 17:21.

11. Galatians 3:28, New International Version. The scholar Stephen Patterson helped me appreciate this aspect of Jesus's meaning. See Stephen J. Patterson, *The Forgotten Creed: Christianity's Original Struggle Against Bigotry, Slavery, and Sexism* (New York: Oxford University Press, 2018).

12. I recount my experience of the Holy Sepulcher in *An American Requiem*, 249–52.

13. Pope Leo XIII declared the Church to be a "perfect society" in his 1885 encyclical "Immortale Dei," available at http://www.vatican.va/content/leo-xiii/en/encyclicals/documents/hf_l-xiii_enc_01111885_immortale-dei.html.

14. My guide was Father Pierre Benoit, a French Dominican priest and archaeologist who lived in Jerusalem. He served on the Pontifical Biblical Commission, which advises the Vatican on biblical issues, for fifteen years.

Part Seven

1. Poetry Foundation, https://www.poetryfoundation.org/poems/42889/hope-is-the-thing-with-feathers-314.

Chapter 22

1. Pope Francis, *The Name of God Is Mercy* (New York: Random House, 2016), 26.

2. James Joyce, *Finnegans Wake* (Oxford: Oxford University Press, 2012), 32.

3. For my account of this experience, see James Carroll, "Who Am I to Judge?," *The New Yorker*, published ahead of print, December 16, 2013, https://www .newyorker.com/magazine/2013/12/23/who-am-i-to-judge.

4. "Pope Salutes 'Saints Next Door' in Fight Against Coronavirus," *The Guardian*, April 8, 2020, https://www.theguardian.com/world/2020/apr/08/pope-salutes -saints-next-door-fight-against-coronavirus-hyprocrisy.

5. Pope Francis, "Urbi et Orbi Address," March 27, 2020, https://www.americamaga zine.org/faith/2020/03/27/read-pope-francis-urbi-et-orbi-address-coronavirus -and-jesus-calming-storm.

6. Francis, *The Name of God Is Mercy*, 9.

7. Ross Douthat, "The Plot to Change Catholicism," *The New York Times*, October 17, 2015, https://www.nytimes.com/2015/10/18/opinion/sunday/the-plot-to -change-catholicism.html.

8. Richard Engel and Kennett Werner, "Steve Bannon and U.S. Ultra-conservatives Take Aim at Pope Francis," NBC News, April 12, 2019, https://www.nbcnews.com /news/world/steve-bannon-u-s-ultra-conservatives-take-aim-pope-francis-n991411.

9. Pope Francis, "Laudato Si'," Encyclical Letter of the Holy Father Francis on Care for Our Common Home, May 24, 2015, http://w2.vatican.va/content /francesco/en/encyclicals/documents/papa-francesco_20150524_enciclica -laudato-si.html.

10. Frances D'Emilio, "Pope Decries That 'Wealthy Few' Feast on What Belongs to All," AP News, November 18, 2018, https://www.apnews.com/c183ed8b926949 9ea0f537d9e8a9f2b6.

11. Carroll, "Who Am I to Judge?"

12. Pope Francis fulfilled at last the promise of Pope John XXIII's "Pacem in Terris" when he renounced nuclear weapons in no uncertain terms. In 1963, as we saw in chapter 14, John had declared that "unless this process of disarmament be thoroughgoing and complete, and reach men's very souls, it is impossible to stop the arms race, or to reduce armaments, or—and this is the main thing— ultimately to abolish them entirely." John XXIII, "Pacem in Terris," Encyclical of Pope John XXIII on Establishing Universal Peace in Truth, Justice, Charity, and Liberty, April 11, 1963, para. 113, http://www.vatican.va/content/john-xxiii /en/encyclicals/documents/hf_j-xxiii_enc_11041963_pacem.html. Francis went further, denouncing the "very possession" of nuclear weapons. During a visit to Hiroshima and Nagasaki in November of 2019, Francis called for "the total elimination of nuclear weapons." Justin McCurry, "Pope Francis Calls for a 'World Without Nuclear Weapons' During Nagasaki Visit," *The Guardian* (U.S. edition), November 23, 2019, https://www.theguardian.com/world/2019/nov/24 /pope-francis-calls-for-a-world-without-nuclear-weapons-during-nagasaki-visit. See also Paul Elie, "The Pope and Catholic Radicals Come Together Against Nuclear Weapons," Daily Comment, *The New Yorker*, November 19, 2019, https://www.newyorker.com/news/daily-comment/the-pope-and-catholic -radicals-come-together-against-nuclear-weapons.

13. Eugenio Scalfari, "The Pope: How the Church Will Change," *La Repubblica*, October 1, 2013, http://www.repubblica.it/cultura/2013/10/01/news/pope_s_con versation_with_scalfari_english-67643118.

14. Francis, "Laudato Si'."

15. Francis, "Laudato Si'," para. 84.

16. Ishaan Tharoor, "The Pandemic Is Ravaging the World's Poor, Even If They're Untouched by the Virus," *The Washington Post*, April 15, 2020, https://www .washingtonpost.com/world/2020/04/15/pandemic-is-ravaging-worlds-poor -even-if-theyre-untouched-by-virus/.

17. Inés San Martin, "Pope Warns of 'Virionic Genocide' If Governments Prioritize Economy Over People During Pandemic," *Crux*, March 29, 2020, https:// cruxnow.com/church-in-the-americas/2020/03/pope-warns-of-virionic-genocide -if-governments-prioritize-economy-over-people-during-pandemic/.

18. John L. Allen, "Pope's Call for 'Obedience' on Mass Restrictions Both Pastoral and Political," *Crux*, April 28, 2020, https://cruxnow.com/news-analysis/2020/04 /popes-call-for-obedience-on-mass-restrictions-both-pastoral-and-political/.

19. Francis, *The Name of God Is Mercy*, 52.

20. Francis, *The Name of God Is Mercy*, 26.

21. Archbishop Carlo Maria Viganò, formerly the Vatican nuncio in Washington, D.C., ambushed Francis during his 2018 pilgrimage to Ireland, publishing a letter claiming that the pope himself had covered up the abusive behavior of clergy. Viganò had done this before, during the pope's 2015 visit to Washington, by arranging a private meeting with the Kentucky court clerk who refused to certify same-sex marriages. Viganò was supported by the pope's American nemesis, Cardinal Raymond Burke, who paired with Steve Bannon in promoting a right-wing school for theological "gladiators" in Italy. Foreshadowing these events was a letter addressed to the pope by thirteen cardinals ahead of a synod in 2015 (and later leaked), warning against any change on the question of divorce and remarriage. Gerard O'Connell, "Dolan Explains Origins of Letter Sent to Pope Francis by 13 Concerned Cardinals," *America*, October 14, 2015, https://www.americamagazine.org/content/dispatches/cardinal-dolan-reveals -background-letter-thirteen-cardinals.

Chapter 23

1. "Gorbachev: US Could Start New Cold War," *The London Daily Telegraph*, May 7, 2008, https://www.telegraph.co.uk/news/worldnews/europe/russia/1933 223/Gorbachev-US-could-start-new-Cold-War.html.

2. J. Anthony Lukas, *Common Ground: A Turbulent Decade in the Lives of Three American Families* (New York: Random House, 1986), 403.

3. "Nun Forced to Quit in Dispute over Mass," *The New York Times*, April 14, 1974, https://www.nytimes.com/1974/04/14/archives/nun-forced-to-quit-in-dispute

-over-mass-symbolic-works-omitted.html. The story quoted me as saying the archdiocesan investigation of Sister Gloria was "the result of the Roman Catholic refusal to admit women to the priesthood. It is an outrage and should be changed. She is a colleague and friend and I support her." In the same issue of the *Times* was a separate news story headlined "Catholic Clergy Declines." See Eleanor Blau, "Catholic Clergy Declines; Protestants on Increase," *The New York Times*, April 14, 1974, https://www.nytimes.com/1974/04/14/archives /catholic-clergy-declines-protestant-on-increase-fewer-joining.html.

4. My failure to more fully support Sister Gloria in the spring of 1974 seems even more questionable in light of what followed that summer and what I did about it. On July 29, 1974, eleven women were illegally ordained to the Episcopal priesthood by four retired male bishops in Philadelphia. The following week, I published an article in the *National Catholic Reporter* supporting the illicit ordination and calling on Catholics to match it. I wrote, "At what point does the order of the Church become idolatry? . . . The regularity with which we [Catholics] hand over conscience to bishops on this and other matters is sinful. . . . The entire structure of Catholic clericalism must be undone. . . . As access to official Church leadership opens to women, the lynch-pin of the whole system of male supremacy will have been pulled. At what point does the 'respect and obedience' due to bishops slip over into yet another failure of moral nerve?" James Carroll, "The Philadelphia Ordination," *National Catholic Reporter*, August 6, 1974. As I read these robust words now, I wonder why I had so much less to say in support of Gloria only a few months before.

5. A. Rebecca Rozelle Stone and Lucian Stone, *Simone Weil and Theology* (London: Bloomsbury, 2013), 24.

6. See Massimo Faggioli, "Benedict's Untimely Meditation," *Commonweal*, April 12, 2019, https://www.commonwealmagazine.org/benedicts-untimely -meditation.

7. Stefano Esposito, "Pope Picks Cardinal Cupich to Help Organize Vatican Sex-Abuse Prevention Summit," *Chicago Sun-Times*, November 23, 2018, https:// chicago.suntimes.com/2018/11/23/18468784/pope-picks-cardinal-cupich-to -help-organize-vatican-sex-abuse-prevention-summit.

8. James Carroll, "The Moral Weakness of Pope Benedict's *Last Testament*," November 15, 2016, TheNewYorker.com, https://www.newyorker.com/news/news -desk/the-moral-weakness-of-pope-benedicts-last-testament.

9. We saw this before, how the very word "clergy," meaning chosen, was first applied to the whole Christian community, not an elite. "But you are a chosen race, a royal priesthood, a holy nation, God's own people, that you may declare the wonderful deeds of him who called you out of darkness into his marvelous light," 1 Peter 2:9.

10. I first wrote about the diaconate as a wedge of change for *The New Yorker*'s website: James Carroll, "After Pennsylvania, What Pope Francis Should Say in Ire-

land," Daily Comment, *The New Yorker*, August 22, 2018, https://www.newyorker
.com/news/daily-comment/after-pennsylvania-what-pope-francis-should-say-in
-ireland.

11. The order of deacon, like that of subdeacon, has long been subsumed as a kind
of transitional way station for candidates to the priesthood, but it has not been a
stand-alone, permanent office in the Church since ancient times.

12. *The Pontifical Yearbook 2017*, https://press.vatican.va/content/salastampa/en
/bollettino/pubblico/2017/04/06/170406e.html.

13. "New papal decree clarifies role of deacons and result of defections on marriage," *Catholic News Agency*, December 15, 2009.

14. Stefano Pitrelli and Terrence McCoy, "Roman Catholic Bishops Recommend
Allowing Married Deacons to Become Priests in the Amazon Region," *The
Washington Post*, October 26, 2019, https://www.washingtonpost.com/world
/europe/roman-catholic-bishops-propose-opening-priesthood-to-married
-deacons-in-the-amazon-region/2019/10/26/671b9ae2-f6a0-11e9-b2d2
-1f37c9d82dbb_story.html. See also Jason Horowitz, "Catholic Bishops Back
Ordination of Married Men As Priests in Amazon Region, a Milestone," *The
New York Times*, October 26, 2019, updated February 12, 2020, https://www
.nytimes.com/2019/10/26/world/europe/vatican-synod-amazon-pope.html.

15. Pope Francis, "Querida Amazonia" (Beloved Amazon), https://w2.vatican.va
/content/francesco/en/apost_exhortations/documents/papa-francesco_esorta
zione-ap_20200202_querida-amazonia.html.

16. Gerard O'Connell, "What's in Pope Francis's Apostolic Exhortation on the Amazon Synod?," *America*, February 12, 2020, https://www.americamagazine.org
/faith/2020/02/12/whats-pope-francis-apostolic-exhortation-amazon-synod.

17. Horowitz, "Catholic Bishops Back Ordination of Married Men." Though en-
couraging a look at women as deacons, the Amazon synod, while proposing the
ordination of married men, refused to contemplate the priestly ordination of
women. That prompted a *New York Times* op-ed: Sara McDougall, "Catholic
Bishops Agree: Anything but a Woman," *The New York Times*, October 30, 2019,
https://www.nytimes.com/2019/10/30/opinion/catholic-married-priests-women
.html.

18. Nicole Winfield, "Pope Creates New Expert Commission to Study Women
Deacons, *Associated Press*, April 8, 2020, https://www.usnews.com/news/world
/articles/2020-04-08/pope-creates-new-expert-commission-to-study-women
-deacons. In 2016, Francis had established the Study Commission on the Wom-
en's Diaconate, but it disbanded in May 2019, with its members reported to
have been unable to achieve consensus on the question. Joshua J. McElwee,
"Francis: Women Deacons Commission Gave Split Report on Their Role in
Early Church," *National Catholic Reporter*, May 7, 2019, https://www.ncronline
.org/news/vatican/francis-women-deacons-commission-gave-split-report-their
-role-early-church.

19. Linda Bordoni, "Pope Francis 'Death Penalty Inadmissable,'" Vatican News,

August 2, 2018, https://www.vaticannews.va/en/pope/news/2018-08/pope-francis
-cdf-ccc-death-penalty-revision-ladaria.html.
20. "Letter from Priests to Cardinal Law," *The Boston Globe,* December 9, 2002,
http://archive.boston.com/globe/spotlight/abuse/extras/priests_letter_120902
.htm. In May 2020, the Council of Priests in the Polish diocese of Kalisz was
called upon by Church authorities to write a letter of support for their bishop,
who was accused of covering up a priest's abuse of children. The Council of
Priests refused—a kind of protest by omission. Monika Sieradzka, "Polish Priests
Defy Bishop Amid Pedophilia Scandal," DW, May 30, 2020, https://www.dw
.com/en/polish-priests-defy-bishop-amid-pedophilia-scandal/a-53634347.

Chapter 24

1. Quoted in *Proceedings of the Massachusetts Historical Society* (Boston: MHS,
1978), 123.
2. Pope Francis, quoted in "Pope Says He Is Worried About Homosexuality in the
Priesthood," AP News, December 1, 2018, https://www.apnews.com/420b7a621
5874971bff9c98577b6c5c5. See also Pope Francis, *The Strength of a Vocation:
Consecrated Life Today; A Conversation with Fernando Prado, CMF* (Washington, D.C.: U.S. Conference of Catholic Bishops, 2018).
3. David Masci and Gregory A. Smith, "7 Facts About American Catholics," Pew
Research Center, October 10, 2018, https://www.pewresearch.org/fact-tank/2018
/10/10/7-facts-about-american-catholics/.
4. The phrase became widely known after the publication of the conservative philosopher Rod Dreher's book *The Benedict Option: A Strategy for Christians in a
Post-Christian Nation* (New York: Sentinel, 2017). He drew inspiration for the
idea from the philosopher Alasdair MacIntyre, who first broached the idea
nearly forty years earlier in his book *After Virtue* (Notre Dame, Ind.: Notre
Dame University Press, 1980).

Epilogue

1. James Joyce, letter to Nora Barnacle, August 29, 1904, quoted in Sean P. Murphy, *James Joyce and Victims: Reading the Logic of Exclusion* (Madison, N.J.:
Fairleigh Dickinson University Press, 2003), 79: "Six years ago I left the Catholic Church, hating it most fervently. I found it impossible for me to remain in it
on account of the impulses of my nature. I made secret war upon it when I was
a student. . . . Now I make open war upon it by what I write and say and do."
2. Matthew 25:40.
3. Matthew 18:20.
4. A Jesuit priest anticipated the pandemic's possible consequence for the Church
this way: "Given the age and low number of priests in the Catholic Church, it
will be impossible for priests to do all the services required by social distancing.

Most services will have to be led by laypersons, most of whom will be women. These Communion services will use hosts consecrated earlier at Masses celebrated by priests. At the Amazon synod last year, there was much talk about a lack of priests and the leadership role of women in local communities. In the pandemic, American Catholics are experiencing the Eucharistic famine that much of the rest of the world has known for generations. The pandemic may make the U.S. church more sympathetic to the changes desired by the Amazonian church, and allow women to share their gifts with the church in a way previously not seen in the States." Thomas Reese SJ, "How Social Distancing May Change the Way We Do Church," *The National Catholic Reporter*, April 22, 2020.

5. Psalm 130:5–6, New International Version.

6. Coleridge wrote that the imagination is "a repetition in the finite mind of the eternal act of creation in the infinite I AM." *Biographia Literaria: Or, Biographical Sketches of My Literary Life and Opinions*, ed. James Engell and W. Jackson Bate (Princeton, N.J.: Princeton University Press, 1985).

Index

✠

JAMES CARROLL served as Catholic chaplain at Boston University from 1969 to 1974. He left the priesthood to become a writer, and for twenty-three years he wrote a weekly op-ed column for *The Boston Globe*. He has written twelve novels and nine works of non-fiction, including his memoir *An American Requiem*, winner of the National Book Award; *Constantine's Sword*, a *New York Times* bestseller and winner of the National Jewish Book Award; and a history of the Pentagon, *House of War*, winner of the PEN/Galbraith Award. Carroll is a fellow of the American Academy of Arts and Sciences. He lives in Boston with his wife, the writer Alexandra Marshall.